GOOD FAT

With 100 Recipes

Fran McCullough

Foreword by Dr. Barry Sears

Originally published as *The Good Fat Cookbook*

SCRIBNER

New York   London   Toronto   Sydney

SCRIBNER
1230 Avenue of the Americas
New York, NY 10020

First Scribner trade paperback edition 2004

SCRIBNER and design are trademarks of Macmillan Library Reference USA, Inc.,
used under license by Simon & Schuster, the publisher of this work.

For information about special discounts for bulk purchases,
please contact Simon & Schuster Special Sales:
1-800-456-6798 or business@simonandschuster.com

DESIGNED BY ERICH HOBBING

Set in Sabon

Manufactured in the United States of America
1   3   5   7   9   10   8   6   4   2

The Library of Congress has cataloged the Scribner edition as follows:
McCullough, Frances Monson, date.
The good fat cookbook / Fran McCullough ; foreword by Barry Sears.
p. cm.
Includes bibliographical references and index.
1. Cookery. 2. Food—Fat content. 3. Low-fat diet—Recipes. I. Title.
TX714.M37926 2003
641.5'638—dc21
2002036545

ISBN 0-7432-2809-X
0-7432-5739-1 (Pbk)

Originally published in hardcover as *The Good Fat Cookbook*.

Contents

Part II: Recipes

GOOD FAT

Foreword

Fat remains one of the most feared words in our vocabulary. For the past twenty-five years, Americans have been told that fat should be avoided at all costs. The U.S. government has spent billions of dollars reinforcing that message, and Americans have embraced the concept. The trouble is that we are now eating less fat than at any time in our history, and in the process we have become the fattest people on the face of the earth. What went wrong?

It turns out that fat was never the dietary villain it was made out to be. In fact, the right types of fat will lead to a longer and healthier life. Fats are simply far more complex than we ever anticipated. There are good fats and bad fats that not only impact weight loss and weight gain, but more importantly help control the expression of your genes. This makes fat one of the most powerful "drugs" you will ever consume. It is the complexity of fats that has made them so difficult to grasp by the medical establishment and the U.S. government, who see them only as the cause of our obesity epidemic. Their response has been to remove as much fat as possible from the diet and replace it with fat-free carbohydrates. Such shortsighted thinking has been the underlying cause of our epidemic rise of obesity that currently threatens the future of health care in America.

So if the best scientists in the world are still confused about fat, how is the average reader able to make intelligent dietary decisions? This is where Fran does an excellent job to begin to explain both the complexity and necessity of fats to the general public. In the first part of the book, many of the mythologies surrounding fats are rapidly put to rest. At the same time, the most recent cutting-edge research on fat nutrition is made easy to understand. In the second part of the book, she also demonstrates with a number of excellent recipes what the French have known for centuries: fat makes food taste better. However, just eating more good fat is not the answer to our health care crisis. Consumption of good fats still needs to be done within a framework that balances protein and carbohydrate as best you can at every meal.

After reading this book, you will be both illuminated and angry. You will be illuminated because you know more about the importance of good fat. You will be angry because you have been lied to for the past twenty-five years, causing both your health and the quality of food you have eaten to suffer needlessly. Take that anger and channel it into making great meals with good fats.

—Dr. Barry Sears

Introduction

You might think that after two million years on this earth, humans would have figured out what to eat. But that seems not to be the case at all, at least in North America, where a debate rages: Fat is good or bad? Carbs are good or bad? More protein or less protein? What should we really eat? And can we have some more french fries while we think about it?

In other parts of the world, such issues usually don't even come up—especially in Japan and France, the two healthiest populations in the world, and good places to find a great meal, which is certainly not the case in America. As we big fat Americans wander through our malls, loading up on junk food whose best claim to taste is actually texture (either crispiness or creaminess), we seem to have lost touch with real food altogether, as well as with our health. To us, health is a huge mystery. If we're good enough, vigilant enough, about what we eat, and vigorous enough about exercise and denying ourselves pleasures like smoking, surely we get to be at the top end of the actuarial statistics. If someone would just figure out once and for all what it is we're supposed to be eating, we'll do it. Just stop giving us contrary advice.

I'm not at all exempt from the whims of dietary wisdom that evolved over the last part of the twentieth century. As a young child, I lived for two and a half years on a tiny remote island in the South Pacific where we had no fresh eggs or milk; instead we had powdered milk (oxidized fat!) or Cocomalt, a canned chocolate milk, and hideous powdered eggs with greenish yolks. I subsisted on SPAM, bananas, and white bread, mayonnaise, and peanut butter sandwiches, sometimes with bologna or liverwurst, washed down with plenty of Coke from the Marine Corps base where my father was stationed. I emerged from this experience ravenous for good food, which I quickly found on my mother's family farm in Iowa, where they still churned their own butter. My mother became an Adele Davis diet devotee when I was in the fifth grade, and although I didn't touch the steamed brains and prayed for the return of lemon meringue pie, being on some weird diet seemed perfectly normal to me.

Once I was an adult, I seemed born to diet. Although I escaped the macrobiotic diet and having my stomach stapled, I've done almost everything else a conscientious dieter might do: I've taken amphetamines to dull my appetite, and I've eaten according to Weight Watchers (a constant struggle), Dr. Atkins (a big success for a while), the Carbohydrate Addict's Diet (that one hour of carbs every day was a huge pleasure but it also piled on the pounds), the liquid diet (fine until my hair fell out), low-fat (I felt constantly bloated, and gained a few pounds), and, finally, my big breakthrough, the Protein Power diet, on which I lost many many pounds (and gained and relost them several times over the same way).

I have a family history of obesity, cardiovascular disease, high blood pressure, and blood clots, so I need to be especially careful about carbs, which shoot up your insulin levels to create not only new fat on your bones but serious problems in your blood vessels. However, I know that low-carb isn't for everyone, and I have a lot of respect for metabolic differences—in fact, there's a fascinating book on this subject, *Biochemical Individuality* by Roger J. Williams (Keats, 1956). Although we're not all metabolically the same, most of the recipes in this book are low-carb because most of us do have problems with insulin, and low-carb eating is the only way to fix that. As a dedicated low-carb eater, I've written two books on the subject, *The Low-Carb Cookbook* (Hyperion, 1997) and *Living Low-Carb* (Little, Brown, 2000).

If you eat low-carb, of course, you end up eating more fat, so the subject is never far from my dinner plate. Through the low-fat era, I've worried like everyone else has about the ultimate health consequences of eating more fat—yet my blood fats are exemplary, much better than they were when I started a low-carb regime. When the idea for this book was born, I was elated, because I wanted to know for myself what the real story is on fats. Frankly, I've been dumb-founded by what I found.

I thought I was a pretty sophisticated fats consumer. I knew that coconut had been the victim of a smear attack—and, in fact, I'd presented that scenario to a group of nutritionists and food writers at a conference in the early Nineties, to blank stares—but I had no idea that coconut is perhaps the best fat of all, the only low-fat fat, and, as well, one that our bodies burn instead of storing and that offers huge immune system benefits. I knew I didn't like the polyunsaturated vegetable oils, such as canola, because they have strange textures and don't taste good, but I hadn't entirely absorbed their devastating effects on our health. Even now, the idea that our good coconut oil has been banished and replaced with these terrible oils—by our government, in the name of our good health—still shocks me.

I was lucky in the Nineties to go to a series of conferences spon-sored by Oldways Preservation and Exchange Trust, a group dedi-cated to the health benefits of traditional foodways. There I first encountered Dr. Walter Willett of Harvard, who made the good fats/bad fats distinction clearly and backed it up with fourteen years of research from the famous Nurses' Health Study. There, also, was Serge Reynaud, explaining the "French Paradox," which extols the health virtues of wine and natural fats. I was an early convert to the Mediterranean diet, and, as a book editor, commissioned the first two books on the subject. I knew all about the wonders of olive oil, which had become my major fat source in the late 1980s.

Still, I was amazed at what I learned in the course of writing this book. I knew fish oil is good and I'd been taking pharmaceutical-grade fish oil for a few months, but until I read Barry Sears's *The Omega Rx Zone* and met some of the researchers doing work on omega-3 fats, I had no idea how central they are to our health. I knew that hydrogenated oils are not good, and that olive oil is very good, but I didn't know the extent of free-radical damage caused by oils like canola and soy and safflower or the cancer-promoting effects of their linoleic acid content. Nor did I fully appreciate the role of antioxidants in controlling those cascades of damaged cells set off by oxidative stress. And, of course, I had no clue to the ways we're programmed to think the opposite of what's true scientifically, by our government (whose health watchdogs take no Hippocratic oath), lobbyists, marketing forces, advertising, and media health celebrities.

Perhaps the biggest surprise was the extent to which whole foods are not in fact whole any longer—even some of the ones you find in the health food store. Tuna can be augmented with something called food glue; butter can have "cream flavoring." Even low-fat milk counts as a processed food these days, with its artificially created tiny globules of fat and its additives of oxidized powdered milk and food coloring.

The fact is, we've been sold a bill of goods about fat. Not only is fat not terrible, but it is the single most important positive influence on our health—if we learn to choose our fats well and support them with good antioxidants from fresh fruits and vegetables. Everything from our brains to our hearts to our potential for developing cancer depends on our fat consumption. This is as true for infants and the elderly as it is for the rest of us, and there's now strong data to support this conclusion.

We're poised at a real turning point in our national consciousness about food and health. Now that we know fat is at the heart of human health and not the destroyer of it, we're in a position to demand good food and good health. The good fats/bad fats issue is complicated, and what I've presented here is an effort to simplify the results of my own research and opinions on the subject. I'm not a science professional, I'm just a cook and an enthusiastic eater who's very aware of the connections between food and health. I approach these issues fork first, and I bring you what seems to me the state of the art at the moment in a form you can use in your everyday life, in the kitchen.

I know the science will change and we'll gradually come to understand a lot of what is presently mysterious about human health and nutrition—which is almost everything. We just don't know very much yet.

That, of course, never stops us from making pronouncements, the most egregious example being our government's thirty-year-long infatuation with the low-fat myth. In those thirty years, we've seen a whole generation raised on low-fat (starting with two-year-olds), not to mention a generation of infants raised on soy milk formulas rather than the highly health-promoting coconut oil that was originally used. The obvious consequences seem clear enough: increased obesity, diabetes, and ADD. Decreased immune function is almost inevitable, as is failure to make good bones and an epidemic of infertility. More subtle problems have yet to emerge, but surely they're there. This scenario is absolutely enraging.

But all is not lost. Your cells are constantly regenerating, and they quickly respond to getting what they need. Barry Sears points out that with good amounts of omega-3 fat, thirty days is all it takes to see dramatic results, verifiable in blood tests. It may take up to two years to lose all the omega-6 fat stored in our body fat (which can be as much as seven pounds), says Bill Lands, a senior researcher with the National Institutes of Health. He points out that these bad fats are lurking in the meantime, waiting to take over if your dietary intake of omega-3 diminishes—another reason it's very important to get your omega-3s from fish or seafood sources every day. Dr. Mary Enig estimates that a year or two is what you'll need to lose your stored trans fats once you stop consuming lots of them. But two years is a relatively short time to change your health status completely, especially if you can eat a lot of great food in the meantime. And that's the deal: good food is actually good for you, as any of our ancestors could have told us.

PART I

CHAPTER ONE

~

The Truth About Fats

What right has the federal government to propose that the American people conduct a vast nutritional experiment, with themselves as subjects, on the strength of so very little evidence that it will do them any good?
—*Phil Handler, President of the National Academy of Sciences, testifying about the low-fat dietary guidelines before Congress in 1980*

To begin, let's consider some basic nutritionally correct "facts," the ones we know so well we could repeat them in our sleep:

- Fat makes you fat.
- A big juicy steak is like a heart attack on a plate.
- Canola oil is the healthiest cooking oil.
- Coconut is a deadly fat that promotes heart disease.
- Eat less fat, and you'll live longer.
- Bacon and eggs is an artery-clogging, killer breakfast.
- The most important thing you can do for your health is to keep your cholesterol level as low as possible.

Actually, none of these widely accepted "truths" is true. Not only are they false, but making food choices based on them will lead to some dire health consequences, despite what the U.S. government prescribes. In fact, almost everything you think you know about fat isn't true, unless you're an especially astute reader of cutting-edge science on the subject. Or unless you happened to read Gary Taubes's

New York Times Magazine cover story on fat that questioned the conventional wisdom on the subject (July 7, 2002). What most of us have believed to be true—and that includes doctors and other health professionals—about fats and health is actually the result of a complex synergy of food industry lobbying, medical celebrity self-promotion, governmental intervention based on no sound science, advertising, a hyperactive health police with media visibility, and our own eager Puritanical desires to deprive ourselves in order to purge our sins of excess and earn the salvation of a healthy old age.

Now that we've had thirty years of margarine, fat-free milk, cheese-free cheese, inedible lean pork, Egg Beaters, dreadful dry chicken breasts, SnackWell's, and approximately fifteen thousand other new low-fat products (high-ticket items that are actually cheaper to produce than "real food" and have a longer shelf life), we should be much healthier. The president of the American Heart Association predicted in 1984 that if everyone ate low-fat, we'd eradicate atherosclerosis, the clogged-artery disease that leads to heart attacks and strokes, by the year 2000. Actually, we were moderately compliant; we did reduce our fat consumption from more than 40 percent of our total diet to 34 percent. Yet only the food industry has gotten healthier.

The incidence of heart disease has not declined, and obesity and diabetes have skyrocketed. We jettisoned our beloved eggs, bacon, cream, cheese, and red meat, and yet we haven't thrived. That's partly because, as we now know, or some of us have noted, dietary cholesterol affects blood cholesterol only by a factor of about 10 percent at most, and blood serum cholesterol is a very different thing from cholesterol laid down in the body's tissues.

High cholesterol levels themselves have come into question as a sure sign of impending cardiovascular disease. In 1991, an American College of Physicians analysis of nineteen cholesterol studies from around the world revealed that for women, the higher the cholesterol, the longer the life. Recent research has shown that high triglyceride levels (over 100), combined with low HDL—the "good" cholesterol—levels (under 35) are much more predictive of heart disease, even if the "bad" LDL cholesterol level is low. (One way to pile on more of those bad triglycerides, as Surgeon General Koop has noted, is to eat a low-fat, high-carb diet.) It's possible to simultaneously lower blood cholesterol and increase the plaque that cholesterol lays down in the arteries—that can be done by consuming polyunsaturated oils, the very ones we've been urged to use for our health's sake. Only one kind of cholesterol actually clogs arteries, and that's oxidized cholesterol. Oxidation is a process a bit like rust. When you expose a cut avocado to the air, it quickly darkens: that's oxidation. You can stop this process quickly by applying an antioxidant—lemon or lime juice in the case of the avocado, just as in the body you can stop the free-radical damage of oxidation by consuming enough antioxidants to disable them. Oxidation has a huge amount to do with your state of wellness, and I'll be discussing it in great detail later.

Why *didn't* eating less fat make us healthier? In his widely ignored first article on the subject, "The Soft Science of Dietary Fat," published in the prestigious journal *Science* (March 30, 2001), Gary Taubes explains that the science proving a connection between dietary fat and heart disease simply was never there in the first place. Hundreds of millions of dollars of research later, there's no proof whatsoever that eating low-fat will improve your health in any way at all. A study commissioned by the Surgeon General's office showed that a woman who died at the age of sixty-five and who had eaten a very low-fat instead of a regular diet all her life might possibly live as much as an extra two weeks—though other studies suggest the number may be more like three days. It's hard to imagine that anyone who likes good food would jump for that devil's bargain: give up a lifetime of delicious food for two more weeks in your mid-sixties! On the contrary, the fourteen-year-long Harvard School of Public Health Nurses' Health Study and its two sequel studies indicate that total fat consumption has *no* correlation with heart disease risk and that saturated fats are little worse, if at all, than the carbohydrates the government's Food Guide Pyramid recommends as the basis of our "healthy" diet (and fat doesn't prompt the addictive response carbs do). And in the Nurses' Health Study, women who ate low-fat had the highest risk for breast cancer.

The Nurses' Health Studies were supported (at a cost of more than $100 million) by the National Institutes of Health, and yet no new dietary guidelines and no new food pyramid have emerged as a result of their findings (for one, that monounsaturated fats like olive oil reduce the risk of heart disease). It is, as Dr. Walter Willett of Harvard, the spokesperson for the studies, says, "scandalous." Perhaps equally scandalous is the fact that Taubes's piece never registered at all in the media, though it was mirrored by a similar investigative piece in the prestigious British journal *Nature* later that year that came to the same conclusions—also completely ignored.

Although some separate elements of the low-fat theory are true (for instance, saturated fats of animal origin do have an elevating effect on blood cholesterol) the overall indictment of fat in general was never more than a theory based on connecting dots and claiming cause and effect—a phenomenon that cholesterol researcher Utte Ravenskov calls false correlation. A benign explanation is that this theory is the result of a very human trait that's almost impossible to overcome. Dr. Dorothy Dinnerstein conducted gestalt laboratory studies at Rutgers University in the 1980s. Over and over again, subjects shown random elements on a field and asked what they saw inevitably connected them into a pattern and often assigned it a meaning as well. The chaos of unrelated elements seems too overwhelming to handle, so we mentally rearrange them. When powerful forces such as industry, the population's urgent wishes, and politics collide on such subjects—the studies on synthetic hormones are a good example—a momentum is established that overwhelms any objections about lack of scientific proof until the proof is undeniable. In the case of the antifat prescription, the motive was a bit dark; although the participants knew, says Dr. Willett, that there were good fats and bad fats, they thought the population wasn't capable of making such distinctions and would be much better served by a more simplistic message, even if it wasn't true—as, indeed, it is not.

In the case of dietary fat, politicians and health officials eager to "do something" about our national health simply plunged ahead and made recommendations, connecting the isolated dots on their own authority with no scientific backup, even though some scientists warned them at the time that this was dangerous. Pete Ahrens at Rockefeller University testified to Congress that everyone responds differently to low-fat diets, so it's a crapshoot (his words were "a betting matter") who may benefit and who might be harmed. But the momentum was already established and the word went forth that fat was bad, very, very bad. Since this new paradigm was hugely to the benefit of agribusiness, relentless marketing did the rest. Spokespeople for various institutions, the ones you always see on television scolding the population for its unhealthy diet, backed up the message, doctors and nutritionists fell right in step, and millions of dollars' worth of advertising did not go for naught. We were hooked.

That's the benign story. To see the nexus of scientists, politicians, and food manufacturers working together to vilify natural fats and convince us that fake fats are healthy—despite plenty of resistance from people like Dr. Paul Dudley White, the famous cardiologist—read "The Oiling of America," by Dr. Mary Enig and Sally Fallon (www.westonaprice.org/know_your_fats/oiling.html). I guarantee a rise in blood pressure. (This article also explains how we got "imitation" foods approved by the FDA that don't require that word on the label.)

The sad-but-true fact is that there are no simple answers—such as, cut saturated fat and you won't have any heart attacks—because no one really knows what causes heart disease. There are at least a dozen credible theories, citing, among them, high homocysteine levels, high insulin levels, excess fibrin, inadequate thyroid levels, low magnesium, inflammation, copper deficiency and iron overload in the tissues. A low-fat diet is suspect for many researchers, as are trans fats (fats gone bad, altered by hydrogen bombardment or high heat and chemical processing). All or some of the theories may work together, or one of them may turn out to be the answer, or the culprit may be something else altogether—we just don't know yet. We do know, however, that eating low-fat resolves *no* health problems, so there's no credible reason to continue doing it—and plenty of reasons not to.

Still, the low-fat dogma seems to have seeped into our very bones and become an article of faith impervious to reason. One simple explanation is that a number of famous careers have been made on low-fat and the investment of these media stars in the perpetuation of low-fat religion is huge. They include fat-phobe Dr. Michael Jacobson of the Center for Science in the Public Interest, who refers to fat in general as "a greasy killer." At least Jacobson, who was a major instigator of the tidal wave of dangerous trans fats (especially those used in fast-food frying) in American food, has had the

A Fats Time Line

Here are some landmarks in our love/hate relationship with fat.

15th- and 16th-century health advice: Fat is very good. The egg is the
  only perfect food.

1825: Jean-Anthelme Brillat-Savarin, author of *The Physiology of
  Taste,* declares in an essay on obesity, "It is only because of
  grains and starches that fatty congestion can occur, as much in
  a man as in the animals. . . ."

1862: William Banting, an obese London undertaker, tries every diet of
  the day and finally is prescribed the lean meat diet (for an ear
  problem), on which he loses a pound a week. His book about the
  diet, *Letter on Corpulence,* becomes a best-seller on both sides of
  the Atlantic. Dieting is called "banting" for decades afterward.

1869: Margarine is invented, in France (!), for the poor, who can't
  afford butter.

1875: Americans are eating thirty pounds of butter per year.

1877: Breakfast cereal is first trademarked in America and begins to
  replace bacon and eggs.

1910: Hydrogenated fats are introduced.

1911: Crisco is born.

1929: George and Mildred Burr, a husband-and-wife research duo,
  discover the essential fats.

1929–1930: Vilhjamur Stefansson, a famous Arctic explorer, is deter-
  mined to document the amazing health of the meat-and-fat-
  eating Eskimos he observed in his expeditions. With a fellow
  explorer, he goes on a voluntary one-year meat-and-fat diet,
  hospitalized and supervised at Bellevue Hospital in New York
  City. They emerge in perfect health, even fitter and with better
  cholesterol blood values.

1953: Dr. A. W. Pennington publishes an article in the *New England
  Journal of Medicine* about his success in treating hefty executives of the DuPont Company with an all-meat diet, supple-

mented by just a few carbohydrates that produced low pyruvic acid in the body.

1955: President Eisenhower has a heart attack; heart disease is thought (erroneously) to be epidemic in America.

1963: Jean Nidetch founds Weight Watchers. Idea is zero fat will make you lose lots of weight.

1972: Dr. Dean Ornish publishes his landmark study of successfully treating heart patients with a very-low-fat vegetarian diet, meditation, and exercise.

1972: *Dr. Atkins' Diet Revolution* is published. Idea is lots of fat and zero carbs will make you lose lots of weight.

1973: The American Medical Association attacks the Atkins diet.

1976: The Pritikin Longevity Center opens. It advocates as little fat as possible, and also cuts out white sugar and flour.

1976: Psychologist David Reuben first intones the mantra heard 'round the world in his book *The Save Your Life Diet:* "Fat Makes You Fat."

1977: With Chairman George McGovern (a Pritikin dropout) at the helm, the Select Committee on Nutrition and Human Needs, which was designed to eliminate malnutrition, takes on over-nutrition. Its dietary report recommends less than 30 percent total fat, less than 10 percent saturated fat. Some scientists object that there is no hard science behind the recommendations, but they are ignored.

1979: Westchester cardiologist Dr. Herman Tarnower publishes *The Complete Scarsdale Medical Diet,* a low-carb approach to weight loss he recommends for his heart patients.

1982: The National Academy of Sciences issues a report on nutrition and cancer, proposing that dietary fat causes cancer.

1984: The National Institutes of Health (NIH) advises all Americans to reduce fat intake. A *Time* magazine cover story announces the end of bacon and eggs in America, because dietary fat is killing Americans—though no data support this conclusion. The Surgeon General's office publishes a "Report on Nutrition and Health," which concludes that fat is the single unhealthiest element in the American diet.

1985: NIH launches the National Cholesterol Education Program, for everyone over two years old.

1985: The National Research Council's Committee on Diet and Health announces that the nation's diet is 89 percent fat and carbohydrate—46 percent carbohydrate, 43 percent fat.

1986: The American Soybean Association sends out "fat fighter kits" to soy farmers, urging them to write their congressmen about the dangers of tropical fats in the American food supply.

1988: A furor over coconut and palm oil is launched. Millionaire heart patient Phil Sokoloff takes out full-page ads all across the country urging his government to protect him against dangerous cookies and crackers. The American Soybean Association, together with the fat-phobic Center for Science in the Public Interest, secures congressional hearings on the subject of the dangers of tropical oils. Dr. George Blackburn of Harvard testifies that there's nothing wrong with tropical oils; Surgeon General Koop calls the whole business "foolishness," but the tropical oils lose. They are banished from the food supply and replaced by soy oil, which is approximately 50 percent dangerous trans fat. This leads to the replacement of healthy coconut oil with soy oil in infant formulas.

1992: The USDA issues the Food Guide Pyramid, which states that fats, oils, and sweets are to be used sparingly because they "provide calories and little else nutritionally." Essential fatty acids are not even mentioned. Idea is to eat more grains (the USDA's real job is to promote American agriculture, after all).

1993: Dr. Dean Ornish publishes *Eat More, Weigh Less*. Idea is that you can eat all you want of anything but fat, and you'll lose weight.

1995: Bacon sales begin to turn around after their disastrous slide in the Eighties.

1996: A Food Marketing Institute and *Prevention* magazine survey finds that 72 percent of those polled make decisions about which foods to buy based solely on the fat content listed on the FDA label; only 9 percent think about the calories.

1997: In a very extensive study of all available information, the World Cancer Research Fund and the American Institute for Cancer Research find no probable reason to believe dietary fat causes cancer.

1999: The four-year Lyon Diet Heart Study shows that for heart patients, the Mediterranean diet results in only one-third as many new heart attacks as the American Heart Association diet (basically the USDA pyramid), and no sudden deaths. Cholesterol levels in both groups are the same. The medical community is flabbergasted.

2001–2002: Gary Taubes writes two myth-exploding articles about the science of dietary fat, explaining that there was no hard science to begin with on which to make wholesale recommendations of low-fat for the entire population. The first article, in the highly respected journal *Science,* is ignored. The second, in the *New York Times Magazine,* which suggests the possibility that Dr. Atkins is right, creates a furor.

2002: The Institute of Medicine reports to the FDA that *no* level of trans fats in the diet is safe, prompting the FDA to mandate trans fat counts on food labels.

Since 1977, Americans have dropped their fat consumption by 17 percent. The obesity rate has increased by 25 percent.

Americans now eat 5 pounds of butter, 11 to 12 pounds of margarine, per person a year.

Since 1925, trans-fat consumption has risen 2,500 percent.

We still eat the same amount of food we ate in 1900, but we eat 127 percent more sweeteners, mainly high-fructose corn syrup, which increases triglycerides and glycation—a major factor in aging and related problems.

2003: Denmark bans virtually all trans fats in processed foods.

The FDA mandates trans-fat labeling in the United States by January 2006.

courage to reverse himself a bit and lobby the FDA for trans-fat labeling. As a result of the imposition of "healthy" fats on fast food, trans fats—the dangerous ones—climbed from 2.4 grams in a typical fast-food meal to 19.2 grams in 1992—not too much in the public interest. *New York Times* columnist Jane Brody has taken on low-fat as a personal crusade, though even she has recently introduced avocados and nuts into her diet and will no doubt write more favorably about fats as the pendulum swings back. Other high-visibility low-fat talking heads include Dr. Kenneth Cooper, Dr. Dean Ornish, and Dr. John Macdougall.

Another reason we haven't heard the truth about low-fat is that most researchers themselves have vested interests in the outcome of their work; usually they know what the results will be before they even get the grant, and there are very few completely openminded people in the health world who are willing to be proved wrong. One brilliant exception is Dr. Mary Enig, a former lipid researcher at the University of Maryland, perhaps the leading fats authority in the country, who has courageously insisted that the data don't support the low-fat assumptions and, worse, that the low-fat diet has had severe consequences for our health because it's deprived us of healthy natural fats and replaced them with dangerous trans fats. Researchers talk about these issues among themselves, and sometimes even publish books about them, but the message isn't heard over the din of the mainstream message.

The emperor has no clothes—but pick up any mainstream newspaper or magazine and you'll read endless articles about the necessity of cutting fat, new strategies for squeezing more fat out of our diets, and admonitions to shape up our fat consumption, or die young. Meanwhile, the population gets fatter and fatter, there's an epidemic of childhood obesity and diabetes, and we all continue to deprive ourselves of delicious food in the hope that we're saving our lives.

One result of our obsession with fat as the major health villain has been a cornucopia of reduced-fat, highly processed food that gives us a huge dose of trans fats, the damaged fats that become, in effect, poisonous, toxic to the cell membranes they're attached to. Studies have shown them to be key factors in heart disease (because among other things they raise LDL—the bad cholesterol—and lower HDL—the good). They also inhibit insulin from binding to the cells, which creates blood sugar problems that lead to diabetes and obesity. About 90 percent of the American food dollar is now spent on processed food, virtually all of it contaminated with trans fats (look for the words "partially hydrogenated" or "hydrogenated," which appear on the labels of everything from peanut butter to cookies and crackers). In 2006 trans fats will have their own line on food labels. In the meantime, there's a list of trans fat–free foods on my website, www.franmccullough.com.

A huge source of dietary trouble is the so-called "healthy" oils that have replaced the good natural saturated fats. That's because these vegetable and seed oil sources of polyunsaturated fats—such as soy oil, corn oil, and canola—are not only full of omega-6, they're very fragile and easily break down if they're not highly processed (and, if they are, they've acquired some trans fats and have lost most of their nutrients). When cold-pressed oils (which have no trans) start to break down (usually in the bottle before they even get to the store), they develop, through oxidative damage, some alarming components called free radicals. These are the body's terrorists, ranging around at will and damaging the chemical structure of cells to produce vascular problems, a vulnerability to cancer, and general havoc. These little monsters are molecules that have lost an electron and are scrambling around to steal one from a molecule on a healthy cell, which then turns into a free radical itself. Free radicals can multiply exponentially this way, and they're capable of altering a healthy cell's DNA, or even killing it. Tobacco smoke and pollutants are major sources of free radicals (breathing itself is a minor source), but the trans fats in food—and especially rancid fats, which we unknowingly consume all the time—can be even more dangerous, both in their own bad effects and in generating free radicals. Trans fats are formed in manufacturing (not at home) when an oil hits 320 degrees in the presence of a catalyst, and most processing takes place at much higher heat levels, 400 to 500 degrees. But oils can also be cold-pressed or expeller-pressed, which means the heat generated is only about 180 degrees. The high-heat processing preserves the oils and keeps them from going rancid while removing most of their natural nutrients; cold-pressing preserves the nutrients but keeps the oil in an extremely fragile state, in which it can easily turn rancid and develop free radicals. These oils may or may not be deodorized.

When McDonald's responded to pressure from the Center for Science in the Public Interest (a name born of marketing genius), among other groups, to dump the very tasty beef tallow they originally used in making french fries (because it was "dangerous" saturated fat), in 1990 they substituted a highly processed fat, trading a neutral natural fat that was relatively resistant to oxidation for a

---

A Little Fat Chat

You don't absolutely have to know all this, but in case you're wondering how it all works together, here's the scoop. One confusing element (among many) is that all fats are mixtures of types; there's no such thing as a completely unsaturated fat (mostly vegetable fats) or a completely saturated one (mostly animal fats)—it's all a question of the ratio. Bacon, for instance, seems like the quintessential saturated fat, but it's not; it's got plenty of the same good monounsaturated fat olive oil contains.

- Saturated fats. There are animal saturated fats—beef, pork, eggs, milk—and vegetable ones—coconut and palm. What they're saturated with is hydrogen atoms, which make them solid at room temperature and very stable. They don't oxidize (think of rust, but in this case the end result would be rancidity) easily, as unsaturated fats do. These are the fats that have been falsely demonized for thirty years, the ones our American ancestors were raised on (albeit in a purer form than what we now consume).
- Unsaturated fats. Unsaturated fats are missing those hydrogen atoms, so they're liquid at room temperature and they're also extremely fragile, vulnerable to light, heat, and oxygen. These include the seed and vegetable oils as well as olive oil (a

toxic one. Almost none of the beef tallow was absorbed by the fries (because saturated oils aren't absorbed), but a huge amount of the bad oil, up to 50 percent, is absorbed. As with all other polyunsaturated fats, soy and canola oil contain linoleic acid, which is known to promote cancer and heart disease, as well as high levels of trans fats if they're hydrogenated, as they usually are. The latest fat at McDonald's, corn plus soy, will increase the amount of fat in the food itself by up to 50 percent over saturated fat—which in any case

fruit oil) and fish. There are monounsaturated fats, such as olive oil, which are called omega-9 fats and generally considered to be very healthful, and polyunsaturated fats, which can be good or not, depending on their processing. Among the polys are the essential fats, the ones we must have in our diets, omega-6 and small amounts of omega-3, perhaps the most valuable fat of all.

- Trans fats. Unsaturated fats can be turned into what resembles a saturated fat—solid at room temperature and stable—by a process called hydrogenation, in which the fat is heated to a high temperature, treated with a nickel catalyst, and bombarded with hydrogen. But these are not natural fats and the body has difficulty with them. Trans fats are in margarine, vegetable shortening, all commercial baked goods, and virtually all processed foods. Cancer cells and bacteria also produce trans fats. Just to confuse you further, there's also a very good natural trans fat called conjugated linoleic acid (CLA), which is in milk and meat.

- Fatty acids. What's a fatty acid, then? These are parts of fats. Each fat cell has some glycerol (glycerin) and from one to three fatty acids hanging onto it in the three different forms mentioned above. Fatty acids—there are more than thirty major ones—have names like oleic, linoleic, and nervonic, but they all fall into those three categories, depending on the degree of saturation (which is to say, how much hydrogen they contain). Confused yet?

protects against trans fat. Is this in the public interest? The same thing has happened to the popcorn at the movie theater: no more butter or coconut oil, both quite healthy natural fats; instead we have a chemical soup of nasty-tasting denatured fats. Processed foods also contain a lot of sugar, especially high-fructose corn syrup, which increases triglycerides (a serious marker for heart disease), as well as small amounts of antibiotics we don't need.

But there's an even more scandalous story. In the late 1980s, the soy industry orchestrated a highly successful scare campaign to eliminate tropical fats (coconut and palm oil) from American food products (and replace them with soy, which now dominates 80 percent of the market) on the grounds that they're "dangerous" saturated fats. The panic they created was so successful that it actually provoked a congressional hearing on the subject. Despite testimony from Harvard's Dr. George Blackburn that there was no evidence whatsoever that tropical oils were dangerous, and Surgeon General Koop's comment—"foolishness"—these hearings sealed the fate of tropical oils. Coconut and palm oils had replaced lard as the fat of choice in commercial baked products because they provided a stable tasty fat with crisping and flaking qualities almost as good as lard's. (The original Oreos were made with lard, which was responsible for their characteristic snap.) As lard went the way of all saturated fats, so did coconut and palm oil, the vegetable saturated fats—which happened to be a three-billion-dollar industry based on healthy fats with no known negative effects. Irony of ironies, coconut fat turns out to be perhaps the healthiest fat in the world. Although it is indeed a saturated fat, like animal fat, it contains a remarkable protective fat called lauric acid, found otherwise only in mother's milk (and in small amounts in butter). It's also known as the low-fat fat, and it has fewer calories (about 2.9 per gram fewer) than all other fats. (See page 57 for the amazing story of what's good about coconut.)

What happened to coconut is not unlike what happened to snake oil about a hundred years earlier. Fats researcher Udo Erasmus (*Fats That Heal, Fats That Kill*) tells a wonderful story about a California doctor, Dr. Richard Kunin, who on a whim decided to see if he could find any snake oil for sale in San Francisco's Chinatown. No problem. When he took it to a lab to be analyzed, he made an amazing discovery: the snake oil really did contain the oil of the Chinese water snake, which has a very high omega-3 content (anti-inflammatory), as well as some other beneficial elements, such as camphor. When the Chinese railroad gangs were building our national rail system, they used snake oil for their aches and pains, and shared it with their Caucasian fellow workers. There was so much excitement about the efficacy of snake oil that word spread quickly, and the patent medicine manufacturers equally quickly started a smear campaign that was so successful, the very idea of using snake oil became laughable.

What we have deprived ourselves of—the delicious, satisfying good fats of traditional diets all around the world—are also startlingly health-protective and offer many other desirable benefits, such as good skin, great hair, a good sex life, fertility, a vital immune system, enough vitamin E for your heart, optimum hormone production, and antiaging properties. Your hormones, which control every cell in your body, don't work properly without adequate fat, and neither does your immune system. Every one of the 60 trillion cells in your body relies on fat—they're actually made mainly of fat—to keep its membranes flexible so that nutrients can enter and toxins can exit, and so it can communicate with the other cells in the body. Fat covers the cell's exterior; if you think of the cell as a house, it's fat that makes the membrane "walls" to separate the "rooms" of different cell functions. Fats, says David King of the Howard Hughes Medical Institute in Berkeley, are essential for cell integrity and survival: "membranes are as important as bones or blood."

According to Dr. Ron Rosedale of the Colorado Center for Metabolic Medicine, fat is the body's preferred fuel, not sugar (in all carbohydrates). He points out that when the body stores excess sugar, it's stored as fat, in a good usable form. Fats not only don't make you fat (unless you eat them to huge excess—and even then, only if you also ingest enough sugars and starches to stimulate your fat-storage system), they're good weapons against obesity.

As the low-fat publicity machine grinds on and on, the actual science of fats has revealed some remarkable new information that should radically change the way we eat, turning the low-fat nonsense on its head. This book explores that research, which includes fatty-acid profiling, and highlights the good foods that give us our best shot at optimal health on the cellular level—the good fats enhanced by good protein sources and a cornucopia of fruits and vegetables jammed with antioxidants (to fight free-radical damage from bad fats) and phytochemicals (plant chemicals) to act as supernutrients. This prescription is for a whole new definition of wellness that affects every organ in our bodies, from our brains to our skin. It's based on health at its most basic: the cellular level.

Best of all, we can drop the food anxiety and once again take pleasure in eating our favorite whole foods (natural foods that are unprocessed and unrefined, in the state in which they grew), with the confidence that taste is a reliable standard for health. When it comes to fats, if it tastes good, it's good for you—or at least not bad for you. Traditional diets, such as the Mediterranean diet and the Asian Pacific diet, all contain excellent sources of the good fats. Only our new "healthy" SAD (Standard American Diet—sad indeed), recommended by the American Heart Association and other health groups, with its heavily processed and fake foods and overemphasis on sugar, is unhealthy. Canola oil (which actually comes from rapeseed—there's no such thing as a canola, nor does anyone eat rapeseed—that's been through selective breeding to remove most of its highly toxic erucic acid) started out as furniture polish, not food. Soy oil was unknown until the 1930s, when it was developed for paint and varnishes because it hardened so nicely on the surface. Linseed (flax) oil had a similar job. Both soy and canola oil, like margarine and "improved" margarines, not only don't taste very good, they're very highly processed fake foods and have lost whatever claim they originally had to healthful properties. There are cold-pressed versions of these fats, but they're so unstable that they're likely to be rancid. They still contain the malevolent omega-6 oil we need to curtail. And even rapeseed oil (canola) has a little very heart-toxic erucic acid—less than 1 percent as allowed by law, but why ingest any? Extra virgin olive oil, coconut oil, and good old butter are not only much tastier, they're also far better health-promoting choices.

Do you now have a license to go hog wild with fats, eating endless amounts of ice cream and homemade fries and other indulgences? No, because calories still count, and there are still a few caveats about the animal-source saturated fats. Saturated fats of animal origin tend to store more easily in the fat cells than other fats. They tend to stiffen blood vessels. And saturated fats and sugars are a particularly diabolical combination that leads to higher triglyceride levels, which we want to avoid at all costs. They also set off a process called glycation, in which sugars bond to proteins and cells lose their flexibility and age prematurely, giving us wrinkles and age spots and general sagginess. For occasional treats, though, these foods are fine, as long as the fats used are natural ones.

If, like me, you tend to gain weight easily and have a family history of cardiovascular problems, you probably have a metabolic disorder called insulin resistance, or Syndrome X, which causes your body to overproduce insulin, the fat-storage hormone. At least 25 percent of the population is estimated to be in this category, so you're not alone. Men who eat high-carb diets shift their cholesterol profiles from normal to Syndrome X. If it goes unchecked, Syndrome X can lead to diabetes and cardiovascular problems. The most effective (indeed, the only) way to deal with Syndrome X is diet, a low-carb diet. (If you have Syndrome X, you need to read Burt Berkson, Jack Challem, and Melissa Diane Smith's book, *Syndrome X,* published by Wiley.) Because I eat that way myself, most of the recipes in this book are low-carb. But here again there's new research; Barry Sears, in *The Omega Rx Zone,* claims that eating enough omega-3 fat (an essential fat found in fish oil and some plants) will cancel out the carbohydrate in, say, a bagel—and there are many other benefits to be had from the omega-3 oil as well.

In this book, we'll explore the "lost" good fats, everything from butter to nuts and avocados and coconut, and show you why—and how—you should integrate them back into your everyday eating. We'll be focusing on whole foods, preferably organic (grown without pesticides), that taste great and offer great pleasure along with their health-promoting elements. And although you should avoid fried foods when you're eating out, even at fine restaurants, because reused oils break down and are full of free radicals and trans fats, you'll learn how to make great fried food at home that's both delicious and safe. Armed with the right information and a willingness to cook some simple, tasty recipes, you can take enormous pleasure at the table *and* know that you're eating very well in every sense of the word.

CHAPTER TWO

~

Rethinking Good Fats/Bad Fats

The fats and oils story may well be the biggest scandal
of ignorance, disinformation and greed in the entire history of food production.

—*John Finnegan,* Facts About Fats

Trying to make your way in the bewildering world of fats is a bit like
being Alice in Wonderland or in a rerun of *Sleeper,* Woody Allen's
futuristic film in which cheeseburgers are the health foods. Not only
is fatsland wildly confusing, with its PUFAS and MUFAS, its long-
chain and short-chain and medium-chain fats, and its double bonds,
it's also completely upside down. Because the food industry and its
lobbying partners have done such a good job of convincing the
media and those in our government responsible for public health
that its products are exemplary, we "know" that saturated fats—and
especially coconut—are evil and that polyunsaturated fats (like
vegetable oils such as canola, sunflower, soy, safflower, and corn oils)
are positively health-promoting. In fact, the exact opposite is true.
The best fat of all is coconut and the worst fat of all is probably soy.
How can that be?

If you think about it, it should come as no surprise that traditional
diets the world over are good for us—we wouldn't have gotten this
far in human progress if they weren't. Major changes in human diet,
however, have been few. They include the discovery of shellfish as
dinner for a group of emergent humans about a hundred and fifty
thousand years ago, a discovery that Barry Sears, in *The Omega Rx
Zone,* credits with the development of the human frontal cortex.

About ten thousand years ago, we discovered agriculture and grains, a new kind of food that for some of us still presents serious problems because we have trouble dealing with excess carbohydrate in our diets. Toward the end of the nineteenth century, we began to eat processed food, sugar, and refined flour. In the twentieth century, we dropped lard for fake fats such as shortening and margarine, discovered the joys of highly processed foods full of chemicals, signed on for fake sugar with huge enthusiasm, and, more recently, reviled fat in all its forms except for the polyunsaturated oils—the most dangerous ones. The flaxseed (a.k.a. linseed) and soy oils that had previously been used only in paints and varnishes because they hardened so ferociously somehow had become our health foods by the end of the twentieth century.

The hard fact is that we know precious little about human nutrition, but we do know that traditional diets the world over have managed to provide their populations with food that makes them flourish. Several excellent books have been written extolling the virtues of the Paleolithic diet, the one we evolved to eat during the time of our great leap forward into civilization. It's a diet of lean protein, greens, and occasional bits of fruit such as berries—no dairy products, no grains except some rare wild ones. And we know too that by and large the food we're eating in the early twenty-first century is *not* making us flourish. There are exceptions, of course: The Japanese and the French, who happen to be the most and the second most healthy people in the world. Both these groups eat quite a different menu from the standard American one, and both their diets are full of good fats (fatty fish and eggs for the Japanese, butter, cheese, duck fat, olive oil, and an occasional treat of foie gras for the French). Right behind these two exemplary groups of healthy populations are the Mediterraneans, whose famous diet, rich in monounsaturated fats such as olive oil, is especially tasty. None of these healthy populations requires a food pyramid like ours to tell them what to eat: they just eat what they've always eaten, with a little interference from American junk food, so relentlessly marketed all over the world. An especially interesting group is the Spanish, southern Mediterraneans who have added lots of meat to their diet recently as they've grown more affluent. The Spanish Paradox is that the more meat and fat they eat, the healthier their profile (researchers speculate it's the antioxidants—the large amount of fruits and vegetables they continue to eat—that are protective).

It seems that every geographical area supplies essential fats for its population in a natural, accessible form. Among the Greenland Eskimos, traditionally there were no reliable supplies of vegetables and fruits, but fatty fish and seaweed provided them a completely healthy diet, perhaps the healthiest of all. In the Pacific islands, there's fish and coconut—that miraculous substance. In Mexico, there are avocados and fish and lard. In Russia, caviar is a traditional miracle cure, prescribed for pregnant and nursing women and anyone whose health needs a boost. Even in the Ireland of the great famine, there were fish and seaweed and wild purslane for the taking.

Only in America, where we insist on having it all, do we have very little of these valuable foods, mainly because we've taken them out of our food supply in the misguided notion that our health will improve as a result. Infant formula, which used to be based on coconut oil (with its uncanny resemblance to mother's milk and easy digestibility) is now made primarily from soy oil, which, aside from containing undesirable omega-6 fat, is known to suppress thyroid function and bind minerals so they can't be absorbed. Possibly this one fact alone explains the epidemic of childhood obesity, ADD, and high cholesterol levels in young children, theorizes hormone expert Pat Puglio of the Broda Barnes Foundation. Soy oil is supposedly healthier because it's not a saturated fat (see page 154 for the soy story).

The fact is that *all* the good traditional natural fats are good for us, some of them—like coconut and avocado and nuts, and olives and olive oil, and fish—especially so. And all of them taste good. In fact, taste is a pretty good index of what's good for us. Who wouldn't choose butter over margarine, or olive oil over canola oil, or a good farmhouse Cheddar over processed American cheese?

Then what's a bad fat?

There are really only three groups of bad fats, and in some cases they overlap: the polyunsaturated vegetable oils, the hydrogenated oils, and the rancid oils. The highly processed vegetable oils made from soy, sunflowers, safflower (which is actually a dye), canola, or corn, and anything labeled "vegetable oil" are unhealthy. Yes, these are the very oils you've been told are best for your health. If you could obtain these oils in a natural way, some of them might be fine (though they all have too much linoleic acid, which in excess promotes cancer and heart disease), but because they're so unstable, it's almost impossible to keep them from turning rancid long before they reach the consumer, creating free radicals. So they have to be highly processed and refined at high heat (400 to 500 degrees), bleached, deodorized, and treated with chemical solvents like hexane, a dry-cleaning fluid. Most of the good qualities—the vitamins and other nutrients—are removed in the process and what remains is "pure" oil, with very little taste and some trans fat. Remember, trans fats are formed at 320 degrees in processing hydrogenated fats, so this high heat is deadly for these oils. Steam deodorizing can also create trans.

Free radicals, those little terrorists racing through the body looking to replace their missing electron with one from a healthy cell, which then in turn becomes a free radical itself, can do a huge amount of damage. The result can become a cascade of altered cells. Free radicals, a.k.a. oxidants, can not only kill healthy cells, they can also damage their DNA, the basic building block of cells. The one thing all cancer cells have in common is their damaged DNA. Free radicals are formed constantly from other sources as well, and the body deals with them, but they can multiply to a point called oxidative stress, beyond the body's ability to neutralize them, and that's when disease starts. To counter free radicals, it's important to consume as many antioxidants as possible (see page 141). The only antidote to trans fats in the body besides antioxidants, says Dr. Mary Enig, is, amazingly, cholesterol, the very element we're trying to banish from our lives in order to preserve our health.

Free radicals increase with consumption of these unhealthy oils and they also increase with age. They do some good work too—like neutralizing viruses and bacteria and controlling vascular tone—and they may even prove useful as chemotherapy delivery messengers, new research shows. But mainly they set off mischief, sometimes very serious mischief, and the only solution is to bring on the antioxidants, the plant nutrients that can stop oxidation in its tracks. The big antioxidant guns—vitamin E, vitamin C, alpha-lipoic acid, lycopene, beta carotene, and squalene from olive oil—make short work of free radicals, and they do it in a charming way: they simply donate one of their own electrons, which stops the hungry free radicals right in their tracks. And the antioxidants don't miss the electron at all. Except for alpha-lipoic acid, you can't make these antioxidants; they all need to come from diet. This war is going on constantly in our bodies, and it's crucial to get the balance right.

If we don't flourish on vegetable oils, it's not surprising that other animals don't do well on them either. For pigs, the mammals most like us in metabolic makeup and in many other ways as well, corn and soy oil are used as feed because they depress thyroid function, so the pigs will grow fatter. Cattle fed vegetable oils developed tumors, so they were taken off it and fed fat from fish and whole soybeans, not oil, instead.

Diseases and health conditions in which free radicals play a part, or even act as a trigger, include heart disease, cancer, stroke, diabetes, arthritis, chronic fatigue, MS, asthma, food allergies, fibrocystic breast disease, Parkinson's, Alzheimer's, kidney stones, gout, and depression, among others. Free radicals depress the immune system, killing off white blood cells. Over time, these molecules have devastating effects on the cells—it's not as if you eat some bad food one weekend and then you get sick. It takes a very long time, and it's cumulative. If this sounds a lot like aging, you're onto something; some researchers think it actually *is* the aging process these bad fats initiate, that aging is in effect a disease. Most of the oxidative damage we suffer, says Bruce Fife, N.D., comes from polyunsaturated oils in food *and* in our tissues. All of these oils, he says, are toxic, regardless of how they're refined (though that process accelerates their damage). It's because they're so unsaturated that they're so vulnerable to oxidation and free radical development. The only defense besides antioxidants our cells have against free radicals are: saturated fats. (There's Woody Allen again.)

The food industry and the health food police, those talking-head health experts with their extensive media exposure, have promoted polyunsaturated fats mercilessly, which is why all of us think they're so good for us. These fats do reduce cholesterol in the blood, but they have a disastrous downside: they increase it in the tissues, which is where it really matters. They are deposited in the vascular membranes, and because they're unstable, cholesterol has to come and pave them over to stabilize them. That's the way, current thinking goes, we get vascular blockage that can lead to a heart attack. But, in fact, only polyunsaturated fats oxidize cholesterol; saturated fat, from animal sources, won't oxidize that cholesterol, which is what makes it dangerous and likely to trigger cardiovascular incidents and strokes. The FDA has gone on record saying it's illegal to claim that polyunsaturated oils can prevent or treat disease. It knows that quite the opposite is true. And for strokes too, according to Dr. Mary Enig, polyunsaturated fats are initiators, while saturated fats are protective.

Although you can and should dump polyunsaturated oils in your kitchen, it's almost impossible to escape them in the outside world. They're in everything from mayonnaise to salad dressing to prepared piecrust (sometimes doubly dangerous because the free radicals are combined with hydrogenated fats, like shortening) and they're the oil (usually; sometimes it's hydrogenated oil as well, a double whammy) used to fry fast food—when they're reused again and again, breaking down their chemical structure further to make them even more dangerous. More irony: FDA tests show that potatoes fried in vegetable oils actually absorb twice as much fat as those fried in animal fat such as tasty lard or beef fat—and, of course, it's dangerous trans fat that's being doubled in each crisp little french fry. That's a good reason to avoid fried foods when eating out—making your own, however, can be healthy.

The second group of bad fats is trans fats. These have been chemically altered, by hydrogenation, to make them more solid and stable, not as fragile as they are in their natural state. Any food label that says "partially hydrogenated" or "hydrogenated" means that product contains trans fats. And we're consuming 2,500 percent more of them now than we did seventy-five years ago—a whopping statistic that applies to no other food, even sugar. Some researchers think this fact alone explains the huge increase in heart disease and cancer rates.

The process of hydrogenation takes an unstable unsaturated natural oil—soy, for example—and heats it to a high temperature, adds nickel as a catalyst, and pumps in some hydrogen. Voilà: you have an unnatural fat that's solid or nearly so at room temperature, one that behaves like a saturated fat and will keep a very long time. Vegetable shortening is hydrogenated, so virtually all baked goods contain trans fats. The most trans fats Dr. Mary Enig, a leading American lipid researcher, has found in extensive studies of the food supply turn up in sandwich cookies, vanilla wafers, animal crackers, and honey graham crackers—favorite treats for kids. Almost all frozen food includes partially hydrogenated fats (and a few antibiotics). Even peanut butter, unless it's completely natural, contains partially hydrogenated oils—though there's a little controversy here: Dr. Enig found trans fats in all peanut butter that contained partially hydrogenated fats, while the USDA found none.

Trans-fat counts on labeling will be adopted by 2006, but in the meantime you can use Dr. Mary Enig's method to deduce to some degree the amount of trans fat by simply subtracting the various elements of fat on the label from the total fat amount. The difference is mostly trans fat (unless there's a lot of monounsaturated fat such as olive oil or lard), plus a little glycerol. It's not a foolproof method, but if you see a lot of grams missing in the count, there's probably a lot of trans fat lurking in there. Because the hysteria about saturated fat continues, that's currently the prominent feature on labels and, unfortunately, it will be under that category that you'll find trans fats. This is a major disservice to saturated fats, which don't belong in the evil fats column. And here's a key point: saturated fats *do not* become trans fats, and they're very slow to oxidize; in the body, they have the opposite effect of trans fats and protect against them. Trans fats, on the other hand, are so solid they can't be broken down by body heat, unlike natural unsaturated fats.

Trans fats are implicated in cancer, heart disease, MS, diverticulitis, and diabetes, among other diseases. All vegetable oils contain trans fats, from 2 percent to about 15 percent (olive oil has only a tiny amount of trans fat). Even butter has a teeny, teeny bit, which comes from the rumen, the first of the multistomachs, of the cow. (There is a good trans fat, conjugated linoleic acid, which comes from milk fat, but more on that later.)

How bad is trans fat? Dr. Kathleen Koehler, an epidemiologist with the FDA, reported at an American Heart Association meeting in 2000 her estimate that removing all trans fat from margarine and just 3 percent of the trans fats in baked items would save more than five thousand lives a year and prevent seventeen thousand heart attacks.

To investigate the effects of trans fats before it approved labeling, the FDA asked the Institute of Medicine (a branch of the National Academy of Sciences) to prepare a report. Three years later, in July 2002, the institute declared that no level of trans fats in the diet is safe. Since hydrogenated soy oil is at least 40 percent trans and canola oil 50 percent (and these oils are absorbed into frying foods at about 50 percent, according to Dr. Mary Enig), here's the smoking gun for what's dangerous about fast food and fried food: the polyunsaturated fats.

Virtually all fake fat, from margarine and Olestra (salatrim, Z-Trim, and Nu-Trim are some other fake fats) to imitation cheese to anything labeled "lite" or "fat-free," is loaded with trans fats. Powdered fats, such as the powdered milk that goes back into skim and low-fat milk, or the powdered eggs that go into baked goods, belong in this category too. The great irony, of course, is that we choose these products to protect our health, while the very act of consuming them jeopardizes it more than any other food we could eat, including pure sugar and pure natural fat. Dr. Mary Enig reports a claim that birds will not eat margarine; they're apparently much better at spotting potential toxins than we are, good canaries in the coal mine. Or possibly margarine just doesn't please the avian palate, as it shouldn't please ours.

In the body, these fake fats not only set the stage for cancer, they also have dire consequences for cardiovascular health—which they supposedly promote. The polyunsaturated vegetable fats oxidize cholesterol, turning it into a dangerous form that can block arteries. On its own, cholesterol is no problem; in fact, it's important for the brain and useful to the body in repairing itself. But when it becomes oxidized, taken over by a process much like rust, its chemical form changes so that it attaches itself to the arterial walls, gradually narrowing them and setting up a situation in which a blood clot can form and then break free to cause havoc elsewhere in the system.

The body doesn't quite know what to do with trans fats, because it doesn't recognize their altered structure as real fats, but it's hospitable nonetheless and invites them right in, elbowing out the natural unsaturated fats—especially if there's a deficiency of omega-3, as there nearly always is, given the American diet. Not only do you get the bad fats this way, you don't get the good fats. Once the trans fats are in, they raise the levels of lipoprotein(a)—a new heart disease marker. This mysterious substance deserves a lot more research, but we do know so far that trans fats are the *only* thing known to raise Lp(a) levels. And saturated fat is the only substance known to date that will decrease them. Trans fats also interfere with the reproductive system, producing abnormal sperm and decreasing the amount of cream in human milk. They weaken the immune system and inhibit the enzymes that metabolize toxic chemicals, carcinogens, and medications. For their crowning achievement, they decrease the response of cells to insulin, setting the stage for insulin resistance and all the terrible things it brings in its wake, from obesity and diabetes (remember, these are now epidemic in this country) to heart disease.

To escape all these disasters, you need to eliminate trans fats as much as possible from your diet and avoid free radicals. To eliminate trans fats, avoid margarine, vegetable shortening, fast-food fries, and other obvious sources. To avoid free radicals, don't use vegetable oils (except for olive oil, which is actually a fruit oil, and unhydrogenated peanut oil); don't use processed food if the words "hydrogenated" or "soy oil" or "canola oil" appear anywhere on the label; and never buy anything labeled "lite," "low-calorie," or "fat-free." Once we have trans-fats food labeling, it will be fairly easy to avoid them. Since you probably won't be able to avoid these foods entirely without becoming a complete neurotic, eat as many fresh fruits and vegetables as you can for their antioxidant potential and take a multivitamin, 400 milligrams natural vitamin E oil with mixed tocopherols and an omega-3 supplement daily, all of which will help to balance out the bad fats. And be sure to eat enough saturated fat to counteract the trans fat. Once you stop eating trans fat, it will take a year or two to get rid of all your stored trans fats.

If you're a vegetarian, you may need to take special care to avoid these oils and fats, which many vegetarians choose because they're not animal fats. Coconut oil, olive oil, and unhydrogenated peanut oil are infinitely healthier choices. Another important thing about coconut: if you're using only plant sources of omega-3, such as flaxseed, you must have saturated fat in your diet to convert this fat into the usable forms of DHA and EPA. If you don't eat dairy products, coconut is essential. In a study of cholesterol levels among vegetarians compared with carnivores, the School of Hygiene and Tropical Medicine in London discovered that although vegetarians had distinctly lower levels of cholesterol, the health profile of the two groups was the same. Vegetarians had slightly higher levels of certain cancers, while meat-eaters had slightly more heart disease.

The third group of bad fats is rancid fats, and it can include any of those in the first group, the polyunsaturated vegetable oils, unless they're partially hydrogenated (not good either, as you remember). Saturated fats can turn rancid too, but they're much more stable and it takes a long time. When rancidity begins with these poly oils, it's often undetectable. Just because you buy an oil in the health food store and it's cold-pressed or expeller-pressed doesn't mean it's good. If it's very fresh and has been handled carefully from manufacture to bottling (in glass bottles) to its trip to the market, it may be fine—but that's the exceptional situation, not the reality. The reality is that we all consume a lot of rancid oils all the time, and they do us a lot of damage. A quite-rancid oil will smell and taste bad, but a going-rancid oil may smell and taste fine. If you heat it and mix it with food, however, you can probably taste the off qualities. If in doubt, pitch it—even if it's truffle oil.

Instead of the vegetable oils, turn to the good natural fats instead: coconut, butter, nuts, avocado, fish, eggs, whole milk and milk products, chocolate, and good old meat. In Chapter 4, I go through them one by one to highlight their health benefits and give you information about how to select and use them. Basically the good fats are the natural ones your ancestors might have consumed at the turn of the nineteenth century, before food processing came into its prime. The other thing they have in common is that they all taste good, my own test for selecting healthy fats.

CHAPTER THREE

~

Essential Fats

It is clear that we could all benefit from eating more "healthy" fats in order to protect our health.

—*Dr. Jose Ordovas, Chief of the Nutrition and Genomics Lab at the USDA Human Nutrition Research Center at Tufts University*

Back in the early 1990s, a famous weight-loss expert put me on an extremely low-fat diet that was, of course, very high carb—just exactly the wrong thing, as it turned out, for me. I didn't feel good, and I was gaining weight, but I was doing what cutting-edge science insisted was the right thing. I had also read a bit about the essential fats, and I was worried that I wasn't getting enough of them. At one point I ran into a friend, a hotshot nutritionist responsible for dietary recommendations at the highest level. I asked her if she thought I was getting enough of the essential fats, since I was eating such a low-fat diet. "You don't have to worry about that," she said, "you get plenty of them. Just worry about your total fat intake." (To be fair, that was the advice in all nutrition and medical handbooks in the Nineties; I should have consulted a biochemist, not a nutritionist, about essential fatty acids.)

Ten years later, the tables are turned, low-fat is on the way out, and essential fats are now recognized as crucial to our good health. And we're still getting way too much of the bad guys and way too little of the good essential fats. As with almost everything else concerning the body, it's a question of balance, and getting the balance right is tricky.

Why are they essential anyway? Because we can't make them, and we have to have them; every other fat can be made by the body itself, so we won't curl up and die if we don't have them on our plates. There are two essential fat groups, omega-3 and omega-6 (fats researcher Dr. Mary Enig proposes a conditional third one, coconut, for its huge health benefits). Both are in the polyunsaturated family. It's the 3s that are the miracle workers, and they are found in fish oil, walnuts, meat (which usually contains the right balance of omega-3 to omega-6 if it's pastured), and leafy greens, especially purslane, a charming weed that's the highest source in the plant world (look for it in your garden or at the farmers' market). Of the meats, lamb has the most omega-3s. Flaxseed is also high in omega-3s, but there are some problems with the oil from flax (see page 50).

The essential fats are the sources of some very important hormone messengers called eicosanoids (these include prostaglandins and leukotrines, among others). These are really our oldest hormones, the ones cells make to go out and see what's up, then return to the cell to modulate things based on the information they've collected. They're the hormones that control other hormones. They also control, among many other things, inflammation and circulation. Lipid chemist Barry Sears, in his groundbreaking book *The Omega Rx Zone*, notes that these two processes are centrally involved in all chronic diseases. Eicosanoids can be inhibited by too much trans fat or stress, especially high cortisol. How well your brain functions, says Sears, depends on how well you control your eicosanoids. That in turn depends on your fat intake and on stabilizing your insulin level through diet. In fact, Sears proposes a new disease paradigm: the failure to communicate through these hormones on the biological internet, cell to cell.

Omega-3s demonstrate an astonishing range of good works through eicosanoids: They reduce the buildup of plaque in the arteries, increase levels of HDL (the good cholesterol), drastically reduce levels of the blood fats called triglycerides (the ratio of triglycerides to HDL is thought by scientists at Harvard to be the most significant predictor of heart attack risk—2 or less to 1 is ideal; more than 4 times more triglyceride than HDL is a red flag), keep our cell membranes fluid for optimum functioning, prevent blood platelets from sticking together to form blood clots, lower blood pressure, and inhibit erratic heartbeat (a primary factor in fatal heart attacks). They may improve ADD symptoms (study results are mixed on this one), and they deal with mood disorders—depression, bipolar disease—better than any known medication. They protect against stroke, can eliminate osteoporosis, encourage weight loss, keep the joints lubricated and functioning well, discourage gout, and protect memory and brain function—the list is almost endless. Cleveland-based nutritionist Lauren Braun finds her patients can delay menopause if they have the right balance of omega-3s, and, indeed, eicosanoids control menstruation. The anti-inflammatory properties are especially important for arthritics and asthmatics. They'll even cure cracked and bleeding heels.

Short-chain omega-3 fatty acids are found in plant sources, such as flax, purslane, perilla, and some greens. They can be converted in the body to the usable, long-chain form, but it's not a certainty.

Long-chain omega-3s come in two forms: EPA (eicosapentaenoic acid) and DHA (docosahexaenoic acid). Both have their source in marine algae and in fish, who eat the algae. DHA is the more neurologically active, EPA the more involved with heart function, but we need both, and the two forms are mixed in fatty fish (though only about 20 percent of the fish's fat contains these two oils; the rest is saturated fat).

The neurological significance of omega-3s can hardly be overestimated. Omega-3s are one of the few substances that can cross the blood-brain barrier. The brain is close to 70 percent fat, so we're literally fatheads, and although it's in every cell in the body, most of the omega-3 is concentrated in the brain and the retina. To promote optimal brain function and visual acuity, you need a steady supply of omega-3s, which also increase blood flow (the brain gets 25 percent of the body's blood). Omega-3s have a profound role to play in Alzheimer's (Sears has had spectacular success treating these patients with high-dose fish oil), dementia, memory loss, mood disorders, and a healthy nervous system.

Unfortunately, we've had a hundredfold increase in omega-6, omega-3's antagonist, in the last one hundred years, says Dr. Joseph Hibbeln of the National Institutes of Health, with enormous implications for heart disease and for depression (clinical depression is the major cause of morbidity, more than AIDS, tuberculosis, and heart disease together). Low levels of DHA are prescriptive for depression, which Hibbeln has found improves 50 percent in just twelve weeks of omega-3 treatment. When combined with diabetes, low DHA and depression make you five times more likely to suffer a heart attack than the average Joe, says Hibbeln.

Dr. Andrew L. Stoll of Harvard, author of *The Omega-3 Connection,* pioneered a study of bipolar patients using fish oil supplements. It was so hugely successful the study was terminated after four months because there was simply no question that improvement was dramatic. Omega-3 won't cure Alzheimer's, which is an inflammatory disease, but it definitely minimizes some of the symptoms. In the famous Framingham study, people with lower levels of

The Long and the Short of It

The links in the chains of fatty acids are comprised of carbons and are divided into groups of short, medium, long, and very long, depending on the number of carbons they contain. The chain length has a lot to do with how our bodies metabolize these fats. The short- and medium-chain saturated fats, for instance—which include butter and coconut and palm kernel oils—get metabolized more like carbohydrates, which is to say they get used right away for energy. They're sent directly to the liver (though they're not deposited there like other fats) and they don't usually end up in the fat cells, either. These fats are easy to digest and have important antimicrobial properties. They also have a stimulating effect on metabolism. They're so good they're sometimes marketed as supplements called MCT oil, which just stands for medium-chain triglycerides (food is a better and cheaper source of these good fats). The long-chain saturated fats (which all come from animal sources) store much more easily and do turn up in the fat cells and also in the liver.

omega-3 had a 67 percent greater chance of developing Alzheimer's. People with the most omega-6 had a staggering 250 percent increased risk for Alzheimer's. Omega-3 improves production of both key neurotransmitters: serotonin and dopamine. Low serotonin leads to depression; low levels of dopamine are characteristic of Parkinson's disease.

Omega-3 (especially DHA) is crucial in pregnancy and post-childbirth, both for the fetus's developing brain and the mother's health (see page 149). In fact, the fetus will steal the mother's DHA if mom's diet is deficient. And postpartum depression is highly correlated with DHA depletion. Omega-3 has shown great benefit for Crohn's disease and even (in one Norwegian study done in 2000) multiple sclerosis. A British researcher, Richard Wiseman at the Lon-

Among the omega-3 fats, the short-chain fat alpha-linoleic acid (this is the fat found in flax oil) is just a precursor to the valuable omega-3 elements—EPA and DHA—the body needs and has to undergo a complicated process of conversion in the body to be useable; EPA and DHA are long-chain fats.

Another important element of fats is their bonds. Double bonds make fats subject to oxidation or rancidity. Saturated fats have no double bonds, so it's difficult for them to be oxidized or turn rancid. Monounsaturated fats such as olive oil have only one double bond, but the polyunsaturates (the vegetable oils we've been told are so good for us) have between two and six double bonds, which is why they turn rancid so easily. The most double bonds belong to the fat that's perhaps the most valuable of all, however, and that's DHA, with six double bonds. This is the fat that's crucial for the brain and vision; it also has a lot to do with the way insulin is received by the cells. Too little DHA is suspected of being a cause of insulin resistance, which is in turn suspected of causing obesity and Type 2 diabetes. Fortunately there's a very stable form of DHA from algae (see Neuromins, page 47).

don School of Hygiene and Tropical Medicine, concluded after reviewing and correlating statistics for all the identified possible causes of breast cancer (such as genetics, environmental toxins, and estrogen) that the only consistent marker is a dietary fat deficiency, which seems to allow some important element to escape the body. Possibly that's omega-3. All the breast cancer patients had low omega-3 levels.

This wonderful fat is woefully lacking in the American diet, because we don't eat enough fatty fish and leafy greens. We get only about 125 milligrams per day, whereas our grandparents got 2,500 milligrams in their daily spoonful of cod liver oil, taken just because, for some reason, everyone knew it was good for you. The Japanese, the world's healthiest people, have omega-3 levels about ten times ours. Researchers in Seattle tracking EMS calls discovered that the odds of cardiac death (but not the number of heart attacks) were cut in half for patients who ate as little as a measly 120 milligrams a day of DHA, far below the optimum levels, and less than you'd get in one omega-3-enriched egg.

The other essential fat, omega-6, works in a seesaw relationship with omega-3. Omega-6 fats are most easily found in the bad highly processed vegetable oils—salad oil, sunflower, soy, and canola—and most of our processed foods. They're also found, in smaller amounts, in whole foods. The omega-6s do exactly the opposite of their omega-3 cousins: the hormone messengers they create cause inflammation, decrease circulation, encourage blood clotting, set the stage for arterial plaque to be laid down in the coronary arteries, et cetera. Too much omega-6 (in the form of linoleic acid) is known to encourage cancer. Still, we need them; like free radicals, they have some important functions in the body (such as blood clotting for wounds), but they must be kept in a beneficial ratio with omega-3s: ideally, 1 omega-6 to 1 omega-3, or 1.5 to 1, the Japanese ratio. The current American ratio varies from 20 (omega-6) to 1 to a whopping 50 to 1, so the bad guys are clearly winning.

Why have our omega-3 levels dropped so much? At the turn of the nineteenth century, we ate much more fish and shellfish, especially oysters, than we do now. Almost everyone took a spoonful of cod liver oil every day. The milling of grains took away some omega-3. Then using bad fats instead of good natural ones contributed hugely to the deficit. And consuming 250 percent more sugar, which interferes with the enzymes of fatty-acid synthesis, keeps us from using whatever omega-3 we do have still in our diet.

Our task at the moment is to dramatically increase our intake of omega-3 and decrease that of omega-6. The single best thing you could possibly do for your health would be to stop using trans fats and vegetable oils (that doesn't include olive oil, which is a fruit oil). These oils are not only full of omega-6s (any omega-3 content is processed away), they're almost always highly processed (because they're so unstable) and therefore oxidized (see page 116). If not, they're very often rancid before you even get them home from the store. If you're ordering a salad at a restaurant, be sure it's dressed with olive oil; otherwise, even if it's a blue cheese dressing, you'll be getting a dose of nasty vegetable oil. Don't worry that you won't have enough omega-6s in your diet if you stop using vegetable oils; you'll get more than enough from the food you eat.

Our average intake of omega-3 fats is a shockingly low 125 milligrams per day. The World Health Organization and the National Institutes of Health recommend 3 grams per day; the American Heart Association recommends two fatty fish meals per week, which would give you about 900 milligrams, a minimal amount. You could get that same amount from eating four omega-3-enriched eggs every week. A mere spoonful of caviar would give you 1 gram of omega-3. Health Canada, the Canadian version of the FDA, recommends from 1 to 1.5 grams omega-3 per day. How do you increase the omega-3s in your diet? There are lots of recipes that include omega-3s in this book. If you eat fatty fish several times a week, use omega-3-enriched eggs, and eat plenty of leafy greens, you'll be covered just by eating good food, the ideal situation. And those same obliging folks who brought you warehouses full of low-fat food are gearing up to bring you more omega-3s, in the form of omega-3 cheese, milk, ice cream, and bread, and even some for Fido, in his food.

If you're trying to counteract a health problem—neurological or cardiac, arthritis, asthma, or bipolar disorder—you'll need to take supplements, since you can't get high doses of omega-3 (anywhere from 8 to 25 grams a day) without taking fish oil, as Barry Sears explains.

SORTING OUT THE SUPPLEMENTS

Fish Oil

Only fish oil—not flax oil or perilla oil, plant sources of omega-3—contains EPA (eicosapentaenoic acid) and DHA (docosahexaenoic acid), the very active elements that influence the hormone messengers. These two fatty acids have slightly different functions; EPA plus DHA is best for cardiac effects, while DHA is best for the brain and the eyes. These two elements haven't yet been tested separately, so we don't know if just one of them will work in a particular way. Although plant oil sources contain omega-3 fat (flaxseed has the most except for purslane), their ALA (alpha-linoleic acid) is just a precursor to EPA and DHA, not the usable form that you need. ALA may have some health benefits of its own, says researcher Bruce Holub, Professor of Nutritional Sciences at the University of Guelph in Canada and a longtime omega-3 researcher, but the jury is still out. The body can possibly use this plant fat to manufacture EPA and DHA, but the process is long and complicated, and there's a great likelihood that it will break down along the way (especially for those with metabolic or inflammatory problems, who probably don't have the necessary enzymes available). Aging is also a factor in the conversion efficiency. You need 10 grams of ALA to produce 1 gram of EPA/DHA, according to omega-3 researcher Artemis Simopoulos, so it's an uphill battle. That's why fish oil is really the best source, except for strict vegetarians, who should use flax or perilla (and see the note on page 37 about the importance of saturated fat in the conversion process). DHA from algae is also a good source.

Couldn't you just take cod liver oil, as our very healthy grandparents all did? Indeed you can, but cod liver these days has high concentrations of toxins as well as vitamin A (which can cause hair loss) in high amounts—plus it tastes bad. A spoonful of cod liver oil gives you about 2½ grams of omega-3, a good maintenance amount. The best sources of DHA (the part of omega-3 that's good for your brain and your vision), however, are not the liver but other parts of the fish, the layer of fat just under the skin and the nervous system. You're better off using health food–grade fish oil (not expensive, less than twenty-five cents a day) or pharmaceutical-grade fish oil (a bit pricey, slightly over a dollar a day). As Bruce Holub points out, the studies showing great benefits were done using health food–grade oil, so it's not a bad choice. In the past, a lot of this oil was rancid by the time it hit the stores, but packaging techniques are much more sophisticated now. To guard against rancidity, buy only fish oil capsules in glass bottles and keep them in the fridge. Every few days, bite the bullet and cut one open to see if it's rancid. If it is (you have to taste it, and you'll know without a doubt if it is) toss the whole bottle, since rancid fish oil not only is not good for you, it's very bad for you. And, although it's much less likely to be rancid these days, health food–grade fish oil can still be contaminated with heavy metals and other toxins such as PCBs, so Barry Sears feels it's best to limit consumption of it to 1 gram a day. However, Consumer Reports tested this grade of fish oil and listed two "clean" products as best buys: the fish oils from Costco and Sam's Club. You can test the quality of health food–grade fish oil by freezing a few teaspoons of it for five hours; if it freezes, it contains a lot of saturated fat and very little EPA and DHA. If it doesn't freeze, it probably has lots of EPA and DHA and is probably pharmaceutical-grade. However, this won't answer the contamination question.

If you're pursuing therapeutic effects, which means you're taking high doses, it's important to use pharmaceutical-grade fish oil, which usually has to be mail-ordered (see Sources). You might think of this as second-generation fish oil. There was a lot of excitement about fish oil in the Eighties, but because it was often rancid and couldn't be used at the high doses recommended today for chronic disease, the results weren't so dramatic. The new pharmaceutical-grade oil has been through molecular distillation, often more than once, to remove these impurities—and it's so pure it has no fishy taste. Some brands of health food–grade fish oil can remind you for several hours after you consume it that you've eaten something fishy. It can also give you a lot of gas and diarrhea, so if you find a brand that doesn't have these drawbacks, stick with it. At the moment, there are only a few sources of pharmaceutical-grade fish oil: OmegaBrite and the Sears formula are the major brands. Another very good one is Neuromins, from Natrol, which is pure DHA (from marine algae, the fish's own source), for brain function. Low-carbers might want to investigate Neuromins because DHA has been shown to increase insulin-receptor sensitivity in the cell walls, which reduces overproduction of insulin. Oddly enough, mood disorders don't seem to respond to DHA—the brain nutrient—very well according to the Harvard mood studies, which is why OmegaBrite includes only a minor amount of it; other researchers, however, disagree.

If you're taking therapeutic levels of OmegaBrite—say 9 grams a day for bipolar syndrome—you'll be swallowing a huge number of capsules every day (also, in summer, you should refrigerate them). The Sears formula is liquid, so 9 grams is a mere spoonful of lime-flavored liquid. If you keep it in the freezer, there's no fishy taste at all. With all omega-3 supplements, it's important to take vitamin E (400 to 800 milligrams daily) *or* 1 evening primrose oil capsule a week (not more). Olive oil is an alternative; if you're using olive oil in the meal, you don't need to take these. All of these antioxidants protect the omega-3 in the body and help it do its job. (Polyunsaturated fats can oxidize in your body as well as in the bottle.) These nutrients are absorbed best with food.

Won't this extra fat in your diet mean you'll gain weight? A maintenance dose for general good health (about 2.5 grams of fish oil) will cost you a mere 40 calories a day. Even at the high therapeutic level, 10 grams, you'd be getting only 200 more calories, which would probably be cancelled out by the good metabolic effects of the fish oil, as it improves your insulin sensitivity and accelerates metabolism. And omega-3 fats aren't usually burned for energy: They have more important jobs to do.

Do omega-3s deliver the goods? Innumerable studies show they do, but there's always biochemical individuality. If you have too much circulating insulin, says Barry Sears, which means you're eating too many carbohydrates, that will interfere with their effectiveness, at least at low levels. And if you're consuming too many omega-6s (from bad vegetable oils), that can knock out the good effects of omega-3s. So the balance of these two essential fats is really important. If you take a statin drug such as Zocor to lower your cholesterol, that will bind all your fats to some degree, not just cholesterol. And there's a new study coming that shows that methyl mercury—in contaminated fish, and perhaps health food–grade fish oil—can interfere with the absorption of omega-3s.

Is there such a thing as too much omega-3? Yes, if you're taking high doses, the balance can go too far and zap your immune system, which is why Barry Sears recommends fatty-acid testing. That's also the way to find out if you have too little fish oil. Another less precise way to tell, he says, is to look at the ratio of your triglycerides to your HDL (good cholesterol) level from a recent blood test, the kind you get at your annual physical. The ideal ratio is 1 to 1; if it's over 2 to 1 in favor of triglycerides, you need more fish oil. Bruce Fife, N.D., offers a way to tell if you're getting too much omega-3: if you notice new liver spots, those dark patches that turn up on your skin as you age, that's an indication your omega-3 is out of balance, which he thinks could lead to too many free radicals circulating in the body (omega-3s are also polyunsaturated, as fragile as all the other oils in this group and as prone to free radical development). Obviously, if you notice new bruises, your omega-3 level is too high.

With omega-3 supplementation, there's some concern about blood thinning to a point where hemorrhagic (i.e., bleeding as opposed to clotting) stroke is a possibility (this is the least common form of stroke—about 15 percent of all strokes). The Eskimos and the Japanese, who have the highest consumption of omega-3s in the world, do in fact have a higher rate of stroke than other populations. But, then, they're not immortal, and since they have to die of something, and it's usually not heart disease, the stroke numbers would be higher. In the Japanese figures, low cholesterol is the suspected culprit. Barry Sears has investigated all the data on that subject and reports there's absolutely nothing in the literature to suggest that this increased hemorrhaging has ever happened. For his own patients, he's used very high levels of fish oil, up to 25 grams for Alzheimer's patients, and has never seen a case of bleeding. It takes a big dose, 10 grams a day, he says, just to get the blood-thinning effect of a single aspirin. I was seriously concerned about this problem, since I have a genetic blood-clotting defect and take Coumadin every day to thin my blood. But adding about 3 grams a day of fish oil has made no difference at all in my blood-clotting test results, which are run monthly.

Other concerns include a rise in cholesterol. Sears says cholesterol levels do sometimes rise a bit, perhaps 5 percent, but that's completely offset by the dramatic lowering of triglycerides and the increase in HDL (good cholesterol).

Omega-3 can slightly decrease immune system function (while omega-6s increase it, by stressing it). That may be one of the reasons it's useful for MS patients and others who suffer from autoimmune diseases, in which the immune system goes crazy and starts attacking its own tissues as though they were dangerous. Calming the immune system down can, at least in theory, mitigate these effects. The many benefits of omega-3 seem to offset the slight possible decline in immune function, but just to be safe, you should be sure to include coconut in your diet (as you should anyway) if you're using a lot of fish oil. Sears says you can avoid the immune system decrease altogether by giving yourself enough GLA (gamma linoleic acid)—just two bowls of slow-cooked oatmeal a week will do that. (More is not better; a bowl every morning is too much.)

Finally, it's a good idea to test yourself (see page 54) to see what's really happening with your blood fats.

Flax

Flax (a.k.a. linseed) has been on the miracle-supplement list for decades now, ever since Johanna Budwig, a German doctor, started curing cancers in her patients with flaxseed oil mixed into a little cottage cheese (Budwig is also a coconut oil fan). For this she received six Nobel Prize nominations—and a lot of scorn.

Because it has more omega-3 fat than any other easily available plant source (the weed purslane has more), flax oil seems like a great idea. But precisely because it has such an abundance of omega-3, it's highly perishable and subject to oxidation. It's really difficult to get flax oil safely into a bottle without exposing it to heat and light and, obviously, air itself, all of which conspire to turn it rancid, even as it sits unopened in the bottle. Buy only cold-pressed oil in dark bottles kept in the refrigerator at the store. Many of the pristine-looking bottles in the health food store are already rancid. Rancid oil not only won't help, it's dangerous. Since flax oil (in my opinion) doesn't taste good anyway, it's hard to know when it's gone off—but any fishy or paint/varnish aroma (remember, this is linseed oil) means you should toss it. Never cook with flax oil; that destroys its valuable omega-3s, turning them into trans fats. Also, flax oil contains no EPA or DHA, the long-chain omega-3s that are the valuable forms. Your body still has to convert the plant-source short-chain omega-3s (ALA, which may have benefits of its own, but they're not yet firmly established) to the usable forms—something that may or may not happen. According to Sears, it takes a whopping 30 grams of ALA to produce 1 gram of EPA; other researchers say it's 10 grams. Fatty fish have already done the work for you, as has their oil.

Lots of flax fans turn to the source, flaxseed. The fat in the seed is well protected by its seed coat and doesn't easily turn rancid. In fact, the seed coat is so tough that if you don't grind the seeds, they will pass right through you with no effects at all. The seed also has some very good things going for it, especially lignans, a plant fiber shown to have very good protective effects against breast, colon, and prostate cancer (lignans aren't in most flax oils but some newer oils do have high-lignan labels). According to the USDA, flaxseed contains 27 identifiable anticancer agents.

If you want to try flaxseed, use organic golden seed, which has a pleasantly nutty taste, and grind it in a coffee grinder just before you use it to protect the oil from oxidation. Be sure to toast the seeds before grinding (250 degrees for 10 to 12 minutes), or use the ground seeds in baking (the temperatures won't rise enough inside the food to destroy the omega-3s); raw flaxseed contains cyanogen, a compound your body turns into thiocynanate, which can depress thyroid function—never a good thing. You don't have to refrigerate the seeds, which will keep well for up to a year.

How much flaxseed? Virtually everyone agrees ¼ cup ground seed is the right amount. You can use it in baking, pancakes, or smoothies, sprinkle it over salads, or tuck it into spreads like hummus or tapenade or even peanut butter.

Not everyone, however, is convinced flax is good, despite all the studies showing benefits. Bruce Fife, the Colorado naturopath, points out that flax's anticancer effects are produced by the free radicals it sets loose—sort of like chemo, the free radicals destroy all kinds of cells, including cancer cells. What may look like great short-term benefits may have dire long-term consequences, since free radicals accumulate and do their worst damage only years later—

What the Experts Take

I asked some of the leading omega-3 scientists if they take fish oil supplements, and all of them do. Here's what they take:

- Bruce Holub, longtime Canadian omega-3 researcher: 3 grams health food–grade fish oil per day (to control his high triglycerides).
- Barry Sears, author of *The Omega Rx Zone:* 9 grams pharmaceutical-grade fish oil.
- David L. Kyle, inventor of the omega-3 infant formula: 2 Neuromins (DHA) a day (200 mg).
- Dr. Georges Mouton, Belgian omega-3 researcher: He takes supplements (and prescribes them for his patients following the same guidelines) according to his fatty-acids profile, i.e., the biological results of his diet and supplements as checked by the Great Smokies lab tests in North Carolina (see page 54); for him, this usually works out to a teaspoon of Eskimo-3 fish oil (a product that's somewhere between health food–grade oil and pharmaceutical-grade oil; see Sources) about half the year. Sometimes his results show he needs flaxseed oil, in which case he takes a tablespoon of an oil from South Africa.

especially, in this case, because flax can also depress the immune system. Researchers are well aware, Fife says, that the anticancer properties of flax oil disappear when vitamin E is given along with it, because the vitamin E stops the free-radical damage and the cancer cells flourish. He likes freshly ground flaxseed better as a supplement than the oil, which is often refined and oxidized, like all other vegetable oils, but only for its lignans.

If you're a flax oil fan, be sure you're getting a really good quality oil. If the oil has been deodorized, that could mean it's been subjected to temperatures of over 500 degrees, which in turn means lots and lots of free radicals. A good flax oil will be expeller-pressed (at temperatures under 180 degrees, which don't seem to damage flax), flushed with inert gas such as nitrogen or argon before sealing to remove the oxygen (which otherwise would promote oxidation and eventual rancidity), and protected from heat and light (look for dark bottles that are kept refrigerated). Omega Nutrition is a good widely available brand, as is Spectrum.

Perilla

Another vegetable-source option for omega-3, but also one that doesn't contain EPA or DHA, the elements you need for good eicosanoid formation, just the oil from which these fatty acids can be made in the body, is perilla oil. It's a product of the beefsteak plant, an East Asian plant that has been used for centuries for its oil and may partially account for the low rates of cardiovascular disease and cancer in those countries.

Perilla is hardly a household word in this country, but the oil shows up in health food stores from time to time and you can mail-order perilla capsules. One very good thing about perilla is that it's more stable than flax, which is why some studies on omega-3 have used it for laboratory work.

You can mail-order perilla from the Life Extension Foundation, at 800-544-4440.

Testing, Testing

Several of the leading fats researchers feel it's important to get an accurate picture of how these fats are actually working in your body. Once you know that, you can adjust your dietary intake and supplements to maximize the health benefits. These tests are probably even more important than the usual blood fats tests, except for those for HDL and triglycerides, which continue to be extremely important markers.

To quote from the commentary that comes with your completed Great Smokies lab test: "A proper balance of fatty acids will lead to mental health and proper nerve function, a healthy heart and circulatory system, reduced inflammation in general, proper gastrointestinal and lung function, a more balanced immune system, and even healthy skin, hair, and nails." Great Smokies is one of two major labs that perform the fatty-acid profile test; the other is NutraSource Diagnostics in Canada, whose test is now available in the United States through Sears Labs. Great Smokies tests the red blood cell membranes; NutraSource feels these oxidize too easily to be accurate, so they isolate the phospholipids in the blood for their testing.

With both tests, the crucial thing to know is the ratio of AA (arachidonic acid), which is dangerous in excess, to EPA, the heart-protective element in omega-3 fat. The ideal is 2 to 1 or lower; anything over 4 to 1 in favor of AA is cause for alarm. The NutraSource test gives you low-, medium-, and high-risk cardiac profiles and will provide dietary guidance and supplement suggestions. Great Smokies provides you with an elaborate printout that even your physician may find bewildering—but spend a little time with it, and everything becomes not only clear but fascinating. While you may never have heard of lingoceric and nervonic acids, they have a lot to do with how rigid your cell membranes are and, therefore, how sensitive they are to insulin and to serotonin, the feel-good brain chemical. In combination with low DHA, cell-membrane rigidity contributes to problems such as insulin resistance, hypertension, diabetes, and depression. Other hormones, such as estrogen and progesterone, bind more tightly to these more rigid receptors, causing stimulation inside the cell—not a good situation for breast cancer. If you came up with such a profile, you'd want to take more DHA to counteract the problem and test yourself again in a few months to see if the additional DHA had made a difference.

For the Great Smokies test, you need a doctor's prescription, and the test results will be returned to your doctor. The hardest part of this test, depending on the state in which you live, may be finding a place that will take your blood and return it to you for mailing to the lab.

The NurtraSource test doesn't require a doctor's authorization and will refer you to a nearby participating lab. They suggest retesting in thirty days to check your progress.

Great Smokies Diagnostic Laboratory
33 Zillicoa Street
Asheville, NC 28801-1074
800-522-4762
www.gsdl.com

Sears Labs
800-404-8171

~

CHAPTER FOUR

The Good Fats

If the USDA were a private organization, I believe that the attorneys general of most states, and the Food and Drug Administration, would prosecute it for violation of consumer protection laws.

—*Edward Siguel,* Essential Fatty Acids in Health and Disease

COCONUT

Though eggs have finally emerged from rehab, coconut may get life plus fifty years before we greet it with the enthusiasm it deserves. Of all the good fats, coconut is not only among the most valuable, but also the most reviled. Over and over again, I have had the experience of telling my savvy, healthy-eating friends about the amazing virtues of coconut, only to be met with a skeptical stare and "Oh, come on, it's not only not good for you, it's the worst fat there is." The reason everyone thinks so is a fascinating story—and a shocking one.

Americans, and by extension much of the Western world, have been brainwashed against coconut by the soy industry—with the collusion of some unlikely bedfellows, the Center for Science in the Public Interest and the U.S. Congress. In the mid-1980s, much of our commercial food supply contained ample amounts of the "tropical fats," coconut and palm oil. These saturated vegetable fats are extremely stable and tasty, so they were extensively used in producing cookies, crackers, other baked goods, and many prepared foods. In 1986, the soy industry saw a chance to claim this strong market for itself. There was a study showing that a cow—a single cow—did not flourish on a coconut diet. That made perfect sense, since no one, not even a cow, could have coconut as the sole source of fat. The essential fats were almost completely missing. The coconut used in the study was hydrogenated, to make it even more stable—and of course all hydrogenated fats are by definition trans fats. And coconut is not a complete fat; it has only minuscule amounts of the essential fats. At the same time, saturated fats had been implicated in the accumulation of cholesterol in the blood, and there was a lot of antifat hysteria brewing. The enterprising soy industry sent out kits to start a grass-roots movement among soy farmers, who were supposed to write their congressmen to complain about the "dangerous" tropical fats throughout the American food supply chain. The letters were written, and an outraged millionaire heart patient, Phil Sokolof, joined the fray with a series of dramatic ads in newspapers all across the country demanding that his government protect him from dangerous cookies and crackers.

Congress responded to these orchestrated alarms and held hearings in 1988 about the safety of the tropical oils and whether they required labeling to warn consumers of their dangers. Even though Dr. George Blackburn of Harvard explained that the study on which these claims were based was meaningless and Surgeon General C. Everett Koop dismissed the entire argument as absurd, the soy industry won the day, and the "dangerous" oils disappeared. Soy oil, with its own very dangerous trans fats, replaced the health-promoting tropical oils (which were also more expensive, so the food manufacturers were delighted by this turn of events). Both the soy industry and the Center for Science in the Public Interest continued to pursue this canard (and do to this day) with releases to media sources about the dangers of coconut and palm oils. All this was based on no sound science whatsoever, simply the single sad cow (plus a mouse study with the same flaws) and the fact that coconut and palm are saturated fats and therefore condemned—though in fact they're entirely different from the animal saturated fats and do not increase blood levels of cholesterol.

In the ensuing years, researchers have quietly proven that coconut is in fact the healthiest of all fats (see "What's So Good About

Coconut," page 64), that it protects against the very conditions it's supposed to aggravate, such as heart disease and cancer. As Harvard's Dr. Walter Willett has noted, "Overconsumption of polyunsaturated oils is more detrimental to our health than saturated fats found in tropical oils." The polyunsaturates he's referring to are the highly processed vegetable oils, such as soy. Dr. Mary Enig, the dean of American lipid researchers, considers coconut so valuable it should be considered a conditionally essential fat. But you won't be hearing much about coconut from the media, because there's no Coconut Council to fund research, send out press kits, take journalists on junkets, and lobby Washington for favorable treatment in the way other elements in the agribusiness food industry cooked up the Dietary Guidelines.

Am I sure coconut doesn't cause heart disease? Yes. In fact, it inhibits platelet stickiness—stickiness can lead to blood clots, which can then trigger heart attacks and strokes—and no other fats inhibit it except the extremely healthy omega-3 fats. All the other polyunsaturated vegetable oils—canola, sunflower, soy—actually increase platelet stickiness because of their linoleic acid content. Soy contains hemagglutinin, a clot-promoting substance that makes red blood cells stick together. Polyunsaturated fats (vegetable oils, but not flax and not fish oil) actually promote cancer and heart disease because they contain linoleic acid and toxic trans fats, so it's completely ironic that we should be turning to them to save us from coconut. The polyunsaturates, says Dr. Willet, are "the most toxic fats ever known." In Sri Lanka, coconut oil is used for most cooking, and people consume an average of 120 coconuts a year, yet they have the lowest rate of heart disease in the world.

Coconut is on the highly exclusive GRAS (Generally Regarded as Safe) list the government maintains; soy is not. (I love British researcher Philip Iddison's comment on the GRAS designation: ". . . a wonderfully vague statement suitable for a litigious society.") Coconut is a "low-fat" fat, and it's the only one: 1 gram is only 6.8 calories, whereas all other fats are 9 calories per gram. It stimulates metabolic activity and it gives you a burst of energy, because it's a medium-chain fat, processed by the body much the same way carbohydrates are, and it gets burned right away. Medium-chain fats (there are very few of them, although butter is about 12 percent medium-chain) don't store very easily in the body, unlike most animal-origin saturated fats and polyunsaturates, the vegetable and seed oils. Butter also has slightly fewer calories than margarine. Coconut has no effect whatsoever on cholesterol (unless, because of its positive effect on metabolism, it may actually increase the good HDL cholesterol and decrease the evil LDL), contrary to anticoconut propaganda. In fact, it's an almost eerily good fat; it seems to do everything but change the oil in your car.

You might think that a lower-calorie fat that doesn't turn to body fat easily and increases metabolic rate would be an ideal candidate for weight loss—and you'd be right. Pigs fed coconut oil (and pigs are closest to us metabolically of all the animals) actually lost weight. Coconut also helps control blood sugar levels, which are so often an issue for dieters. In the Polynesian islands, where coconut may compose up to 60 percent of the diet, obesity is rare, as is heart

Jennie's Macaroons

It seems too good to be true: this brand offers a tasty cookie that gives you a huge energy boost along with an immune system boost so profound that HIV–AIDS patients use it therapeutically on a daily basis. These macaroons are gluten-free, wheat-free, lactose-free, and sulfite-free, with a huge dose of lauric acid, the mother's milk nutrient. One big cookie, available at health food stores, has 7 grams of lauric acid; Jennie's also produces cans of smaller cookies. These cookies are basically a wad of coconut with honey mixed in, and quite sweet, unfortunately. And, in fact, they *are* too good to be true; but if you can afford their 310 calories per big cookie and 34 grams of sugar, they're a pleasing way to get your coconut. If you're about to engage in high-energy sports, an individually wrapped Jennie's macaroon would burn off with no problems and give you great energy in the bargain. Find out more about them at www.redmillfarms.com.

disease. Among the hefty Samoans, it's a diet in excess of 4,000 calories a day that causes the weight gain, and even coconut can't protect enthusiastic eaters from the consequences of that. Bruce Fife, who probably knows more about coconut than anyone else in America, has devised an entire dietary regimen based on coconut (detailed in his book *Eat Fat, Look Thin*).

But that's only the beginning of coconut's great virtues. It's a rich source of lauric acid, a fantastic immune system booster, which is otherwise found only in mother's milk (almost 50 percent) and (to some degree) butter and the seeds and leaves of the bay laurel tree. AIDS patients have used monolaurin, a derivative of coconut, with success; it can attack viruses (herpes, flu, hepatitis C, HIV) with a fatty covering and destroy them by "melting" their protective fat layer. Monolaurin is also in some infant formula and used as an antiviral, antibacterial, antifungal agent elsewhere. It acts as an antioxidant to enhance the efficacy (by about 100 percent) of the essential fatty acids (omega-3 and omega-6 fats) and protect them in the body. In fact, if you're taking fish oil supplements, you may need to have your fatty-acid profile checked (see page 54) if you're also consuming coconut on a regular basis—it's that effective at increasing their potency.

Coconut is especially valuable for people with low levels of thyroid hormone (hypothyroid), who have low metabolism as well. Because it increases the metabolic rate, it restores energy and improves general health, since the thyroid hormone affects every cell in the body and determines the uptake of nutrients in the cells. For those who, like me, have lost their gallbladders, coconut is especially important, because it's so easily digested (that's because it bypasses the pancreas and liver and is used immediately for energy). If you haven't been digesting fats properly, you may find you have lots more energy not only from the coconut itself, but also from the improved efficacy of the fat-soluble vitamins that may have been passing through your system unused.

The stability of coconut is entirely remarkable; it's the most stable of all the fats, the most resistant to oxidation. On your kitchen counter, a jar of coconut oil will keep for 2 to 3 years. That quality makes it not only superior for commercial food products (though it's almost completely disappeared from those now, thanks to the success of the tropical-fat phobes), but also excellent as a cooking oil, since it can take heat up to about 350 degrees without breaking down as other fats do. Like all other saturated fats, such as lard, it isn't absorbed into fried food as vegetable oils are, so it doesn't contribute extra calories to fried food. It also browns foods beautifully.

Cracking Coconuts

Fresh coconut isn't a frequent guest in most American kitchens; here's how to handle it. Once in the market, coconuts are fresh for only two to three months at best, so there's a chance you may get one that's gone off. Some cooks buy two at a time for this reason. Be sure there's plenty of liquid sloshing around inside the nut and no moldy patches anywhere. To crack open a fresh coconut, first freeze it for an hour; this seems to help separate the meat from the shell. With an ice pick or a sturdy nail, tap into two of the eyes of the coconut. Drain the thin liquid off and take a taste; it should taste sweet (if it doesn't, chances are the coconut is rancid). Wrap the coconut in a towel and whack it on a hard surface—a sidewalk is perfect—with a hammer or the back side of a cleaver around its waist until it cracks open (or better yet, use an Australian coconut knife—see Tools). Pry the meat away from the shell with an oyster knife or any dull knife. You can refrigerate the meat, well covered, up to several days. You don't really need to peel the brown skin off (a vegetable peeler is the tool of choice) unless it would ruin the look of your finished dish; it's full of fiber and looks pretty in some dishes. Fresh coconut also freezes perfectly; just grate it and seal it tightly in a plastic freezer bag.

Coconut is hard to grate, but a food processor works very well. There are various coconut-grating gizmos on the market and the heavy-duty ones work well for a while, then give up the ghost after a brief life.

Pregnant women or women who might become pregnant should take coconut routinely as part of their diet to confer the maximum immune benefits to their babies. Cooking with coconut oil is also a good idea for pregnant women, since the trans fats present in vegetable oils can be passed along to the fetus. And all minimally processed vegetable and seed oils are to some degree rancid by the time they're on the shelf at the health food store, because they're so unstable and vulnerable to oxidation. Replacing these dangerous fats with coconut is both easy and highly protective.

All forms of coconut, with the exception of sweetened dried coconut and coconut cream (it's the sugar that's a problem) are good. Coconut has a lot of fiber as well as its very healthy fat—three times as much fiber as broccoli. One tablespoon of dried shredded coconut has 2 grams of protective lauric acid; a tablespoon of coconut oil has a whopping 7 grams. A pharmacologically active form of monolaurin is available from www.lauricidin.com: it's called Lauricidin®. To check on which products have the most lauric acid at the moment, go to www.lauric.org; at this writing, it's Grace coconut milk, with 3.5 grams per 2 ounces.

How much coconut oil should you consume? For weight loss or other therapeutic effects, 3½ tablespoons a day, with meals, says Bruce Fife. This amount of coconut will also protect you from many passing germs and some viruses—and give you gorgeous skin and hair as a bonus.

There's only one coconut caveat; if you feel you're not thriving on coconut, it might be because your blood type is O. Dr. Peter J. D'Adamo, author of *Eat Right for Your Type*, says coconut is not good for those with type O, the oldest blood type, which is most like that of our Paleo ancestors.

Coconut milk isn't the liquid inside the coconut (that's coconut water); it's made from grated coconut mixed with water—a blender does this well—and strained. Canned coconut milk has a creamy topping; just mix it back into the milk. Diluted coconut milk is a great dairy substitute in shakes and smoothies, it's good in soups and stews, and it's very useful in desserts. It's also surprisingly good over cereal or fresh fruit. All of which is a good thing, because once the can is opened, the coconut milk won't keep for more than a few days, a week at most. Freeze leftovers. If you have access to a good

Asian store, look for frozen coconut milk, which is very fresh and delicious.

Chaokoh brand canned coconut milk from Thailand is probably the best canned coconut milk of all, and it can be found in Asian markets as well. Taste of Thai is a reliable supermarket brand. Coconut milk can contain several things that don't have to be listed on the label, such as cornstarch. Sometimes you can find unsweetened blocks of coconut cream, especially in West Indian markets (Grace is the best brand). It needs to be diluted half and half with hot water and used only in cooking, but it's delicious. Canned cream of coconut is another thing altogether, sweetened and meant for paper-parasol cocktails.

Dried unsweetened coconut can be found at natural foods stores

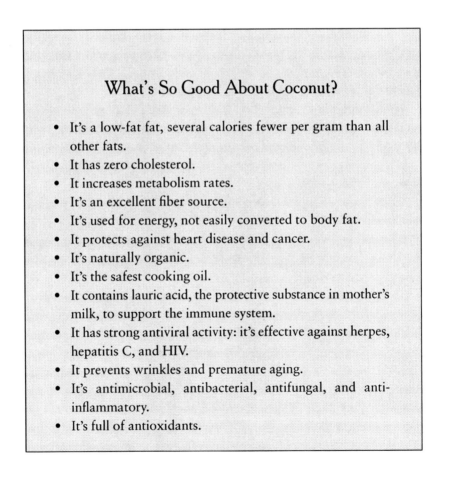

What's So Good About Coconut?

- It's a low-fat fat, several calories fewer per gram than all other fats.
- It has zero cholesterol.
- It increases metabolism rates.
- It's an excellent fiber source.
- It's used for energy, not easily converted to body fat.
- It protects against heart disease and cancer.
- It's naturally organic.
- It's the safest cooking oil.
- It contains lauric acid, the protective substance in mother's milk, to support the immune system.
- It has strong antiviral activity: it's effective against herpes, hepatitis C, and HIV.
- It prevents wrinkles and premature aging.
- It's antimicrobial, antibacterial, antifungal, and anti-inflammatory.
- It's full of antioxidants.

and Asian markets (where it's sometimes called coconut strings), but it tends to be very dried out. To rehydrate it, mix it with a slightly smaller quantity of water and let it sit for an hour. The coconut will reabsorb water and you can use it for cooking.

You may see dried powdered coconut milk in the market; just pass it by. It's a low-quality product in which the fat has been oxidized to some degree.

If you're looking to add coconut to your diet on a regular basis, using coconut oil for cooking is one of the best ways. Although some brands of coconut oil—the so-called virgin ones—have a mildly sweet coconut flavor, most are almost flavorless (these are usually more refined). It's strange but true that sometimes coconut itself (some coconut milks in particular) doesn't taste very coconutty, especially in baking. If you want that flavor, get some good-quality natural coconut flavoring, not imitation coconut (King Arthur is a good source—800-827-6836; www.kingarthurflour.com—and it also has high-quality dried shredded unsweetened coconut that's moist).

BEST

- High-quality coconut oil, sometimes called coconut butter or virgin coconut oil (which has a slightly higher level of lauric acid, 53 percent), available at natural foods stores. Omega (800-661-3529; minimum order $30), Tropical Traditions, an artisanal oil (866-311-2626; www.tropicaltraditions.com), and the truly delicious Coconut Oil Supreme (800-922-1744) are excellent brands. These premium coconut oils have the sweet smell and taste of the coconut water from a just-opened coconut. They make superb moisturizers as well and work against wrinkles and precancerous lesions; in fact, it's worth keeping one jar in the kitchen and another in the bathroom. Bruce Fife says that coconut oil applied topically is absorbed into the system in the same way as coconut products you've digested—though it's hard to know how much you're getting, since some of the oil may disappear onto bed linens or clothing.

  These oils are solid at room temperature (so they don't work for salad) and melt at around 76 degrees. You don't have to refrigerate them, but if you do, they'll keep even longer than their 2 to 3 years of stable shelf life—but they'll also be rock hard. They're good for baking, stir-fries, fried potatoes, fried onions, and making popcorn.

- To address a serious medical condition such as a virus or fungal infection, you need to use Lauricidin® from Med-Chem Labs (www.lauricidin.com).

GOOD

- Plain coconut oil (Spectrum is a good brand; although it's refined, it's expeller-pressed, i.e., cold-pressed) in natural foods

---

More Coconut, Please

It takes a lot of fresh or dried coconut to supply the good fat, so the easiest source is to use coconut oil (3½ tablespoons per day is the recommended amount) for cooking and coconut milk in place of cow's milk. Here are some ideas on how to increase your coconut intake.

FRESH OR DRIED UNSWEETENED COCONUT

- Use it in cereal, hot or cold.
- Sprinkle dried coconut over salads.
- Grind it in the food processor and mix it in with hamburger meat, to both lighten and flavor it—½ cup dried unsweetened coconut is the right amount for 1½ pounds ground chuck, to serve 4.
- Add chopped dried coconut to baked goods; if you grind it very fine in a food processor, you can substitute it for some of the flour.

---

stores. Spectrum also makes a coconut oil that's labeled for body moisturizing, but it's okay to cook with it. According to Bruce Fife, the coconut guru, the fat contains so many natural antioxidants that they balance out the negative effects of refining—which include heat and solvents. Because regular coconut oil is made from copra, dried coconut that sits out in the sun and can attract insects and fungus, it must be highly processed. But better some coconut oil than none, and if the best is not in your budget or you can't be bothered to mail-order it, it's worth using regular coconut oil. This is a good oil to use for deep-frying, up to 350 degrees.

COCONUT MILK

- Dilute it a bit, emulsify it in the blender, and use it in place of cream over fruit or cereal. You can sweeten it with a little honey or Splenda (the alternative sweetener that's so new we don't know anything terrible about it yet) if you like, or add a jot of vanilla.
- Replace some of the cream in soups with coconut milk.
- Use diluted coconut milk in smoothies and protein shakes instead of yogurt or milk.
- Use it instead of cream in ice cream and puddings.
- Use it instead of milk for hot chocolate.

COCONUT OIL (BUTTER)

- Use it in stir-fries.
- Use it in place of butter or olive oil for cooking vegetables; it's great for browning them.
- Use it for making popcorn.
- Use it instead of other fats in pancakes, muffins, and quick breads (use 25 percent less coconut butter by volume to replace another fat in a recipe).
- Use it instead of butter on toast, or mix it with butter.

- Canned coconut milk from Thailand is usually very reliable, especially the Chaokoh brand (13.5 ounces) and Mae Ploy (which comes in a 19-ounce can). For some reason—possibly the guar gum it contains, as many brands do (without the label saying so)—the Thai Kitchen brand is almost solid in the can; you'll probably need to dilute this brand a bit with water. Thai Kitchen also has a premium coconut milk with higher fat than the regular product. Sometimes you can find small 5-ounce cans of coconut milk at Asian markets; these are very convenient. Asian markets also have dramatically lower prices for dramatically superior coconut milks—worth a trip. Don't buy "lite" coconut milk, which not only doesn't taste good and is missing the good fat, but also may have flour added to thicken it (the label won't tell you that). Leftover coconut milk can be stored in the fridge or frozen, well sealed, for a couple of days or up to a week—taste is your most reliable guide to whether it's still good.

AVOID

- Moldy coconuts or those that don't have sloshing liquid inside when you shake them.
- Lite coconut milk.
- Sweetened coconut—it's candy.
- Imitation coconut flavoring is nasty.
- Powdered coconut milk isn't good for much.

Note: If you're allergic to sulfites, the preservative that often appears in food and wine, look for coconut and coconut milk in the natural foods store.

BUTTER

People are too afraid of a little butter these days.

—Julia Child

Among the many victims of the low-fat police, it's hard to decide which good fat suffered most: butter, cheese, coconut, or eggs? I'm voting for butter, since it's just beginning to make the most tentative of comebacks and people still apologize for adding butter to their food—even though it's only 80 percent fat.

For those few hardy souls who managed to endure the margarine era without actually consuming margarine, you're the ultimate winners. You've given yourself the benefit of a healthy fat (see "What's So Good About Butter," page 72) and avoided at least some of the terrible health problems inflicted on us by fake fats. In fact, historically, when butter consumption is down, the incidence of coronary heart disease and cancer is up—just the opposite of what you might think. The partially hydrogenated margarines can easily be rancid (they're deodorized, so you'd never know), and they're also full of trans fats, the most dangerous fats of all. And researchers at the Royal Children's Hospital in Australia have linked the dramatic increase in childhood asthma to increased consumption of polyunsaturated fats, especially margarine.

What about all those new margarines that flow like catsup or claim loudly that they have no trans fats? If you ate a spoonful of those instead of a spoonful of butter, you'd save yourself 20 calories and get none of the benefits of real butter, not to mention its glorious taste. The fat you'd consume in the margarine would store in your fat cells more easily than butterfat, which, because it's a short-chain fatty acid, doesn't tend to end up on your hips. And margarine supplies no nutrients whatsoever beyond its fat calories. If you melt diet margarine, it disappears by half because it's half air and water. Is this a good deal for 20 calories?

What about cholesterol-lowering margarines like Benecol and Take Control? These are made out of oils from ground-up trees and soybeans (never a good thing; see page 154), which contain plant sterols, the active ingredient here that binds cholesterol. The sterols do this by tricking your intestines into thinking they're cholesterol, ready to be absorbed, but in fact they block the sites where choles-terol is absorbed, which lowers cholesterol by about 10 percent. This mission is accomplished at a cost about four times that of butter. Plant sterols may or may not turn out to be a good thing in the end, but, in any case, margarine isn't the way to consume them. These margarines can also contain trans fats. Sterols snatch some very important fat-soluble vitamins (A, D, E, K, and beta carotene) and keep them from being absorbed, producing a deficiency of these vita-mins (which has negative implications for both cancer and heart dis-ease rates over the long term) of as much as 25 percent. And it takes 3 tablespoons a day of plant sterol margarines, about 250 calories, to have the cholesterol-lowering effect. Butter, on the other hand,

Ghee and Clarified Butter

To make ghee, heat a pound of butter in a saucepan over medium-high heat for about 15 minutes, or until the surface is covered with a film over large flat bubbles. Lower the heat to medium-low and cook for another 15 minutes, or until the milk solids at the bottom of the pan turn golden—not brown, or the flavor will be ruined. Strain the butter through a fine-mesh strainer lined with a clean kitchen towel or a coffee filter. Store the ghee in a tightly closed jar. It will keep a very long time in the refrigerator and for days or weeks at room temperature. Use ghee for cooking foods at a high temperature.

Clarified butter doesn't have the slightly nutty taste of ghee because the milk solids aren't cooked until golden, but it's even eas-ier to make. Preheat the oven to 300 degrees. Cut the butter into 1-inch cubes. Place them in a small ovenproof dish and cook until the butter separates into two distinct layers, the white milk solids on the bottom and the clear yellow liquid on top. Carefully pour off the clear oil on top and discard the milk solids. Store in the same way as ghee.

enhances your store of those very vitamins, and a tablespoon of butter goes a long, long way, and costs just under 100 calories (butter is only 80 percent fat).

Just a little butter can do wonders for almost any vegetable, especially greens like spinach, as can olive oil, of course. Mixed together, they allow you to sauté foods at a higher temperature than you could with butter alone, as well as provide some of the good antioxidant benefits of olive oil. If you want a buttery flavor for cooking at high heat, use ghee or clarified butter, butter that's had the water and milk solids removed. Ghee is the oil of butter, not quite as healthful, since it's missing some of the nutrients that stay behind in the milk solids, but it lasts forever, is easy to make, and has stood the test of a very long time. People with milk allergies usually aren't allergic to ghee.

Although butter will keep in cold storage for years, it's best when it's freshest. Butter connoisseurs think fresh sweet cream butter goes off as quickly as cream itself; French chef Jacques Pépin thinks the flavor stales after three days. To keep butter at its spreadable best, get one of those gizmos called butter bells that are widely advertised. This clever idea comes from Normandy, home of great butter: you spread softened butter inside a ceramic container with

Better Butter?

Although I think there's nothing wrong with butter at all, if you insist on having some margarine-like spread, you can make a really good one out of natural fats. Just mix room-temperature butter with an equal amount of olive oil in the food processor until it's well combined and creamy. Taste for salt: a little sea salt does wonders for this spread.

Keep the spread in the refrigerator and it will always be the right consistency for spreading. If you leave it at room temperature, it will ooze into a big mess.

holes in it, then invert that into a small crock of cool water. The water seals the butter completely from oxygen, the enemy of all fats, and keeps it cool but soft enough to spread. You don't usually need to refrigerate the butter, and it will keep for several weeks at room temperature, but you should refrigerate it in warm weather; just change the water occasionally and make sure it's covering all the

What's So Good About Butter

Aside from containing about 12 percent lauric acid, the immune-protective element in mothers' milk, butter is full of some very good things—and it's only 80 percent fat:

Vitamin A
Vitamin D
Vitamin E
Vitamin K
Copper
Zinc
Chromium
Selenium
Iodine
Lecithin
CLA (conjugated linoleic acid)
Oleic acid (which is also in olive oil)
Glycosphingolipids
Methyl butyrate (a liver cleanser that promotes leanness and
    muscularity in cows—as it does in humans)
Myristoleic acid (an antiarthritic compound; destroyed by
    heat)

Butter also contains short-chain fatty acids, which don't store easily as body fat.

holes. To serve, you simply invert the butter keeper and set it on a plate. The best version I've seen comes from a potter named Hervé Coffig in Normandy, and it's called a *beurrière conservateur.* Hervé makes a gorgeous speckled blue clay butter keeper, a work of art in itself, which he sells along with many other ceramics at his website (http://perso.club-internet.fr/hccoffig).

If you keep butter in sticks in the refrigerator, you may notice it acquiring a waxy darker yellow coating, sort of like the wax on cheese. This coating doesn't taste good, and it's actually oxidized fat, so remove it before using the butter. If butter has little white specks in it, that means the rinsing process was incomplete—choose another brand next time.

Like most "whole" foods, butter can have nonbutter things in it, such as cream flavoring or other "natural flavoring," as Land O' Lakes Ultra Creamy Butter does. Sometimes these additives actually appear on the label.

Sweet (unsalted) butter or salted? Gourmets like sweet butter (an American invention to differentiate our butter from the cultured European butter, implying that butter is sour) and many think it's fresher, since salt can somewhat disguise rancidity. That's not usually a problem, however, so you can freely choose whichever taste you like.

Our butter choices have skyrocketed in the past couple of years. Now we have high-fat butters (regular butter has 80 percent fat) such as Plugra (82 percent fat), a chef's darling, and Land O' Lakes Ultra Creamy, a mild butter with 83 percent fat. Vermont Butter and Cheese's butter tops the scale at 86 percent, and some luxury butters can go as high as 90 percent. Left to its own devices, butter naturally has 80 percent fat. What's good about high-fat butters? They're very good for making pastry, for one thing. And the moisture in butter cooks off in any case, sometimes creating steam where you don't want it. These butters can take higher temperatures without burning. If you're making ghee, you'll have less milk solids to contend with when you're straining it. Most of these high-fat butters are also made with care, so they're higher quality than the usual run of the dairy case butters.

American gourmets are starting to have a taste for cultured butters in the European style as well. Cultured butters are made with cultured cream and aged at a very cold temperature. They may emerge with a distinctive fresh, nutty taste—or they may be a bit rancid. You'll have to go by brand, and find one you like. If you choose a European brand, it will have no antibiotics or hormones used on the pastured dairy cows that gave the cream, which is a definite plus. American organic butters are also quite good and some of them are cultured in the European style, which is to say the French style. Cream is infused with a starter, like yogurt or cheese, which develops a complex flavor before it is churned. In fact, butter really is a form of cheese, which is a useful way to think about it if you're spreading a generous amount on bread. If you live in or near a state that allows it to be sold, raw butter is especially delicious and valuable nutritionally.

Sometimes you can find Anchor butter from New Zealand (it's widely distributed in the Caribbean), which has a distinctive deep yellow color and a distinctive taste, the result of cream from grass-fed cows. This is pure, very traditional butter. In Europe, the spring butter from grass-fed cows is considered too strong to be used at the table. If you like it, though, this butter is full of all sorts of special nutrients.

If you're not going to use all the butter you've bought in a short time, either freeze it, wrapped well in foil, or turn it into ghee or clarified butter. If it just sits in the back of the fridge for a while, it will pick up off flavors and the lack of freshness will be noticeable.

FISH

Of all the portentous health dictates issued in the past few decades, perhaps only four remain unassailable: smoking is bad for you, exercise is good for you, fruit and vegetables are good for you, and fish is good for you. How good the fish actually is will depend, however, on how big it is, where it grew, and what it ate, as we shall see. Not all fish has a clean bill of health.

In traditional societies, however, the big fish eaters are always the healthiest groups. That's thought to be the reason the Japanese are the healthiest people in the world, though their fascination with the Western diet is tarnishing their crown a bit. Whether it's people in the Outer Hebrides eating mainly fish and oats and seaweed, or modern societies like the Japanese, the fish eaters win. This fact was first noted when researchers studied the Inuit, a Greenland Eskimo group with very limited food resources and a very high fat diet. Their health, however, was entirely remarkable; there was virtually no cardiovascular disease, even though the Inuit ate more fat than any population studied. Clearly something in that fat was protective—and indeed, that turned out to be the omega-3 oil in the fish. Since that time, a number of studies (including two major Harvard studies in 2002) have confirmed that fish—or omega-3 supplements—have dramatic benefits for heart patients and very positive benefits for everyone. Beyond their heart benefits, fatty fish can be protective against prostate cancer, according to a thirty-year Swedish study, which found that men who ate a moderate to high amount of fish (and in Sweden, most of the fish is fatty fish) had a two- to three-times lower risk of developing prostate cancer. The combination of good protein with omega-3 fats—all fish have them, but in varying amounts—makes them the healthiest protein source.

In America, fish eating is confined mainly to the coasts. Most Midwesterners don't much like ocean fish (or lamb, for that matter). Although there are abundant fish in the Great Lakes, and they're much beloved by the locals, pollution has so thoroughly contaminated them that pregnant women are urgently warned not to eat them.

Pollution is also a large problem in the coastal waters, where industrial waste and contamination from ship traffic as well as mercury and PCBs provide a lot of toxins that inevitably wind up in the fish who live there, usually bottom-feeders (which are low-fat fish). Aside from the question of where your fish lived and how fat it is, the biggest factor in its relative healthfulness is what it ate. Since most fish are the marine equivalent of cannibals (though they also eat a lot of algae and other microorganisms, and some of them, like herring, are vegetarian) what they ate includes generations of what-they-ate—a minnow gets gobbled by an anchovy who's dinner for a sardine and so on, all the way up to the very large fish, who accumulate toxins all along the way and thus end up with a large amount of it in their fat. And you're that last rung on the food chain, so you get all those toxins too, which get stored in your fat. For this reason, you can eat all the anchovies and sardines and other small fish at the bottom of the food chain you want, but because of mercury and other toxins such as PCBs, we're advised not to eat large fish such as tuna, swordfish, shark, and king mackerel more than twice a week. Mercury, which turns into methyl mercury once it hits the water, can also negate some of the good omega-3 fat, according to a new study.

The most valuable fish from an omega-3 standpoint are the ones in the "blue" family, with mackerel, a fish most of us hardly ever eat, leading the pack. Herring, bluefish, salmon, trout, tuna, and swordfish are also high on the list. These are fatty fish that thrive in cold waters and, except for most of the salmon and trout on the market, they're wild fish. Their high fat content makes them good candidates for smoking or grilling, but they're also very good baked or broiled.

Because our seas are so overfished, every hatchery everywhere is depleted—and the European Union has proposed drastically cutting fishing fleets to deal with what looks like an impending disaster—farming has come to the rescue. More or less. Controversy about fish farming rages, though a third of the world's fish is now farmed, and estimates are that by 2010 fish farming will surpass beef farming. Fish grown in cages in close proximity are as vulnerable to disease as caged chickens are, so they're often heavily treated with powerful antibiotics and other drugs (although these drugged fish supposedly spend a year swimming around in clean water to ditch all the chemicals). Is fish farming actually sustainable (i.e., does it spare natural resources)? Maybe not—if it takes at least 2 pounds of fish (in the form of ground-up fish, the best feed—which is not fish meal that's had its oil extracted) to produce a pound of farmed fish, it doesn't seem likely to continue too long. Gourmets disdain the taste and texture of farmed fish; environmentalists worry about the contamination of the sea and genetic mingling of farmed and wild fish. Although farmed fish are generally freer of mercury and other toxins than wild fish, farmed salmon generally has lots of PCBs and there are other serious pollution problems: farmed shrimp from China and Vietnam have been found to be contaminated with a dangerous antibiotic (because disease is a big problem with farmed fish) called chloramphenicol, which can cause childhood leukemia, among other diseases, in humans. Chloramphenicol is banned in the United

States and in Western Europe. It should be easy to stay away from these shrimp by checking the source for your shrimp, but, alas, testing shows that the antibiotic has turned up in some packages of domestic origin as well, because shrimp, like olive oil, can be "from" wherever it's packaged, never mind the actual geographical source. Still, the FDA assures us that all shrimp sold here is safe to eat; meantime, they're rigorously checking imports from China and Vietnam.

Fats researcher Dr. Mary Enig says that farmed fish have more antibiotic residue than any other farmed animal, including beef. Disease-resistant bacteria have turned up in farmed fish, says Barry Estabrook, a journalist writing in *Gourmet*. It's possible for these bacteria to jump species, from fish to humans, which could mean a powerful antibiotic such as Cipro could be rendered useless.

Fish farmers are getting their act together and any day now, we'll have branded farmed fish so we'll know exactly where it's from and what it ate, but in the meantime it's a bit of a crapshoot. If, say, farmed salmon are eating ground-up anchovies or algae, then their omega-3 content should be good. In fact, the FDA lists farmed salmon as higher in omega-3s than wild salmon, which seems a bit unlikely until you realize the farmed fish are much fatter, by about 20 percent, than their hard-swimming wild cousins. But that doesn't mean all their extra avoirdupois is just bonus omega-3; if the fish are grain-fed, their extra fat includes a lot of saturated fat, for which we have no need and much tastier sources in any case.

If these salmon are eating wheat or corn or soy meal, which is highly likely, their omega-3 content will be low. And, going lower; new strains of soybeans are being bred now that will have less than half the omega-3 of regular soybeans (so they'll last longer on the shelf). But they'll still have the same omega-3 count on their labeling as soybeans have always had, so you won't know they're deficient. Farmed fish that don't eat fish meal and are given grain instead sometimes actually develop cardiovascular disease, says Artemis Simopoulos, a leading omega-3 researcher. Grain-fed fish need fish oil for flavor as well as their own (and our) good health. If you can, it's always best to avoid grain-fed fish and fish that's not from sparkling clean cold water such as Norway or Canada, countries that also have very good regulations in place. But you usually don't have that choice.

Farmed fish with high omega-3 levels are salmon and trout. Coming soon is a wonderful fish called cobia (ling), a sportfish caught in the Gulf and along the Southeast Atlantic coast. Cobia has a sweet, lobsterish taste and texture, with good amounts of fat. It takes well to aquaculture, and it's on its way to us.

Finding wild fish is getting harder and harder. In America, wild salmon is available only from May through September, and this gorgeous fish usually comes at a very high price. Many of the oysters in America are farmed, as are almost all of the Southern clams and catfish (fed almost exclusively on grain). But no one's farming sardines or anchovies yet; these little fish are always reliably wild and full of great levels of omega-3, with almost no accumulated toxins.

Is there a case to be made for eating *no* fish? From an ecological perspective there certainly is, since fish everywhere are danger-

Fish for Breakfast

In other parts of the world, fish for breakfast is standard fare, or used to be—kippers in England and Scotland, herring and eel in Holland, all sorts of fish in the Middle East, and of course smoked salmon and whitefish here. It's a great idea, and a great way to get your omega-3s up and running for the day. The following are good on toast (try mackerel on rye toast), including low-carb toast, and almost all of them are good with scrambled eggs.

- mackerel canned in olive oil, drained
- gravlax
- smoked trout
- smoked salmon
- kippered (hot-smoked) salmon
- whitefish (sable)
- salmon caviar

ously overfished (check out www.seafoodchoices.com for the latest information on endangered fish), and perhaps from an economic perspective as well—fish is expensive and easy to ruin by overcooking. Pollution is another serious concern as is antibiotic and other drug pollution in farmed fish. If you just don't like fish, especially oily fish, there's no reason to force yourself to eat it. So far no studies suggest that it's better to have a food source for fish than a supplement source; we know the supplements work. On the other hand, if you like fish, it's a great protein source, with the bonus of high levels of omega-3. Your choice.

Here are the fish with the highest levels of omega-3 fat, the healthy fat.

Salmon

Aside from canned tuna, salmon is the fish most Americans love best—even in its bland, somewhat mushy farm-raised form. Salmon in all its permutations—smoked, fresh, canned, or caviar—has plenty of omega-3 fat in a highly palatable package.

Vanity is a good reason to eat salmon. Yale dermatologist Dr. Nicholas Perricone (*The Wrinkle Cure*) likes his patients to eat it twice a day and calls it a facelift on a plate. It's the omega-3 and especially DMAE, a nutrient that promotes muscle tone and inhibits skin-sagging. Salmon has more DMAE than any other food.

If you've never tasted wild salmon, you owe it to yourself to try it in season, which is May through September. It has a completely different texture from farm-raised salmon because this is working salmon that swims in the ocean and then makes its way back up into rivers to spawn. Its fat content is highest just before it makes the trek. Instead of the wide chevron designs you're used to seeing in the salmon in the supermarket, separated by big white stripes of fat, this salmon has tight small chevrons and just a thin streak of white fat separating them. Its color is much richer (though farmed salmon is given carotenoids in the feed to pump up the color). But the big deal about wild salmon is its firm texture and the sensational taste: luxurious, buttery, the essence of good fish.

Almost all of our wild salmon comes from the West Coast: Oregon, Washington, and Alaska. The first wild salmon to hit the market every year are often Copper River salmon from Alaska, which have a high fat content and firm texture. This delicious salmon also has a finely tuned publicity machine behind it, which is just as well, since its season is only about three weeks long (end of May to early June). King salmon, a.k.a. chinook, makes its big splash in May as well, and it has the highest fat content of all the salmon— you can hardly believe a simple plainly cooked piece of it isn't drenched in butter.

Among the wild salmon with medium amounts of fat are the sockeye, which is vividly red, and the coho (a.k.a. silver), not as tasty and more likely to flake, because it doesn't have a very firm texture. These two and the pink, which is a low-fat salmon, are the ones that usually get canned. One of the surprises in the fish world is that although wild salmon is very rarely available fresh in our markets, canned salmon is actually wild. On the West Coast, several packers sell high-quality wild salmon in cans; among them is Katy's Smokehouse, which has a superb canned king salmon.

Good canned salmon—king (chinook), sockeye, or coho is fine and the skin and bones are good sources of calcium and other nutrients. This salmon is fine for salmon burgers, salmon salad, and salmon loaf.

All of these wild salmon are Pacific salmon. You may think Atlantic salmon is also wild, but it almost never is; it's actually just a species of salmon, the one most likely to be farmed, and it can be farmed anywhere from Norway to Chile. In fact, most of our farmed Atlantic salmon comes from Chile. Wild Atlantic salmon has declined 75 percent in the last thirty years.

If you're buying salmon fillets, get center cuts. The skinny part toward the tail has less fat, so it will be tougher. All salmon benefits from a little salt before cooking, preferably sea salt. Leave it to season for from 20 minutes up to 2 hours, then film the surface with some good olive oil. If you're grilling salmon, which is delicious, either grill an entire fish or put the fish in a grill basket—otherwise it tends to fall apart while it's cooking.

BEST (ALL WILD)

- Wild salmon in season (May through October)
- Artisan-smoked salmon from Ireland or Scotland or the Pacific Northwest (see Sources)
- Canned king (chinook), coho, sockeye, or red salmon
- Salmon packed in pouches (though the bones and skin are missing)
- Frozen-at-sea salmon

GOOD

- Fresh firm farmed salmon raised on fish or algae oil in cold clean waters (Norway and Ireland are good sources)
- Smoked salmon from good suppliers

AVOID

- Soft, mushy farmed salmon
- Canned pink salmon
- "Supersalmon" from Canada, which has been raised on growth hormones

Tuna

Virtually every American child—and almost every American cat—dearly loves tuna. Rich, delicately fishy, almost sweet, canned tuna is the only fish many of us eat on a regular basis. Old-timers may have noticed that canned tuna isn't what it used to be, and that's because the food regulations changed several decades ago so that tuna prices could be kept low. We used to get firm steaks of tuna or big chunks, and although that's sometimes still the case, more often we get flakes of tuna, bound together with soy protein, casein, and onion powder to make "food glue," binding tiny bits of fish into what look like chunks of tuna. (Chicken nuggets are produced in the same way.) These additives are quite legal, and the FDA doesn't require them to be listed on the ingredients label. Tuna can also be treated with tripolyphosphate (TPP), the same chemical that's used on scallops kept in short-term storage. TPP binds with water to bulk up the fish so that it fills the can completely—sometimes you can barely fork it out. By such magic, you get only 4.4 ounces of actual tuna in a 6-ounce can. If this sounds odd, how much odder is it that most American tuna is canned in American Samoa, and it's frozen before it's cooked and canned?

Ordinary supermarket tuna is often frozen and then cooked twice. The whole fish is cooked, the oil is removed and sold separately (including some omega-3s, unfortunately), and then the tuna is cooked again in the can with some vegetable broth.

The Mercury Question

Since pregnant and nursing women have been urgently advised not to eat various large fish—shark, swordfish, tuna, king mackerel—on a regular basis, the question arises as to whether these fish are good in anyone's diet. And it's problematic, because three of these fish are excellent sources of omega-3, the very fats these women need to eat.

But mercury toxicity is a serious problem that can result in neurological damage. Although there has always been a certain amount of mercury in the ocean, where it concentrates from the air, industrial pollution has intensified the environmental levels, especially in the Great Lakes, in rivers, and along the coastline.

How much mercury gets into the fish? It's impossible to say, though, in general, fish caught in shallow waters has more, and the larger the fish, the higher the concentration. In the case of tuna, for instance, there are giant fish and there are small fish. The small fish, unless they're living near the coastline, are much less likely to be contaminated, and those are the fish that usually end up in cans of tuna.

The two major agencies in charge of such things have, amazingly enough, different guidelines for mercury consumption—and even different fish on their lists. The FDA has an upper limit of about 20 micrograms of mercury per day per 100 pounds of body weight. The EPA has an upper limit of 4.5 micrograms, meaning close to five times

So choosing a good canned tuna is a serious undertaking. The spectrum ranges from nasty flakes of tuna jammed in the can with vegetable broth or an inferior oil—soy or vegetable oil—to superb imported and domestic tunas that are among the most delectable fish imaginable. Great tuna is caught far offshore, perhaps twelve hundred miles out to sea, where the waters are cleaner. In the boutique brands, it's usually sashimi quality, which is to say the absolute best, and often it's line-caught and hand-cut as well. A buzzword in the tuna world is *ventresca* (which just means "belly" in Italian),

stricter. There's a huge safety margin of about tenfold even in the FDA guidelines, which should mean that most people are not at actual risk from eating a fair amount of fish from time to time. According to the FDA, a single week's consumption of a lot of fish won't cause a big increase in mercury levels in the body, but a second week might start to cause a problem. For fish not on the danger list, consumption of up to 12 ounces a week is fine, says the agency. If you're feeding kids or if you're pregnant, be especially cautious.

According to a *Consumer Reports* study of canned tuna, mercury levels are twice as high in white tuna as in light tuna. How much mercury you can safely absorb depends on body weight. A 132-pound woman can eat one can of white tuna or two cans of light tuna a week with no ill effects.

If all this makes you uneasy, fish oil or DHA is the way to go—pharmaceutical-grade fish oil has no mercury or other toxins and all the benefits of omega-3 fat.

There's some optimistic mercury news as well. A study (*Science*, 2003) on mercury compounds in fish discovered that it's not methyl mercury, as had been widely assumed, but probably thiol-mercury, which is only about one-sixth as toxic as other mercury compounds.

Secret weapon: alpha-lipoic acid, the very powerful antioxidant, also clears mercury and other toxins from the body. If you eat a lot of fish, it's a good idea to take 200 milligrams a day, with a B-complex vitamin supplement.

thought to be the most succulent part of the tuna, with a rich layer of fat just under its belly skin. Great Spanish and Italian tuna is usually caught during the harvest when it's the fattest because it's ready to lay eggs. Once landed, this great tuna is then speedily canned in olive oil, often extra virgin olive oil. A salade Niçoise made with this type of tuna is sensational.

Varieties of tuna make a difference too. Albacore, the "white" tuna, has the most omega-3 fat, but it is, to my taste, dry and boring. It also has twice as much mercury as light tuna. With just a little less omega-3, light tuna (which means light in color only) is much tastier, especially if it's packed in olive oil. If you have a choice, look for yellowfin, tongol (which has a very mild flavor), and bluefin (the fattest, most prized tuna, but also the biggest one, so a good candidate for mercury content, a particular concern for pregnant women). Otherwise, most canned tuna is skipjack, not a particularly fine fish but, on the other hand, a smallish tuna, not so likely to have large stores of mercury. Lots of cheap tuna is caught close to shore, where it's likely to pick up off flavors from diesel fuel and other contaminants you'd prefer not to eat.

Is there any advantage to water-packed tuna? If you like it, it's fine. A 1998 article in the *New York Times* explained, however, that oil-packed tuna actually has less fat than water-packed tuna. That's hard to swallow, but the reason is logical. Fat doesn't mix with water, so almost none of the tuna fat goes into the packing water. But some of the tuna's fat *does* mix with the oil that's drained off, so it's lower-fat. I think olive oil–canned tuna is much tastier, and, besides, the antioxidants in the oil protect the omega-3s in the fish to some extent.

If you drain oil-packed tuna very well, say 20 minutes, an amazing amount of oil comes out of it. Unless it's boutique tuna, toss the oil. If you have boutique tuna, packed in glass jars, be sure to keep it in a dark place so the fragile oils aren't depleted by light.

Aside from its good protein and omega-3 fat, tuna is a rich source of selenium. Ridha Arem, M.D., author of *The Thyroid Solution,* says that free radicals can actually destroy thyroid tissue, but only if there's a selenium deficiency. Tuna also has more DHA, the brain-food part of omega-3, than other fish. Tuna is on the mercury list, however, though some researchers say it is less likely to have mercury contamination than the other big fish, depending on whether it's deep-sea tuna or caught offshore (tuna travels a lot) and whether it's small (skipjack, bonito) or large (bluefin).

Fresh tuna steaks are wonderful quickly panfried or cooked on the grill. Sashimi quality tuna can even be eaten raw—though that's always a bit of a gamble unless you have an impeccable source. You can make your own preserved tuna—called tuna confit (see page 244)—if you run across some great-looking tuna at the fish market.

Great fresh tuna is bright colored and doesn't have any brown areas or rainbow colors—that would mean tuna that's been hanging around too long. Because of its relatively high omega-3 content, tuna spoils very quickly. Ask your fish market when the tuna comes in and buy it that day; have steaks freshly cut, the dark oily stripe removed, and cook it the same day. Tuna tastes best undercooked in the center; in fact, it can be almost raw in the middle. If it's cooked all the way through, it will be dry and uninteresting, whereas almost-raw tuna is very succulent and delicate.

BEST

- Sashimi-grade fresh tuna
- Imported boutique tunas: Ortiz bonito belly (*ventresca*) from Spain (The Spanish Table, www.tablespan.com); L'Antico Sappore Trancio di Tonno and Flott, from Sicily (www.esperya.com)
- American boutique tunas: Katy's Smokehouse (www.katyssmokehouse.com) and Lazio (www.laziotuna.com), both albacores; Katy's is roasted in the can with just its juices, Lazio, a favorite of Julia Child, is packed in olive oil. Dave's gourmet albacore has lots of aficionados; it's sold at Whole Foods Market stores or through the website www.davesalbacore.com.

GOOD

- Genova (yellowfin) or Progresso chunk light tuna packed in olive oil

OKAY

- Supermarket tuna
- Tuna in pouches (which has been minimally heated, unlike

canned tuna, so in theory it retains more omega-3s); it's dry and relatively tasteless, however

AVOID

- Flaked tuna
- Tuna packed in soy oil or vegetable oil

Swordfish

Although it's a good source of omega-3 fat, swordfish has a few things going against it. Because it's such a huge fish, it's high on the mercury list. It's also expensive and overfished. But it's mighty tasty; if you like swordfish and it's not on the endangered list, great. Give it a try with the milk soak on page 211, which brings out a lovely sweetness in the fish.

Trout

Virtually all the trout you see for sale in the market are farmed, but they can be very good, depending, as with everything else, on what they ate. Trout raised on soy taste like cardboard, declares one fish expert, and so they do. They're also not good sources of omega-3s. So once again, taste is a good indicator of what's good for you—a delicious trout is one that was raised right, which means it will have a good amount of omega-3.

Wild river trout are still around, of course, and people catch them all the time. Their flavor is lovely and delicate. Lake trout may be polluted, but they're especially high in fat, so their omega-3 content is enhanced—if you know the source is clean, they're good for you, but they may have a muddy taste.

My favorite way to eat trout is smoked.

To choose fresh trout, ask at the fish market what its feed was—if it was grain-fed, pass it by. If it was raised on fish or algae oil, however, it should taste very good and have good amounts of omega-3. Look for a slippery fish with a clear layer of slime (unappealing, but a good sign nonetheless) all over it. As with shrimp, however, you're probably better off with a flash-frozen farm-raised trout than a well-traveled fresh one, which may be way too old by the time it reaches your kitchen.

BEST

- Wild trout
- Smoked trout, especially the apple-wood smoked trout from Walden Farms in Virginia (www.waldenfoods.com)

GOOD

- Farm-raised trout fed on fish or algae oil

AVOID

- Farm-raised trout fed on grain
- Lake trout, unless you're sure the source is pristine; it can have a muddy taste and may have concentrated pollutants

Mackerel

Mackerel are abundant fish almost everywhere yet completely unappreciated in America except for a few enlightened outposts such as New Orleans—though they sometimes appear on restaurant menus as amberjack. They're the big winners in the omega-3 competition, so they're definitely worth a second look.

Because they're so oily, mackerel must be pristinely fresh, preferably cooked the same day they're caught. If you can manage that, you'll have a terrific fish that's not only full of the good fat but also almost delicate in flavor. Panfried or broiled, so that the skin gets crisp, these fresh, fresh fish are delicious. A mackerel that's a few days old, however, is the fishiest of fish, the one that embodies everything you dread about fish, as Irish chef James O'Shea likes to say. O'Shea also points out that mackerel, like all the other oily fish, even salmon, has a dark strip of flesh that's filled with fat of a slightly bitter nature. Unless you remove that strip, which not all fishmongers do, you'll be left with something quite ferocious on your plate.

Mackerel have a season: they're best of all in the fall, after they've plumped up during summer. In the spring, they're at the end of a long fast, so they're not nearly as fatty. But there are mackerel available all year long, with varying degrees of fat content.

Especially good eating is the king mackerel, a big gamefish that usually turns up in the market as mackerel steaks. Don't try to marinate these—can't be done. But king mackerel is high on the mercury list, so it shouldn't be a constant part of your diet. Spanish mackerel are much smaller and rank right up there with the tastiest fish around. They're great almost any way you can think of to cook them, from grilling to smoking to roasting to broiling. If you love fish, Spanish mackerel should be on your shopping list.

If you've ever eaten canned mackerel from big cans, chances are you won't want to be doing that too often. Although it's a good cheap protein source, with lots of omega-3, to my taste, it's very reminiscent of cat food.

On the other hand, mackerel fillets canned in olive oil in small cans are quite delicious, and some omega-3 seekers even eat them for breakfast. If you can't find them at your market, look in the kosher section, where they sometimes turn up.

If mackerel scares you, an easy way to approach it is to find a good brand of smoked mackerel, which is quite delicious.

BEST

- Spanish mackerel and king mackerel steaks, impeccably fresh
- Canned mackerel fillets in olive oil, in small cans

GOOD

- Atlantic mackerel

AVOID

- Big cans of mackerel
- Any mackerel over a day old

Herring

You'll probably never see fresh herring for sale in an American fish market, but pickled herring and herring fillets in sour cream turn up from time to time, especially in East Coast delis, and they have the good fat.

Herring is much beloved in Europe, but it has never caught on across the pond. You're more likely to see it canned, in the form of kipper snacks (definitely an acquired taste) or herring fillets. I find either one a tough go—herring can have a very strong, superfishy taste—but some people love them.

The one way you may find fresh herring is labeled as fresh sardines, about 3 to 4 inches long. These are great on the grill (see the recipe on page 242).

Sardines

Of all the great sources of omega-3 fat in the sea, sardines are the purest and best, not to mention the cheapest. Because they're so young, they haven't had time to build up toxins in their fat in the same way big old fish do. The word *sardine* just means small fish, and some sardines are actually herrings—which are vegetarian, so they don't have the toxicity problem at all. Because you eat them whole, they provide extra nutrition beyond their good fat and protein; the bones are a great source of calcium, and eating the whole fish means you get a higher concentration of DHA, from the nervous system, than you do with, say, a fish fillet.

Sardines (including canned ones) are great on the grill, and they're also great smoked. My favorite sardines in the can are the tiniest ones, lightly smoked and packed in two layers in olive oil (don't buy sardines packed in linseed oil, a.k.a. flax, which doesn't taste good and is far too perishable; it can't take either the heat of canning or the extra oxygen involved in the process). Gourmets think the finest sardines come from Portugal, which is a rich unpolluted source, or from Norway. In France, canned sardines are considered a special delicacy, and they're kept to age in their tins—a twelve-year-old can of sardines of good pedigree is like a great fine wine.

If omega-3 fat rather than taste is your main concern, look for sardines packed in sardine oil. Otherwise, olive oil is the best fat. Sardines that are packed in soybean oil or cottonseed oil have too many omega-6s, the very fats you should be avoiding, and cotton is not a food crop in any case. If you prefer them, water-packed sardines are also fine.

Before you run screaming out of the room at the very idea of sardines, give them a chance. Although they don't have as much omega-3 as whole sardines, the skinless, boneless kind will taste less fishy. Better yet, choose a good brand such as Season Brisling sardines (sprats) in olive oil, drain them well, give them a good squeeze of fresh lemon juice, and eat them atop a slice of just-toasted whole-grain bread with a slathering of good butter and a slice of sweet onion, if you have any. If this doesn't taste good to you, you really don't like sardines.

Sardines also have a great affinity with crackers. Manhattan chef Gabrielle Hamilton loves sardines on Triscuits so much she serves them with drinks at Prune, her very hip restaurant.

Lots of Europeans eat sardines several times a week, and they've come up with charming sardine utensils to deal with them. One is a little perforated shovel to pull the sardines out of the can minus the oil; another is the British classic sardine fork, a short flat fork with

---

What's So Good About Sardines

- They have 40 percent more omega-3s than salmon and 500 percent more than tuna.
- Sardines with bones are great sources of calcium. One serving gives you half your daily calcium requirement, more calcium than a cup of milk.
- They're the least polluted of all the omega-3 fish except for anchovies—especially those from Norway.

stubby tines. You'll see these in antique markets such as Portobello Road in London, and they're actually very useful.

BEST

- Portuguese or Norwegian sardines packed in olive oil, the smaller the fish, the better (Mediterranean sardines have more mercury)
- Lightly smoked sardines (delicious)
- Water-packed sardines
- Sardines packed in sardine oil, which are higher in omega-3 fat
- Some good brands: Angelo Parodi, Season, and King Oscar

AVOID

- Sardines packed in soy, cottonseed, or flax (linseed) oil
- Sardine fillets (the bones are very good for you)

Anchovies

I know, you either love anchovies or you hate them. But chances are, if you hate them, you couldn't detect their presence in a dish where they're not staring you in the face. That's because their deliciousness goes straight into the food they're enhancing, while their fishiness just vaporizes. You can make them even less fishy using the trick on page 211.

Caesar salad, Worcestershire sauce, and Asian fish sauce are all based on anchovies—so you may be more familiar with these tasty little fishes than you think.

Anchovies come out very high on the omega-3 scale, but that's misleading, because they're always compared ounce for ounce with other fish. No one I've ever heard of would think of sitting down to eat as many anchovies as would balance the scale with a piece of salmon (three tins' worth)—it's just not possible, because the flavor is so concentrated and they're so salty. Still, they have lots of omega-3, they're not contaminated in any way by anything, and their deliciousness factor is so high that you should welcome them into your kitchen.

Chefs love anchovies packed in salt, but these are hard to find in the market, and they require boning and extensive rinsing in any case. Chefs can also order vacuum-packed pizza-size packages of already cleaned, delicious anchovies that are preseasoned with a great variety of flavors, everything from olive and olive oil to vinegar and herbs. You may see white anchovies for sale or on a restaurant menu—these have been bleached by a long rest in vinegar, and they can be an alarming surprise: they're extremely punchy.

For a home cook, the best bet is anchovies in jars, preferably from Portugal. These need just rinsing and perhaps mellowing, using the trick on page 211. Anchovies in tins are good too; look for the ones from Portugal packed in olive oil. A lot of anchovies come from Peru, and they're not as tasty.

Although they seem to keep forever in the refrigerator, anchovies quickly lose their delicious flavor. If you're not going to use them all up in two or three days, make anchovy butter (just chop and mash anchovies into softened butter) and freeze whatever you don't use within the week.

BEST

- Salt-packed anchovies, which have to be rinsed and cleaned, then put in olive oil (one big salt-packed anchovy equals an entire small tin of anchovy fillets)
- Talatta Sicilian oil-packed anchovies (www.citarella.com)

GOOD

- Portuguese or Spanish anchovies packed in olive oil in glass jars

OKAY

- Tinned anchovies packed in olive oil from Portugal

Caviar and Fish Roe

In Russia, caviar is health food as well as a gourmet delight. A spoonful of caviar is just what any Russian doctor or grandmother recommends for childbirth, any kind of illness, or a fragile constitution. In the absence of loads of greens and other vital produce, Russians make do with caviar (which contains vitamins as well as omega-3s), as they have for a very long time. Until the recent economic disaster, an ordinary Russian family might enjoy half a pound of caviar every month.

Most Americans have never even tasted caviar, and of those who have, aficionados aren't instantly born. Still, this is very good stuff—a mere spoonful gives you a full gram of omega-3s and no doubt other nutrients we're unaware of to date. If you like caviar, here's a green light to eat more. If you don't like it, try some of the milder forms listed below. These are the major caviars, beginning with the different species of sturgeon.

> Beluga: This is from the famous giant sturgeon, the one that's in danger from overharvesting. It comes from the Caspian Sea, and it is quickly put into cans or jars with little processing. This is the Rolls-Royce of caviar, but not everyone agrees it's the best tasting. It's definitely the most expensive, upward of $50 an ounce.
>
> Osetra: With a more aggressive taste than beluga, this firmer caviar is also considerably less expensive.
>
> Sevruga: These eggs are much smaller than beluga caviar, and it costs only half as much. Some people like it best of all, however.

Imported sturgeon caviars can be found at a great bargain in the wholesale clubs such as Costco year-round, and especially around the holidays, and they're very good quality. Salmon caviar can be very good and can be used almost exactly as regular sturgeon caviar is used. It's very high in omega-3 fat, like all caviars.

The word *caviar* is like "Champagne"—there's only one source of real caviar, the sturgeon, and you're not allowed to call anything else caviar. So it's quite incorrect to call salmon eggs, for example, caviar, but everyone does. A really lovely caviar comes from Pacific salmon. If the source is chum salmon, it will be pale yellow and a bit soft. The caviar from king and coho salmon is the bright red one, and it's a bit firmer.

There are also American caviars, produced in the Pacific Northwest (especially good whitefish caviar) and in Louisiana (American sturgeon), from the Mississippi River. These taste a lot like sevruga, and are usually a comparative bargain.

Fish roe is delicious and full of omega-3. If you can find smoked cod roe in a tube, buy it—it's sensational on crackers. Regular cod roe is very good too, essential for taramasalata, the delicious Greek spread (for a recipe, see page 179).

All caviars are extremely fragile because of their high omega-3 content once the jars are opened. They don't keep: you might be able to stir some caviar from last night into your morning scrambled eggs, but anything beyond the next day will be very disappointing. Arrigo Cipriani of Harry's Bar, the famous Venice landmark, thinks caviar is such a luxury that you should have it only very rarely, buy the best, and buy a lot to consume with toast, butter, and good Champagne.

BEST

- You have to suit your taste to your purse, but I'd start a caviar adventure with sevruga from a good source. "Malossol"—which means very lightly salted—is a good thing to look for on labels.

GOOD

- American sturgeon caviar from the Mississippi
- American whitefish caviar from Tsar Nicoulai, especially Tiger Eye, which has a beluga-like character (www.tsarnicoulai.com)
- Salmon eggs from the Pacific Northwest

AVOID

- Lumpfish caviar (or any other pasteurized fish eggs) from any source; if it doesn't need to be refrigerated, don't buy it except for cod roe in a tube.

SHELLFISH

Although they have less omega-3 than the fatty fish, shellfish are still very good sources, better sources than the leaner fish. Shrimp, oysters, and mussels are the leaders of the pack. Shrimp is definitely the crowd pleaser of the group. Shrimp production has increased three-fold in the last decade, primarily because of shrimp-farming, but our taste for shrimp is also at an all-time high.

Shrimp

There's almost no actual fresh shrimp for sale in America, unless you happen to live in the shrimp belt. But frozen shrimp that's been properly handled may be even better than fresh, because it's frozen right away at the proper temperature, so it doesn't get a chance to deteriorate on its way to market. The shrimp you see piled up at the fish market is actually thawed shrimp, which starts to deteriorate as soon as it's thawed. So you're better off doing the thawing yourself.

You can buy shrimp in big frozen blocks or individually frozen in bags—which is more convenient, because you can just pull out a few shrimp and leave the rest in the freezer for a month or two (wrap them very well, in a couple of layers of plastic wrap and foil). To defrost, you'll get the best flavor if you do it slowly in a bowl of well-salted water in the refrigerator. If you buy already thawed shrimp, toss them with kosher salt or sea salt and let them rest in the refrigerator for half an hour before you thoroughly rinse and prepare them—this will freshen them and develop their flavor.

Big shrimp are obviously easier to prepare than little ones, but size is no indication of flavor; sometimes the little ones are completely delicious. There are some fantastically good little red shrimp along the northern east coast in the spring and summer, caught in water off Maine (Maine reds) and Connecticut and Rhode Island (Stonington shrimp). They're always fresh, not around long, and so full of flavor you may think you've never tasted shrimp before. Rock shrimp are sold without their shells, which makes them appealing, but they're also appealing because of their succulent lobsterish flavor. You can make a great mock-lobster roll with rock shrimp.

Remember, while origin is important, lots of Asian shrimp (which may have the problematic bacteria) get mixed in with American shrimp, which is in short supply, so it's not a guarantee.

Oysters

Along with the spoonful of cod liver oil Americans were downing in the nineteenth century, they were also enjoying another big omega-3 source, the oyster. Oyster houses flourished all along both coasts and barrels of oysters even made their way to aficionados in the Midwest. These ordinary oyster eaters weren't having their oysters on the half-shell with a little lemon as gourmets do today, they were cooking them.

But oysters are strangers in most kitchens today, which is a shame. And the majority of oysters we have are farm-raised; some of them have been through a cleaning process called depuration, to take away sand and other impurities. There are only six depurating plants in the United States, so only a small percentage of shellfish is treated this way. But those that are will be visibly cleaner—mussels will have no beards, for instance. All shellfish comes to the market with a health tag indicating its source of harvest (well, most of the time; those Asian shrimp do sneak in) and the date. If it's been depurated, it will have the letters DP at the end of its health tag ID code, which begins with the abbreviation of the state of origin; Maine, for instance, has health tags that begin with ME. Some fish markets display the health tags; if they don't, you should ask to see them, to find out how fresh the seafood is.

If we've lost our taste for oysters, it may be because they're such hard work to get into—unless you're expert, bloody fingers are the rule. But here are a couple of tricks to make oyster work easier. The first involves not an oyster knife, which doesn't work very well, but an old-fashioned church key, the beer opener with the triangular head. This is the perfect tool to gain entry to the oyster. Hold the oyster securely on the countertop and insert the point of the church key at the hinge. Press down, just enough to open the oyster. Slip a paring knife in the opening and slide it along the inside of the shell to find the muscle that holds the top of the oyster to the shell, being careful not to cut into the oyster itself. Lift off the top shell. If you see a little black spot by the hinge, carefully remove it—it's bitter and it tastes bad. Slide the knife under the oyster and cut the lower muscle, freeing the oyster. Try not to spill any of the juice. You might fearlessly serve the oysters on the half-shell: arrange the oysters, still in the bottom shells, on a bed of cracked ice to serve. I don't recommend this, however; there are rare incidences of bad oysters and the consequences of eating just one can actually be fatal.

Oyster method number two is the idiot's way of doing it—just heat the oysters briefly, and they'll pop right open. This can be done in a covered grill, in a pan in the oven, or in a covered pan on the stovetop. The key is to do it briefly, just a couple of minutes, until you hear the shells clacking open. The oysters inside will still be raw unless you let the oysters stay over the heat too long.

If you get truly fresh oysters from the harvester, with the harvest date noted (check the health tag at the market), you can keep them for up to ten days in the refrigerator, covered with a damp towel.

Oysters are famous for their aphrodisiac potential—interesting, since they themselves change sex several times at least during their lifetimes, sometimes more than once a day.

BEST

- Wild oysters, especially from Oregon and Washington, Rhode Island, or Louisiana

Mussels

Mussels are a great favorite in Europe, but here they have a very small fan club, even though they're cheap, good to eat, and very easy to cook. Again, the problem may be their preparation and nervousness about whether they're good or not. A single bad mussel can do a lot of damage.

The old days of endless scrubbing and dealing with huge amounts of grit, however, are over. Farmed mussels don't need extensive cleaning and many of them have been depurated, which means they have almost no grit and are very clean.

Keep mussels refrigerated, covered with a damp towel to keep them moist. You're going to cook them live, so don't clean and debeard them until just an hour or two before cooking. Toss any mussels that look the least bit unalive; open shells are a dead give-away.

There are freshwater mussels in American rivers, especially the Clinch River in Virginia, but because mussels are great filters for low-level contaminants and because their life span is about the same as ours—which may make you think twice about eating them—they can be seriously contaminated.

Especially noteworthy are the big sweet Mediterranean mussels grown in Puget Sound (a place they got themselves to from the Mediterranean, though now they're farmed). These big, juicy, sweet (actually higher-carb) mussels from Taylor Shellfish Farms come into season in the summer, unlike all other mussels, right after Copper River salmon departs the scene.

BEST

- This is one case in which farmed is better than wild.
- Mussels are best in the fall, winter, and spring, except for the Mediterranean mussels from Taylor Shellfish Farms (www.taylorshellfish.com), which are summer mussels.
- Small mussels are tastier than big ones, except for the Mediterranean and the large New Zealand mussels, which are delicious.

AVOID

- Mussels you or a friend have harvested, or freshwater mussels; farmed mussels are carefully checked, but wild ones can be contaminated, and there's no way you can tell.
- Summer mussels—they're not mussels at their best, and most of their good nutrients will be in scant supply.

OLIVE OIL AND OLIVES

Olive Oil

When I was first learning to cook as a teenager, there was only one olive oil to be found in the supermarket, Pompeiian, which came in a tiny pyramid-shaped bottle. Rumor had it that Italians used this stuff as hair pomade, and it was generally viewed with suspicion, a fit companion for garlic and other bad actors. But the advent of pizza and pasta changed all that. Today in my kitchen there are about six olive oils (which is too many), all but one of them extra virgin. The sixth oil is a light olive oil I use just for frying. I use these oils or coconut oil for virtually all my cooking. My mother would be astonished to see me making a cake with olive oil.

By now the word has gone out: olive oil is the best oil of all for our health, and it's the most delicious oil as well. In fact, as with most real foods, taste is a reliable indicator in olive oil of how healthful the oil is: the more delicious, the better its health profile. So what makes olive oil so healthy?

The first news on this subject came from Ancel Keys, a researcher who was looking all over the world for the healthiest populations. His Seven Countries Study, done in the 1950s, studied twenty-two populations in seven different countries; Crete and Japan emerged as the healthiest. Because in the Fifties heart disease was the most feared illness, that and longevity were the subjects of the study. A very small group of men on the island of Crete were not only very healthy but also very long-lived. This study of what they ate and how they lived is the origin of the Mediterranean diet, a construct of American health researchers to reap the benefits. Except for the Paleolithic diet humans have flourished on for millennia, it's still the best diet around, and because the food is so delicious and so easy to prepare, it's a simple and enjoyable way to eat.

Olive oil is the centerpiece of the Mediterranean way of eating, and it should be the centerpiece of ours as well—not so much to replace butter, but to replace the vegetable and seed oils, such as canola, sunflower, soy, and corn, that have taken over our food supply and pose such dangers to our health (see "Bad Cooking Fats," page 116). Unlike those polyunsaturated oils, olive oil is primarily a monounsaturated oil, so it doesn't stiffen cell membranes like saturated fat of animal origin and it doesn't contribute to the dangerous oxidation that sets the stage for vascular disease and other health disasters.

In fact, olive oil comes with its own natural antioxidant package. The olive oil antioxidants are a thousand times more powerful, weight for weight, than vitamin C. The antioxidants are basically sunscreen, the result of the olive tree's efforts to protect itself from the hot sun, and they're in the leaf of the olive as well as the fruit. The leaf (sold as olive leaf extract in capsules) contains some very powerful antioxidants, capable of killing some viruses, such as Epstein Barr. It can also lower blood pressure without any side effects. Inevitably some of the leaves get into the oil during pressing, which adds some pepperiness and more antioxidants to the mix. Most of the vast store of natural antioxidants, however, is lost when the olives are cleaned before pressing (the cleaning water is usually discarded). Enough, however, remain to make olive oil your best choice at the table and in the kitchen. And even when olive oil is refined, enough antioxidants survive the processing so that they protect the oil from completely breaking down at high heat, such as in frying, if it doesn't go on for a long time. You can actually taste the antioxidants in olive oil; they are highly concentrated in the slightly bitter *olio nuovo,* the new oil that's pressed every fall and bottled right away. You can see them too: the new oil is green (though some other oils are also green). But these antioxidants are fragile and the oil mellows quite soon—some would say deteriorates.

A University of Milan study in 1994 discovered that oleuropin, a key element in olive oil, actually inhibits the oxidation of LDL cholesterol—the process thought to lead to atherosclerosis, hardening of the arteries. Important as antioxidants are for antiaging and cardiovascular health (not only decreasing LDL, the bad cholesterol, but also increasing the good kind, HDL, by about 7 percent), perhaps their most valuable asset is their activity against neoplasms, new growths on cells that can lead to cancerous cell growth. Olive oil seems to be specifically protective against breast and prostate cancers, as well as endometrial cancer. It also inhibits blood clotting, so it protects against stroke and heart attack. There is a much lower incidence of osteoporosis in areas where plenty of olive oil is eaten as well, and the same is true of dementia. When you consume lots of olive oil, your cell membranes remain fluid, able to receive nutrients and toss out their cellular garbage—good health at its most basic level. Because it's so healthful and so easily digested, it's great for both children and the aging. Extra virgin olive oil is usually one of a baby's first foods in Italy—and one of the last foods of the departing.

Of the three main categories of olive oil—extra virgin, virgin, and what's sometimes called pure olive oil—I'm sure you know that extra virgin is the best, and the most expensive: it's pressed without using heat or chemicals (unlike all other vegetable and fruit oils) and it's from the first pressing of the olives, the cream of the crop. Maybe. Unfortunately, in America there are no actual regulations beyond the acidity level (less than 1 percent, though the standard may shortly become more rigorous, dropping down to 0.8 percent). As long as the acidity and chemical analysis requirements are met, some of the oil can still be chemically extracted—or some of it can be not olive oil at all but nut oil or even the dreaded seed oils. Some of it will undoubtedly be real extra virgin oil, but if the price seems too good to be true, it probably is. The way around this is to buy good estate-bottled oil, which is more expensive and usually more delicious, or find a merchant you can trust. And be guided by taste: the adulterated oils just won't taste as good.

The acidity level of virgin olive oil can be up to 2 percent, twice as high as extra virgin, but the oil is still not processed with heat. It doesn't have as much flavor, so it can be used in baking and frying.

Plain or pure olive oil is a blend of a little extra virgin oil with a lot of highly refined oil (usually refined with hexane, a dry-cleaning chemical that's also used to refine soy and canola oils). The extra virgin is added because the refined oil has almost no flavor of its own—so it's often sold as "light" olive oil (a marketing ploy), meaning without flavor, not with lower calories or fewer fat grams. This stuff is the dregs, frankly, though there are even worse dregs, the solvent-extracted residue called pomace, which is used almost exclusively in institutions and some restaurants and not foisted off on the rest of us in the marketplace. (Though I've recently seen pomace, in a charming little bottle that sells for about $3 per cup, in one of Manhattan's finest gourmet markets.)

Olives pressed for oil can be harvested at several stages, from unripe, in which case the oil will be bitter, to mature, which produce a buttery oil. Greek Kalamata olive oil has traditionally been a buttery oil, but now it's changing to a more bitter one, to please the tastes of fans of Tuscan olive oil. The oil from unripe olives will have a slightly greener color, but otherwise color is meaningless.

The oil of the olive has become so coveted that gourmets speak reverently of it and carry on about its fine points and complexities as though it were wine—with which, in fact, it shares many characteristics. Olive oil is alive in the same way wine is, and a huge number of factors conspire to create its distinctive taste, as they do with wine. In Italy alone there are more than four hundred varieties of olives. So where do you start looking for a good oil? To muse about all the possibilities, or some of them, take a look at Deborah Krasner's *The Flavors of Olive Oil,* which characterizes some distinctive oils on a country-by-country basis and notes a few bargains.

Olive oil is like salt; if you can afford the really good stuff, get it—it will make a huge difference in your cooking and perhaps in your health as well. The good stuff is often estate-bottled, made in small quantities with great care. My top three picks for the good stuff are mild French oil, expensive but great for making mayonnaise and other delicate dishes; estate-bottled Tuscan oils, such as Cappezzana; and fine Arbequina olive oil from Spain. If I see unfiltered oil from a good source, I get it—these oils have a wonderful complexity and no doubt are full of some interesting elements we don't yet know about. (I'll never forget finding a brilliant unfiltered Arbequina oil from Spain at Costco for about $1 per cup; every time I walk in the store, I hope I'll see it again.) Although we know of more than three hundred elements that conspire to produce the aroma in a given oil, new discoveries of micronutrients are constant in the olive oil world.

Country of origin isn't always a good indicator of what you're looking for, although French oils are almost always more delicate. Spain is the largest producer of oil, some of it excellent, and some of it—along with Greek oil—destined for Italy, where it's bottled and sent to us as Italian oil, sometimes even as Tuscan oil. For a good everyday oil, I choose a good Greek oil such as a Kalamata from the Avia Cooperative (which appears here under various labels, but Avia will be listed somewhere on the label)—these are good bargains and usually wonderful. Iliada is another good Kalamata oil that's widely available. Price clubs such as Costco have some excellent extra virgin oils; if you have access to Trader Joe's, their organic oils are also very good. If you just want a good supermarket oil, try Colavita, which a number of professional cooks use as their house olive oil for general cooking.

Should you choose an organic oil? Olive trees do have a lot of pests, and they're usually controlled with chemicals. Besides, organic oils tend to be labors of love, so you may end up with a product far superior to what its price would suggest.

There are two specialty oils worth knowing about. *Olio nuovo*, from the first pressing of the year, is jammed with antioxidants and much prized by the locals. Savvy Italians go to the mill to taste the new pressing; they love the burn at the back of the throat these new oils have—the more peppery and burning, the better (and the healthier). The new oil is really more of a condiment, wonderful on bread and vegetables and fish. Despite all its antioxidants, this oil is a bit fragile and best used up within a few months. Look for *olio nuovo* in the spring.

Perhaps the most singular olive oil comes from Armando Manni, an impassioned amateur producer who wanted to create a perfect olive oil for the health of his newborn son, Lorenzo (no, this isn't Lorenzo's oil . . .). This had to be Tuscan oil, from a rare cultivar, and Manni wanted it to have the maximum polyphenol (antioxidant) content possible. The best oils have a polyphenol content of between 100 and 250 milligrams per liter. Manni's oil sometimes exceeds 450 milligrams, and it is always at least in the high 300s. For his child, he also wanted a delicate, light-on-the-palate oil. Manni's friends so loved this oil that they wanted their own, adult version, a bit fuller in taste, so of course he obliged.

Besides their polyphenol content and their superb taste, these very expensive oils are preserved with an amazing freshness, so that opening a bottle is like trying just-pressed oil. Almost all the damaging UV rays are screened by the glass of the bottle and special gases are used to minimize oxygen inside the bottle. If you want to learn more, go to www.manni.biz.

The quality of the oil you choose is only partly dependent on the producer; the minute you open the bottle, you become responsible for its quality thereafter. The enemies of olive oil, and all fragile oils, are UV light (which turns out to be much more damaging than previously thought), heat, and oxygen. Oxygen enters the bottle right away when it's opened, and from then on the process of deterioration is in full swing. Actually the oil is deteriorating slowly on its way to the market and on the shelf in the market, but the pace picks up once it's opened. It needs to be tightly sealed (no cute little countertop metal pitchers with open spouts, and definitely no copper), stored away from light and heat, and not left open after you use it. If it's in a clear (not dark) glass bottle, covering the bottle with foil is a good idea. You could keep it in the refrigerator to stall the inevitable a bit, but gourmets feel that's not a good idea for optimum flavor and texture. A trick I learned decades ago seems to be a good idea: when you open the bottle, add the contents of a capsule of natural vitamin E oil and stir it in well, to boost the oil's own vitamin E. In theory olive oil is good for two years after harvesting, but in fact it's a good idea to use it all the first year. The younger it is, the tastier, and the more antioxidants. Although there's no standardized labeling, look for a harvest date and count forward—or a "best by" date and count backward. If you need to use up a bottle before you thought you might, make some tuna confit (see page 244).

Different oils have different lives in the bottle; delicate Arbequina oil from Spain can go off as quickly as three or four months after the bottle is opened. How do you know if your olive oil is rancid? If it smells nutty (which sounds like a good thing, but isn't), or fishy, or like bananas, it's rancid and will do you harm. With all unsaturated fats, it's a struggle against oxidative rancidity, which turns them into trouble. Olive oil is much more protected by its own antioxidants than other oils, however, which is why it lasts longer.

You can use olive oil for almost everything you do in the kitchen, including baking. In fact, it's wonderful for baking, because it gives a good texture and good keeping qualities as well as some flavor— but you don't taste the cake and think, wow, that's olive oil. You can also use less oil when you bake if you're substituting it for butter or hydrogenated vegetable fats like Crisco—just use one-quarter less olive oil. If you're replacing other liquid vegetable oils, use olive oil measure for measure. This is the one time you might consider using a light olive oil, if you want no olive flavor at all; it's a better choice than the bad vegetable oils.

BEST

- Estate-bottled extra virgin oils from France, Italy, and Spain
- Tuscan *olio nuovo*
- Boutique extra virgin oils from California (like the Tuscan oils, these are expensive)

GOOD

- Kalamata extra virgin oil from Greece
- Kirkland extra virgin oil from Costco
- Trader Joe's organic extra virgin oil
- Iliada extra virgin oil

OKAY

- Colavita extra virgin oil

AVOID

- Pure olive oil, which is highly refined and tasteless—but okay for deep-frying
- Light olive oil—"light" just means pale, i.e., very refined and deodorized; use only for frying and baking, if you need a flavorless oil

Olives

Olives have, of course, all the benefits of olive oil, but they have even more of the good things, because a lot of antioxidants go down the drain when olives are cleaned for making oil. Green olives have more antioxidants than dark ripe olives. All olives also have fiber, and calcium, magnesium, and potassium, plus some nutrients that vary depending on the type of olive.

If it's good to have some nuts every day—and it is—it's also good to have some olives every day. Possibly this is why Europeans often serve nuts and olives with wine as a prelude to the evening meal. If you want something more interesting, serve warmed seasoned olives (see page 171) and spiced nuts, which offer a big bang for almost no work.

You should taste olives before you serve them to anyone, because very often they're overly salty, especially Kalamatas. Give them a really good rinse and if that doesn't do it, give them a soak for 15 minutes and then a rinse.

Buy olives in bulk if you can, and ask for a little extra brine after they're weighed so you can store them at home in the fridge for several weeks. Or, once you get them home, drain the brine and toss the olives with olive oil to cover—they should keep for a month at room temperature and they'll taste better than refrigerated olives. But all olives go eventually; that little container at the back of the refrigerator may have mold growing in it, and even if it doesn't, the olives may be too soft and missing some of their flavor. To use up olives that might otherwise go off, make some tapenade (page 173) or olivada (page 172).

It's not hard to pit olives—sometimes you can do it with just your thumb against a cutting board—and you should always buy them with the pits intact. The flavor starts to go the minute they're pitted, so buying pitted olives is not a good idea.

NUTS

The fact that nuts are on average 50 percent fat is probably hardwired into every dieter's brain. In the old fat-makes-you-fat era, nuts were definitely off the plate. So conscientious dieters missed out on their huge health benefits, which include very good protection against heart disease, prostate cancer, and possibly the development of Type 2 diabetes. They also have countless vitamins and minerals and antioxidants and phytochemicals and phytosterols—all extremely good for you. And, on top of all that, nuts help you *lose* weight: a study at Brigham and Women's Hospital, overseen by the Harvard School of Public Health, discovered that dieters who ate nuts were not only more satisfied with fewer calories, but also lost weight faster and kept it off longer than low-fat dieters. All of the above virtues are also true of peanuts, which are actually legumes that grow underground. Although peanuts have a bit more omega-6 than we'd like them to, their other benefits are so important that they shouldn't be shunned.

Several excellent studies show heart benefits from nut consumption. The USDA Human Nutrition Research Center at Tufts University showed that just a few nuts can lower the risk of heart disease by from 25 percent to 39 percent—a few nuts being 5 ounces a week. The Nurses' Health Study at Harvard discovered that women who ate 5 ounces of nuts a day had a 39 percent lower risk of fatal heart attack (these women tended to have healthier habits in general, but once the statistics were adjusted for other risk factors, nuts were the element that made the difference). A 2001 study at UC Davis looked only at walnuts, and the results are striking: just 5 ounces a *week* cut the risk of cardiovascular disease by 30 to 50 percent. For some reason not yet understood, walnuts are especially protective because they affect the metabolism of fat differently from other omega-3 and omega-6 fats, such as fish and soy. An ounce a day seems like a good compromise—that's just ten walnut halves.

Why do nuts have these good effects? All of them (except peanuts) have very deep roots that pull up minerals; all of them have good fiber counts; and some of them have some specific elements that are valuable. For high vitamin E content (a major antioxidant), it's almonds, peanuts, and hazelnuts. Vitamin E is protective for the blood vessels against attack by free radicals. Peanuts and hazelnuts also contain folate, which lowers blood levels of homocysteine, thought to be a major risk factor for heart disease. Walnuts have the omega-3 ALA, which seems to prevent heart arrhythmia and interfere with excessive clotting. Arginine, which converts to nitric oxide in the blood to widen the arteries and lower blood pressure, is found in walnuts, hazelnuts, peanuts, and almonds. All these nuts also have protein, calcium, copper, potassium, magnesium, phosphorus, thiamine, and zinc—not to mention loads of phytochemicals and phytosterols, which are natural chemicals with cancer-fighting properties. Peanuts also have reserveratrol, the magical ingredient that's in the skin of red grapes and red wine, a powerful antioxidant that may protect against some cancers such as colon, prostate, and breast.

But surely macadamia nuts are really bad for us? Not at all—they have a fatty-acid profile that's quite similar to olive oil's. A University of Hawaii study in 2000 showed that mac nuts don't increase weight or cholesterol or triglycerides. Because they're high in oleic acid, like olive oil, they actually lower cholesterol. And they're the only food with significant amounts of palmitoleic acid, another good monounsaturated fatty acid.

If you're eating an ounce of nuts a day, how does that work out? You can count that at about 180 calories, half of which should come off your carb budget. Pistachios, peanuts, and cashews are the lowest in calories, but even the highest are only 40 calories more per ounce, so you can choose your favorite or a mixture, to get the benefits of all the different nuts. Here's how it sorts out for an ounce of nuts, i.e., how many nuts you get for your ounce:

Nutting Up

You can take your ounce of nuts in some very pleasant ways.

- Sprinkle chopped nuts over your cereal (there's a great low-carb cereal from www.lowcarbcorner.com).
- A handful of chopped nuts in a green salad is lovely, especially if it's dressed with some cold-pressed oil from the same nut.
- Nut crusts for fish are delicious; try some roughly chopped almonds on fish fillets.
- Add some nuts to your tuna salad.
- Nuts and honey on morning yogurt is classic.
- Chopped toasted nuts are wonderful with vegetables such as green beans, broccoli, asparagus, and chard.
- Nuts can be added to virtually any cookie with excellent results.

Peanuts—28
Pistachios—47
Walnut halves—10
Macadamia nuts—10
Hazelnuts—20
Cashews—18
Brazil nuts—6
Almonds—26

Needless to say, all bets are off if the nuts are rancid, in which case they're very bad for you. All nuts will keep for a month in the fridge and in the freezer for at least a year, carefully sealed. But a lot of nuts are already rancid in the store. If you don't have a good source, it's worth mail-ordering them (see Sources) to be sure they're fresh. Nuts that are already roasted and salted are often rancid too, but their main drawback is that they've usually been tossed with soybean oil or some other highly refined bad-fat oil. Just toast your own raw nuts as you use them (see page 169); it's a snap, and the results are much more delicious than store-bought roasted nuts.

Nut butters can be very good nut sources or bad ones; it all depends. Good sources are marked "natural" and will not have been hydrogenated, so the oil is separated out and you have to stir it back in. (It helps to turn the jar upside down every time you use it so the oil will slowly work its way in the opposite direction.) Marantha almond butter and macadamia nut butter have no sugar, no trans fat, and nothing chemical added. Supermarket peanut butters that don't separate into an oil layer and a nut butter layer (because they're hydrogenated, a bad thing) can also have all sorts of additives, from molasses to cornstarch. Natural peanut butters such as Arrowhead Mills, Smucker's, and Laura Scudder (a West Coast brand) are the ones to look for—tasty and with nothing nasty in them.

What about aflatoxin, that mold peanuts can get that's so deadly? The peanut industry claims there hasn't been a single incidence of aflatoxin in peanut butter in years and an aflatoxin expert, John Groopman at Johns Hopkins, agrees that there's almost none in the United States. In Africa and Asia, however, aflatoxin is a huge problem, and it's suspected of setting the stage for liver cancer.

The only problem with nuts is eating too many, because they're so incredibly tasty and moreish. Anything over an ounce a day should be factored into your total calories for the day. You can easily eat less carbohydrate to compensate, and you'll feel so much more satisfied with nuts that you won't be tempted to indulge in sweets.

BEST

- Very fresh raw nuts, from the natural foods store or stores with high turnover whose nuts are always fresh (price clubs often have very good buys on very fresh nuts)
- Natural nonhydrogenated peanut butter such as Arrowhead Mills

AVOID

- Preroasted, salted nuts—do it yourself
- Nut butters that are hydrogenated—check the label

AVOCADOS

The name *avocado* comes from *ahuacatl,* meaning "testicle tree" (the fruit hangs in pairs), which may be why avocados have always been considered an aphrodisiac. In fact, they first got their marketing boost in the Twenties, when growers had to issue a public statement to refute the rumor that they aroused desire in the eater— and sales soared. During the antifat era, they were condemned for their high fat content and pretty much ignored, except for guacamole.

But now avocados are back like gangbusters, and that's because they've earned their place in the health pantheon. They have twice as much vitamin E (the potent antioxidant) as was previously thought (which was already lots); plenty of B vitamins, including folate (the one that lowers dangerous homocysteine levels in the blood); more protein than any other fruit (which is not to say a lot); more fiber than any other fruit; more lutein (a carotenoid very beneficial for the eyes); lots of glutathione (another antioxidant); magnesium; and 60 percent more potassium (which helps to prevent stroke and high blood pressure) than bananas. They're high in fat, but it's the healthy monounsaturated fat, which helps to lower cholesterol. They have four times more beta-sitosterol, a nutrient that reduces the amount of cholesterol we absorb from our food, than any other fruit. And they have zero cholesterol.

Preliminary results from a Japanese study show avocados may protect against liver damage from hepatitis C, results persuasive enough that the head researcher added avocados to his diet.

Beyond their nutritiousness, avocados are very easy to digest—in fact, Israeli babies are weaned on them.

And, of course, all this goodness comes in a very delicious package. Avocados are endlessly adaptable, and they can even be heated—but they can turn bitter if overheated.

Hass avocados are, to my mind, the most delectable, and they're in season all year long. These are the black pebbly skinned ones. The bigger green-skinned Fuertes can be good in the spring for slicing, but they tend to be bland and watery, much less nutty and buttery. In some markets, you may see tiny cocktail avocados, which are tiny Fuertes; if you do, grab them—some people eat them skin and all; in the center there's just a little quill instead of a pit.

The biggest problem with avocados is having a ripe one ready when you want to use it. A perfectly ripe avocado is gently yielding but not soft at the stem end. You'll usually see unripe avocados at the market, and they'll take 3 to 4 days to ripen at home at room temperature. You can hasten the process a bit by putting them in a paper bag with a ripe banana, whose gas will ripen the avocado. Use the paper bag even if you don't use the banana; it will still help in the ripening. In an emergency, you can take a nearly ripe avocado to an acceptable taste and texture by microwaving it for a minute. The heat will soften it and bring out the buttery quality.

The other big problem is that you need to prevent a sliced avocado from turning brown, so you either have to cut it at the last minute or douse the cut flesh with lemon juice or lime juice. A way of bypassing all that is the clever trick used by supercook Diana Kennedy, of slicing the avocado through the skin into the usual vertical slices, but leaving the fruit intact and the skin on until the last minute; then you just peel off the skin slice by slice. There's also an avocado slicer (see Sources) that works really well, though slicing avocados is hardly a problem that needs solving.

If you're stuck with too many ripening avocados, you can freeze avocado puree: just add a tablespoon of fresh lemon juice for each 2 avocados, seal tightly, and freeze for up to 1 month.

Wonderfully good as avocados are for you, it may seem as if avocado oil is the dream oil—a smokepoint of 500 degrees, plus all those other great attributes. And it says "cold-pressed" on the label, so you know it's a good oil. Not so fast. Pressed avocado oil is very bitter and unpalatable, so it has be refined and deodorized before it turns into that lovely clear liquid in the bottle. That means it isn't a healthy oil at all anymore, because of free radical and trans-fat problems. So stick to the fruit and pass by that great-looking oil.

COOKING FATS AND OILS

As we've seen in earlier sections of this book, a lot of the choices for cooking are extremely problematic (see "Bad Cooking Fats," page 116). Since this is one of the most important health choices you can make, it's a good idea to clear out everything that's not health-enhancing from your kitchen cupboards and start anew. It's also a good idea to date oils when you buy them, since anything over a few months old, except for olive oil and coconut oil, can be a problem. Light, heat, and oxygen are the enemies of fragile oils, so you need to buy them from a market that doesn't display them in full sunlight.

Fat Insurance

When you eat a lot of rich food at a single meal, you can dramatically increase the amount of fat in your blood—a temporary effect, but not a positive one. Drinking a spoonful of vinegar (not lemon juice, which doesn't give the same result) will eliminate this phenomenon.

If you get an improperly stored oil, it will be well on its way to rancidity before you even open the bottle.

The good fats for cooking are in the oleic family, sometimes known as omega-9 fats, which include both animal and vegetable sources: butter, lard, olive oil, hazelnut oil, and peanut oil. Avocado oil seems to belong on this list too, but since it's impossible to bottle it without heavy refining and deodorizing (because it's bitter and needs refining), you should leave it on the store shelf. Canola oil (a.k.a. genetically modified rapeseed oil) is also high-oleic, but it suffers from the same problems as avocado oil and also has too much omega-6. (The Spectrum brand of canola and soy oils is guaranteed not to be genetically modified and is expeller-pressed.) Some safflower and sunflower oils have had a small amount of monounsaturated oil added—they're labeled high-oleic.

Here are the very best fats and oils to use, bearing in mind Dr. Mary Enig's advice that you shouldn't confine yourself to just one oil. Good oils are all full of good nutrients—unless they've been removed in processing—and you need a broad spectrum.

NOTE: Avoid oils in plastic bottles. Tins or dark glass bottles are best.

- *Olive oil.* Use extra virgin from a good source (see page 105) for general cooking, in salads, and as a dressing for vegetables whenever a distinctive olive flavor is appropriate. Olive oil is good for baking (use 25 percent less than solid fat such as butter than the recipe specifies); extra virgin oil is fine for baking unless you want a flavorless oil. But use mild or light olive oil for deep-frying; although this is a highly processed oil, it still retains a few of its antioxidants and in frying, very, very little of the fat gets into the food, if it's properly fried (see page 226). Olive oil also tends to form a crust on the food as it's frying, which protects against absorption.

  It's essential to protect olive oil from light, heat, and oxygen by storing it tightly sealed in a cool, dark cupboard. It's a good idea to stir in the contents of a capsule of natural vitamin E oil when you first open the bottle (ideally a dark bottle, to protect the oil inside) to boost the antioxidants. If you're not going to use it often, it's okay to store olive oil in the refrigerator and just bring it to room temperature before using, though the texture will suffer a bit (but this isn't a good idea for the best estate-bottled oils).

- *Coconut oil (a.k.a. coconut butter).* This is very good for sautéing, baking (use 25 percent less than the amount of fat called for in the recipe, or the food will be greasy), frying, and for popcorn. It's not suitable, however, for salads or as a dressing for vegetables unless the weather is very warm, so the coconut oil will be liquid. Solid at room temperature, coconut oil melts at 76 degrees. Extremely stable, it will keep for at least a year at room temperature, and up to two years in the refrigerator.

- *Unhydrogenated peanut oil.* This excellent oil is great for frying because it has a very high smokepoint. Roasted peanut oil, such as the excellent product made by Loriva, is delicious on salads

Mix It Up

You're not confined to using a single oil for a single purpose. Lots of cooks routinely mix butter with olive oil, especially for sautéing vegetables. You can heat the butter to a higher temperature (butter by itself can't be heated over 325 degrees) this way, and you'll also get some of the good antioxidant benefits of olive oil. Coconut oil is also a good mixer with other good fats, such as olive oil.

Dr. Mary Enig suggests a mixture of equal parts coconut, sesame, and olive oils, which needs to be liquid when it's mixed (since the coconut butter will be solid at room temperature it needs to be slightly heated) and thereafter refrigerated. This combination works very well for light frying and sautéing and products are already coming onto the market that ape this blend. Some of them are marketed as MCT oils, medium-chain triglycerides that don't easily store in the fat cells. Because they're metabolized in the liver, they're burned like carbohydrates for energy. Coconut is usually the base for these oils—and they're not superior to your own blend, though they're much more expensive.

and as a dressing on some vegetables, like greens and broccoli. Peanut oil has a similar good high-oleic profile to olive oil, though it has more omega-6 than olive oil. Partially hydrogenated peanut oil will have trans fats, however, and plenty of free radicals, so avoid it—it will say on the label if it's partially hydrogenated.

- *Sesame oil.* Like olive oil, this oil has its own natural protection against rancidity. The Asian toasted sesame oil turns rancid easily, though.
- *High-oleic sunflower oil.* If you desperately need a flavorless oil that's not light olive oil, this is your best candidate, as long as it's expeller-pressed (cold-pressed, without high heat), not hydrogenated, and stored carefully. Still, this is a fragile oil with no particular health benefits beyond its high-oleic additive. It's about 4 percent trans if refined.
- *Nut oils.* These are delicious, mild oils, best used as vegetable dressings—you can heat them a bit, but don't cook with them, and go easy on the walnut oil, which has a lot of linoleic acid. European nut oils are the best. In Europe there's a great tradition of roasted nut oils, and they're very carefully cold-pressed

Lard from Scratch

Start with good pigfat, preferably from a naturally raised pig, one raised without hormones or antibiotics.

Preheat the oven to 325 degrees. Chop the pork fat into small cubes, discarding any bits of tough skin. A handful at a time, mince the fat in the food processor.

Place the fat in a heavy ovenproof skillet on the top shelf of the oven and bake for 20 to 25 minutes, or until the fat has rendered out. Strain out the crunchy little bits and give them to the birds— or keep them for a cook's treat; they're nice in a salad. Pour the lard into a container, seal tightly, and keep in the refrigerator. It will keep almost indefinitely.

and handled. The nuts used are first-grade, not the second-rate nuts used in most American oils, which are already well on their way to breaking down. Spectrum has a line of these European-style nut oils; another good brand is Loriva. Store these oils in the refrigerator, because they're still very fragile.

- *Butter.* You already know how good butter is and how ghee, or clarified butter, can be used as the "oil" of butter to cook at higher temperatures (see page 70).
- *Tea oil.* New on the market, old in parts of Asia, tea oil is an interesting, healthy oil with less saturated fat than olive oil. Cold-pressed from tea seeds, it's good for sautéing and drizzling over vegetables and salads. It has a light fragrance and a delicate taste. Tea oil has a very high smokepoint, so in theory it should be

Bad Cooking Fats

Bad fats are basically damaged fats or fake fats, like margarine and Olestra, Oatrim, Z-Trim, and other nameless fats of dubious origin. All natural fats in their natural state are good for you (except high omega-6 oils or oils that have been stored badly or too long). You can tell they're good for you because they taste good. Bad fats don't taste good, and they can have some very serious negative effects in the body. But bear in mind that rancid fats, the worst fats of all, don't always taste rancid; if you suspect an oil may have gone off but it still smells okay, heat it and mix it with a little food—the bad taste may emerge.

- Trans fats: anything partially hydrogenated, which includes margarine, vegetable shortening, and all fake fats. Check labels; don't buy it if it's partially hydrogenated or hydrogenated or if it says "low-fat" or "lite." These fats have been altered, bombarded with hydrogen and usually treated with hexane, a dry-cleaning solvent, and aren't recognized by the body as food. They're extremely bad for your health.
- Highly processed oils: soy oil, canola oil, safflower oil, veg-

great for frying—but it's expensive, about $14 for a medium-sized bottle. This is a designer oil, a novelty that's a nice addition to vegetables, especially Asian ones. To find out more about it, check www.therepublicoftea.com.

- *Rice bran oil.* Has a delicate flavor, a high smoke point, and lots of antioxidants.
- *Lard.* Yes, lard. Pigfat (and that includes bacon) actually belongs in the high-oleic group, with a similar profile to olive oil's. Sardinian cooks add some lard to frying oil for extra crispness. Bonus: lard has some antimicrobial properties. If you have a yen for commercial potato chips, you could seek out some old-fashioned chips cooked in lard or peanut oil, such as Grandma Utz's handmade chips from Pennsylvania or Tim's Cascade

etable oil, salad oil, and light olive oil (except for occasional frying). These oils are highly processed to stabilize them, because in their natural state vegetable and seed oils are extremely fragile, vulnerable to light, heat, and oxygen. The stabilizing process involves high heat and often chemical deodorizing as part of the refining process. In the process, the good nutrients are lost, free radicals and trans fats are formed (this begins to happen at 320 degrees in the presence of a catalyst). These oils also depress immune function. They can be used in "good" natural foods where you might not expect them, such as nuts or dried berries, in which case they have a negative effect.

According to Dr. Mary Enig, canola oil is particularly to be avoided. Although there are no long-term human studies on canola, animal studies indicate that it's not good for the cardiovascular system because it's associated with fibrotic heart lesions, negative changes in blood platelets, and vitamin E deficiency. Because it's known to retard growth, the FDA does not allow it to be used in infant formula. Some canola has been heavily deodorized, creating a problematic form of trans that affects the prostaglandin pathways (which influence metabolism, among other things).

Chips from Washington. Because it's also a somewhat saturated fat, lard doesn't break down in frying the way the vegetable oils do, so it's the best choice for frying chicken or other hearty food. Lard is the best fat to use for piecrust, and it's also very good in other baked goods, such as gingerbread. But supermarket lard is highly processed and nasty-tasting, so avoid it. To make your own lard, see "Lard from Scratch," page 115.

- *Palm oil shortening.* Made by Spectrum, it is organic and has no trans fats. It's a good substitute for partially hydrogenated shortenings.

- *Duck and goose fat.* These are absolutely delicious fats that also

Smokepoints

The smokepoint of an oil means just what it says, and it also means the point at which the oil is damaged, broken down, and unhealthy to use—though the breakdown begins at much lower temperatures. In sautéing and shallow-frying, this isn't a big issue, but for deep-frying it's essential to have an oil with a relatively high smokepoint, such as peanut oil.

A special case is olive oil. The smokepoint varies tremendously from oil to oil and harvest to harvest, depending on the level of acidity—the better the oil, the lower the smokepoint (between 200 and 240 degrees)—which has given competing oil manufacturers the opportunity to list olive oil's smokepoint as extremely low (280 degrees), when in fact a nonvirgin olive oil has a very high smokepoint, up in the mid-400s like peanut oil. Extra virgin oils, however, will "break" at a much lower temperature.

Peanut oil: 425 degrees
Olive oil: 200 to 425 degrees (see note above)
Canola oil (partially hydrogenated): 440 degrees
Safflower oil: 318 degrees
Sunflower oil: 450 degrees

belong in the oleic family, but they're hard to come by, unless you roast your own duck or goose. If you do, be sure to save the drippings. They're wonderful for frying potatoes and onions, or for enriching a soup at the last minute, or for cooking the vegetables for a stew. French goose fat should be available at the natural foods store. Chicken fat also fits this good profile to a lesser degree; if you like it, use it.

- *Inexpensive truffle oil.* It has nothing to do with truffles; it's based on a chemical invented at the University of Manchester in England. Real truffle oil is insanely expensive—and delicious. Use it as a condiment; don't heat it.

DAIRY PRODUCTS

Of all the foods in the world, none, except possibly soy, is quite so controversial as milk. Screeds against milk are all over the Internet, and plenty of people think there's no reason anyone should drink any milk after they emerge from toddlerhood. These milk-phobes say milk causes rheumatoid arthritis, obesity, and diabetes—oddly enough, the very conditions milk fans say it cures. Paleo diet aficionados say milk is very recent in our evolutionary past, just three thousand years old, so we shouldn't indulge since our ancient ancestors didn't—that's the diet we evolved to eat. Detractors also point to America as the only country where milk drinking is an adult pastime, a sort of infantilizing habit that makes no sense. It's unthinkable for a sophisticated Frenchman or Italian to down a cold glass of milk with, say, some brownies. But researchers worry that nine out of ten women aren't getting their daily calcium requirement (by about 50 percent) because they don't eat enough dairy products (seven out of ten men don't either) and that children's bones are suffering because they've substituted soda and fruit juice for milk. A new worry is that women are getting too much calcium from all the supplemented foods, which plays havoc with their metabolism and binds iron, a benefit for men but a possible problem for menstruating women.

Possibly everyone is right: according to the Weston A. Price Foundation, which is devoted to traditional foods and their place in our health, contemporary supermarket milk does have a lot of problems, while raw milk, the milk humans have been drinking for about three thousand years, does not. People who are allergic to milk, for instance, are usually not allergic to raw milk. Milk fat is complicated; it has more than five hundred different fatty acids and, in its whole form, antimicrobial factors.

Regular old milk is one of those "whole" foods that seems like it's just pure goodness, in this case, pure cow. But in fact it can be pure milk plus antibiotics, growth hormones, pesticide residues, a little bleach from the milk lines, coloring, and tiny milk-fat globules from homogenization that can easily enter the bloodstream and increase free radical activity. Because skim milk tends to have a blue cast, it's artificially colored. Low-fat milks, 1 and 2%, have spray-dried milk powder, which has oxidized cholesterol and is likely to contain rancid fat as well as lots of nitrites, added to bulk them up. (The Straus dairy in the San Francisco Bay Area is a notable exception. They use a process of reverse osmosis, which basically removes water and condenses the milk. The result is delicious low-fat milk with no additives.) Many cows are treated with recombinant bovine growth hormone (rBGH), a fact that should be noted on the labels of their milk, but since it's undetectable in milk itself, hormone-treated milk can turn up in all kinds of products without being identified as such. Research at Tufts University has suggested rBGH milk may actually trigger the growth of cancer cells.

What upsets critics of commercial milk most is the very fact that it's pasteurized. We have pasteurization as a result of World

The Japanese Take on Ice Cream

Aisu kurima is a new darling for the Japanese, and they're busy creating wildly imaginative new flavors. What they all seem to have in common is their nonsweet high-omega-3 profile. New *aisu kurima*s include: fish ice cream, octopus ice cream, squid ice cream, and crab ice cream . . . but no sardine ice cream yet, and no Cherry Garcia.

War II, when dairy farmers and cheese makers went off to war and were replaced by inexperienced workers who let safety and quality practices deteriorate as they geared up to supply huge amounts of cheese for the war effort. People did in fact die from consuming raw milk products. So in 1949, pasteurization became mandatory. It involves heating milk to a temperature of 170 degrees to destroy bacteria. Taste suffers mightily; raw milk is much more delicious, and once you've tasted it, you'll recognize the "cooked" flavors in pasteurized milk. In the process, say critics, there's a huge nutritional loss for a marginal gain—the problems pasteurization protects against are salmonella, a mild form of E. coli, and listeria, not very serious illnesses unless you're immune-compromised. But people do still get mildly sick from drinking raw milk, however infrequently, even if it's rigorously inspected and tested. On the other hand, raw milk seems to be safer than water; according to the Centers for Disease Control, more than one million people nationwide are made ill by the water in their own homes, and some of them—thousands—die.

Here's a partial list of what's lost in pasteurization, according to Thomas Cowan, M.D., of Noone Falls Health Care, Peterborough, New Hampshire:

- Lots of colloidal minerals and enzymes, which are used in the absorption and utilization of sugars and fats in the milk
- A cortisone-like factor in the cream that's heat-sensitive and aids in combating allergies
- Beneficial bacteria and lactic acid, which implant in the intestines and contribute to a balanced immune system

In addition, he says:

- The heating process produces minerals that are precipitated and so can't be absorbed, sugars that can't be digested, and fats that aren't healthy.
- The process also interferes with calcium absorption, one of the main reasons to drink milk in the first place.
- Heating milk causes changes in the milk protein that have been associated with blood clots.

- Raw milk is useful for treating eczema and arthritis, and it was used to treat diabetes before insulin.

Raw milk is both unpasteurized and unhomogenized, with a lovely cream layer on the top. It's delicious, and it makes ordinary supermarket milk seem boring in comparison. In California, it used to be for sale in supermarkets under the Alta-Dena label, but now it's only sold in natural food stores. It has a shelf life of only seven days, so it presents a problem for commercial distributors. It's a state-by-state question whether it's legal or not.

Whether it's raw or processed, there's a lot to be said about the health benefits of milk. Calcium has become a hot nutritional factor, and it's clear that the best source is milk (except for the bones in canned salmon and sardines), despite all the fortified products on the market. Calcium is, of course, crucial for preventing osteoporosis and for forming good bones in young children—but both children and teenagers have drastically reduced their consumption of dairy products in favor of sugary drinks such as soda and fruit juice. And it's not only bones that calcium's good for: in a 1999 study at Creighton University in Omaha, dieting women who got 1,000 milligrams of calcium a day (the recommended amount) lost 18 pounds more on average than those who didn't. Researchers theorize that the calcium turns off one of the hormones responsible for storing fat. Women who consumed at least three servings of dairy foods per day turned out to be the least likely to become obese, an 80 percent reduction in risk at any level of calorie intake. Michael Zemel, Ph.D., of the University of Tennessee, theorizes that calcium affects the way fat cells do their job, causes them to make less fat, and turns on the machinery to burn fat.

A 2002 *Journal of the American Medical Association* study is perhaps most fascinating of all. It tracked more than three thousand young adults over a ten-year period to determine their habitual intake of dairy foods. Some of these subjects turned out to be overweight, but among them, the ones who consumed the most dairy products had a lower risk of developing insulin resistance, the Syndrome X problem that low-carb eaters are trying to overcome. The overweight individuals consumed fewer dairy products than normal-weight eaters, but those who consumed the most had a whopping 71 percent lower incidence of insulin resistance—and all types of dairy foods, both low-fat and high-fat, were found to provide the benefit. And that includes ice cream (but not soft-serve ice cream, which is full of bad fats, oxidized fats, and high-fructose corn syrup).

Insulin resistance clearly has a genetic component, and it can be controlled by rigid low-carb dieting (such as the Atkins and Protein Power diets) and by alpha-lipoic acid, but until this study, there'd never been evidence that it could be avoided to some degree by simply indulging in some very palatable foods. If weight problems run in your family, you should be sure your kids eat a lot of dairy products.

Researchers couldn't really explain why dairy foods had an impact on insulin resistance, but they noted several earlier studies that linked dairy foods and components such as calcium, magnesium, and potassium to reduced risk of high blood pressure, heart disease, stroke, and Type 2 diabetes—a constellation of ills that are primarily associated with insulin resistance. What's particularly remarkable about this study is that apparently overweight subjects seemed to be protected by dairy products from becoming obese and developing insulin resistance, key risk factors for Type 2 diabetes and heart disease—a finding that could have an important health impact on our ballooning population, removing a lot of the risk of being pleasingly plump.

As if all this weren't exciting enough, there's major research coming in about CLA (conjugated linoleic acid), an omega-6 fat that's in beef and especially dairy products and to a much lesser degree in other animals, such as chickens. You'd think CLA was a bad-fat candidate, since it's an omega-6 fat and a trans fat too. But CLA is actually the only *good* trans fat, and it's becoming a star, because it behaves in the body like an omega-3 fat. Among its benefits are heart health, vein health, and good cholesterol profile as well as low triglycerides. It has anticancer properties, antioxidant actions two hundred times more powerful than beta carotene, and good effects in controlling blood sugar and promoting fat loss. At Harvard Medical School, a supplement called CLA One inhibited the growth of colon cancer and prostate cancer cells in test tube studies. CLA also builds muscle and reduces fat.

The health-enhancing aspects of CLA were discovered by accident at the University of Wisconsin in 1979, when researchers were studying the cancer-causing elements of overcooked food; in fried ground beef, the CLA turned out to be protective. Many, many animal studies later, and a few human ones, it seems the benefits are indeed true, especially for breast cancer. There are different forms of CLA, and some results have depended on which form was used. Currently, three-year studies on human subjects are under way in Scotland, so we should know soon exactly how good CLA is. So far we know that the natural form, in dairy foods, is anticarcinogenic but doesn't seem to offer the heart benefits of the supplement. The most potent CLA, by a factor of three, is pasture-raised cows' milk—but, of course, most of the cows providing milk for your local supermarket have never seen a pasture. A piece of cheese has a lot of CLA; in fact, you'd have to eat fifteen chickens to get the same amount, according to CLA researcher Dr. John Wallace. All ruminant animals, including sheep, produce milk with high CLA levels.

It's striking that all dairy products have these good effects, from milk to cheese to yogurt to crème fraîche (which is especially rich in enzymes) to ice cream. Raw-milk cheeses such as real Parmesan and Roquefort have, of course, all the good elements of raw milk, and they've sat for at least sixty days, which allows the enzymes to destroy any bacteria that would be harmful. (All other raw imported cheeses also have the sixty-day restriction, and they are endangered by American proposals to ban them altogether on the grounds of food safety.) Although gourmets insist these cheeses are better younger, they're still absolutely delicious, and American artisanal cheeses are now rivaling some of the famous European ones—except for Parmesan; the real stuff is unrivaled. And its lactose has been so thoroughly digested by enzymes that two-year-old Parmesan is given to babies in Italy (along with a trickle of extra virgin olive oil) as one of their first foods.

Cheese is the most concentrated source of milk's nutrients, which include high-quality protein, vitamin A, vitamin B_{12}, phosphorus, and zinc. B_{12} also appears in meat, fish, and poultry, but it's best absorbed from dairy products; deficiencies lead to anemia, dementia, and nerve damage. And, of course, cheese is a great source of calcium, deficiencies of which are widespread, according to an article published in 2000 in the *American Journal of Clinical Nutrition.*

Yogurt, especially full-fat yogurt with active cultures, has always had a reputation for healthfulness. Both yogurt and cottage cheese have been considered diet foods for decades now, possibly because of the phenomena described above.

Milk fans think the good things in milk are actually in the fat itself (and certainly that's where the CLA is). Aside from cheese, cream is the best milk-fat source if you can afford the extra calories—but not ultrapasteurized cream, which has nearly eternal life and not much flavor. Its microfat particles easily get into the bloodstream and promote free-radical reactions, not a good thing. Organic cream that's not ultrapasteurized just thickens as it ages into a lovely concentrated form like the Middle Eastern kaymak. For a day or two, that is; then it does, of course, eventually develop off flavors and get moldy and sour.

Just because a dairy product is labeled organic doesn't mean the cows who produced it ever saw a pasture or grazed on one. The larger the company, the more likely it is that the cows were factory-farmed, albeit on organic food.

It would seem there's no point in choosing a low-fat milk, with its unhealthy additives. If you're interested in raw milk, check out the website at www.Realmilk.com, which will give you a state-by-state rundown. That's also the place to find out about cow-shares, a sort of cow co-op in which you and your partners share a cow's milk production.

BEST

- Full-fat organic milk, a relative bargain
- Raw-milk cheeses, American or imported, preferably organic (European raw-milk cheeses can be ordered from www.fromages.com—very expensive, and very good)
- European dairy products, which have no hormones
- Products from small artisanal dairy farms
- Organic yogurt and cottage cheese with active cultures
- Raw milk from a dairy with a good bill of health (in California, look for Organic Pastures, www.organicpastures.com)

- Full-fat milk with no rBGH (a milk-production stimulator)
- Cheeses with no preservatives
- Milk in waxed cardboard cartons; great as it looks, milk in glass bottles can easily lose its riboflavin, a very important nutrient

AVOID

- Imitation or low-fat cheeses—these are full of trans fats
- American cheese
- Processed cheese spreads
- Low-fat dairy products
- Ultrapasteurized cream
- Soft-serve ice cream
- Sweetened yogurts, which are often full of cornstarch too

EGGS

Eggs had to bear the full brunt of the anticholesterol hysteria, and they're just now beginning to recover. When I did some volunteer work in the pediatric department at Harlem Hospital, I'd sometimes get into diet conversations with the parents, and inevitably they had two fixed ideas about health: eggs are bad for you and margarine is good for you. No amount of reason could dislodge these opinions: they "knew" to avoid eggs and butter.

In fact, eggs are the most nutritious single food in the store. The list of their nutrients looks like the label of a very high-ticket multivitamin, at bargain basement rates. The cholesterol scare was based not on eggs themselves, but on powdered eggs (which were of course oxidized) and on crystalline cholesterol, at huge intakes (1,500 to over 4,000 milligrams a day), way beyond anything a human would eat in a day. These were pharmacological studies, not food studies. There are, in fact, exactly zero studies showing a link between actual eggs and heart disease. Who eats the most eggs in the world? The Japanese, the healthiest people in the world, who eat about 340 eggs per person a year. Even the American Heart Association has backed down on eggs, though they haven't exactly trumpeted the news. They moved gradually up from recommending four eggs a week to seven eggs a week, but it's only on their website you discover there are now no specific restrictions on eggs at all. In fact, twelve eggs a day would be fine, but no one's studying that.

The only thing wrong with eggs is their very high omega-6 levels, which isn't the chicken's fault but entirely due to the feed it usually gets. That feed ratio is about 20 to 1 omega-6 to omega-3. But now the problem's been solved. The big new rage in eggs is omega-3-enriched eggs, which is actually a very good idea. Chickens themselves, like pigs, are low in omega-3s, so they can use the extra nutrients. Feed for these eggs can come from flaxseed, algae, or fish oil (rarely)—depending on the source, their eggs can taste good or very fishy (the chickens raised on algae feed). But omega-3 eggs are a very good deal. Chickens have already done the work of converting the fats to the usable form, which in the case of eggs is DHA, the brain-protective form. Two eggs, depending on the source, can offer you about 600 milligrams of DHA.

Free-range eggs sound like a great idea, but in fact "free-range" has no actual definition. Maybe the chicken could possibly stick its head out a window, or maybe it's scratching around in the barnyard. Free-range chickens can be sort of like New Yorkers who gaze out their third-story windows, wondering what it's like to be "out there." In theory, running-around birds get to eat bugs and seeds and other flavor-enhancing things, but they may also peck at droppings from wild birds and rodents, picking up some unfortunate diseases. If the flocks are carefully managed, free-range is great, but it's far from a guarantee of much of anything. "Organic" is a much better sign to look for on the label. Real free-range chickens, like those in Greece, have lots of omega-3, from pecking on wild greens and flax. If you have a small-farm source of real free-range chickens, they should have lots of omega-3 naturally.

Eggs are great sources of two hot new nutrients. Choline is a new essential nutrient (proclaimed so by the National Academy of Sciences Institute of Medicine) that's crucially important for the developing fetus's brain and good for the rest of us. Two large eggs a day meet the requirement. Lutein is great for your eyes, and the usual highest source recommended is spinach. But eggs have twice the lutein content of spinach, and that's because in eggs the lutein has high bioavailability, which is to say your body can actually absorb the nutrient easily. The chicken has taken the nutrients from corn and alfalfa and processed them for you. Lutein, by the way, is what gives egg yolks their bright color—and I'd swear a bright orange egg is a delicious egg, as well as a lutein-rich one.

Nutritious as they are, eggs are also a bit fragile. They quickly pick up odors in the refrigerator, especially strong odors like cabbage. (They also absorb good odors, like truffles.) It's a good idea to give them a sniff before you use them, especially if they'll be appreciated for their own flavor in the finished dish. A good egg will be good for about two weeks in the refrigerator; if the yolk has an opaque film over it, the egg is too old and should be pitched.

As with all proteins, you shouldn't cook eggs at very high heat, or they'll toughen. Don't literally boil hard-boiled eggs, for instance; dropping them into a gently simmering pot of water for exactly 10 minutes, then plunging them into ice water will give you a firm but tender egg.

The best eggs I've tasted in America are from New Zealand, home of all wonderful foods (New Zealand apples have half the level of pesticides of American ones). The label is Frenzs, and they turn up at Whole Foods markets on the West Coast, though not yet on the East Coast. The chickens that produce them not only go out, they run around in a pasture and eat all sorts of interesting things that contribute to their flavor. They have the bright orange yolks that are the hallmark of all truly delicious eggs.

BEST

- Organic eggs, preferably omega-3-enriched

GOOD

- Supermarket eggs that are truly fresh

AVOID

- Cracked or smelly eggs
- Low-cholesterol eggs
- Egg Beaters

RED MEAT

Perhaps the guiltiest pleasure of all is our passion for meat—juicy steaks, succulent burgers, bacon, a magnificent roast beef. In our current nutritionally correct climate, ordering a steak at a restaurant is often an occasion for apology to one's fellow diners. Certainly there are a lot of issues about meat raising—such as sustainability and environmental impact, antibiotics and hormone use, humane practices, and the crucial issue of feed—but cholesterol is the least of these and should really be off the table now as a major scare factor. Vegetarianism may be a necessary choice for people with religious concerns or sensitivity to meat from a physical or spiritual perspective, but it's not a choice to make for health reasons. The good, easily absorbable form of iron, heme iron, is only in meat, and B_{12}, a crucial nutrient, is nearly impossible to find in vegetarian sources. Vegetarian children can have problems growing adequate bone structure unless their diet is carefully supervised.

And why is that? First of all, as so many researchers have pointed out, meat is what we were designed to eat and what brought us to the peak of civilization. Plant foods are good for ruminant animals, like cows and sheep, who have more than one stomach, but we single-stomached folk only partially digest plants, and it's a bit of a strain on our systems. Although people often complain that a meat meal gives them a heavy feeling in the stomach, it's probably the fat that's producing a feeling of fullness and satiety; a salad can be much harder on human digestion. Dr. Melvin Anchell, author of *The Steak Lover's Diet,* says that everything we need can be found in meat, including vitamin C. But we already know that from the year-long study done on early-twentieth-century Icelandic explorer Vilhjalmur Stefansson, who lived with Arctic Eskimos for five years and joined them in their exclusive diet of fish, meat, and fat. Stefansson was amazed at the health of the Eskimos and at his own after indulging in their regime. And as has been noted over and over again with heavy meat eaters, there were no dental problems among the Eskimos. Stefansson was so enthusiastic about the diet that he persuaded Bellevue Hospital in New York City to supervise him and a fellow explorer while they continued the diet for a year, adding no vegetables, fruits, or starches. The scoffing among medical authorities was overwhelming, but so were the results: at the end of the year, the intrepid explorers emerged in perfect health. The only glitch was that in the first few days of the supervised diet they felt ill, but Stefansson quickly realized that the meat was too lean, and as soon as more fat was added, they once again thrived.

Meat includes a lot of excellent nutrients beyond its protein. It's a great source of B vitamins, such as B_6 and, especially, as mentioned above, B_{12}, hard to find elsewhere, which cuts homocysteine levels, a risk factor for heart disease. Meat also has a lot of B_2, calcium, iron, copper, and some antioxidant minerals such as selenium and zinc, which are part of the enzyme system for antioxidant action. Iron and copper can go both ways—they can be either pro-oxidant or antioxidant, that is, depending on a lot of other factors in the body. Dairy products are a very good source, but meat is an excellent source of the hot new nutrient CLA (see page 123), which looks in preliminary studies like a strong protector against cancer, heart disease, and weight gain. Meat (and spinach) contains alpha-lipoic acid, which lowers blood sugar levels by 10 to 30 percent and improves insulin function, according to a 1997 study—important especially for low-carbers. At feedlots, many cattle also are given vitamin E, to retard browning on the meat in the supermarket—but, of course, the E also has antioxidant properties in the meat itself.

What about the fat? That high CLA content of meat is *only* in the fat, for starters. Although people routinely call animal fats saturated, in fact they're actually less than 50 percent saturated. And of the saturated part, a third of that is stearic acid, a good fat that behaves like a monounsaturated fat such as olive oil—rapidly converting to oleic acid, lowering cholesterol levels by about 14 percent, and inhibiting platelet clumping, according to a 1988 study reported in the *New England Journal of Medicine*. The Stefansson study shows that the fat is important, but you don't need to ingest a huge amount of it to get the benefits. The marbling fat in a steak—a major sign of quality—mostly drips away in the cooking, as does much of the fat in grilled burgers. Roasts need just a thin layer of fat to baste them and give them added flavor. But pork now has about the same fat profile as chicken—not a good thing, necessarily, because it's lost a lot of flavor and texture in the process. Market demand for low-fat meat has meant a steady decline in meat's palatability, especially for pork. Dr. Mary Enig notes that meat has a good ratio of omega-3 to omega-6 fats, especially in its natural grass-fed state.

From Michael Pollan's fascinating article in the *New York Times Magazine* on beef-raising practices ("Power Steer," March 31, 2002), we know that the feed determines almost everything else about meat, from its nutritive value to us to its own health and its consequent need for antibiotics. Cattle and sheep are ruminant, meant to be pastured so they slowly fatten on grasses, as wild animals do (and that's the meat we're really designed to eat). The goal in the mass-production feedlots that supply most of the meat in America is to simply get the animals as huge as possible as quickly as possible, so that the small profit margins can be preserved. That means grain, especially corn, but it can also mean some eyebrow-raising protein feed, such as chicken manure, "feather meal" (also used occasionally in fish farming), and blood products—all "natural" and perhaps even organic. But because these animals weren't born to eat grain, it creates some major health problems that require antibiotics (most of the antibiotics produced in America are given to animals) and their meat often undergoes irradiation to be sure the problems aren't passed along to us.

This state of affairs wasn't always the case, of course. It was only about three decades ago—about the same time tuna standards changed (see page 81)—that the USDA began a program to increase the number of animals raised and boost dairy production. There was even a slogan for this project: "Get Big or Get Out." The huge industrial agribusiness of meat raising we live with now was a deliberate choice on the part of the government. To make this leap, they encouraged farmers to pack livestock indoors instead of pasturing them, pumping them full of cheap feed such as grains and junk like chicken manure. Dairy cows were overmilked. It's those factory-farming practices that have not only compromised the quality of American meat and milk, but also brought us the huge number of hormones and antibiotics necessary to raise animals this way.

Of American cattle, 60 to 90 percent are given hormones: the natural hormones estrogen, progesterone, and testosterone, as well as some synthetic ones. When the European market refused to accept American beef on the grounds that it is tainted with hormones, the U.S. government was outraged and brought in a consultant, Dr.

Samuel Epstein, to prove that there were no excessive levels of hormones in animals, and that, in any case, they're entirely safe. To his astonishment, the expert discovered that the USDA had never checked a single animal for hormone contamination, so they literally had no idea whether these hormones were present or not. They were indeed present as it turned out, sometimes over forty of them in a single animal. The government insists these hormone levels are safe, but there are almost no studies to prove that one way or the other. The pro-hormone argument is that any hormonal residue ends up in the kidneys and liver, not often eaten, or in the fat, which shouldn't be eaten (but of course is). Hormone-treated cattle are a big bargain; they eat less yet gain much more muscle and come to

---

Burger Tricks

Burgers have come to represent our biggest anxiety about meat and how good it is for us. But as the CLA research has proved, burgers aren't nearly as bad for us as researchers previously thought, because their CLA (see page 123) is protective against the HCA carcinogens they release when they're grilled—which some experts say are the equivalent of a pack of cigarettes, while others say they're minimal. Just in case CLA doesn't do the trick, though, here are some more strategies:

- Michigan University researchers advise adding antioxidants to the burger meat in the form of a 400 IU capsule of vitamin E for each pound of raw meat. Just stick a pin into the capsule and squeeze it into the meat. Cook as usual.
- If you panfry burgers, say scientists at the Lawrence Livermore Laboratories in Berkeley, you can eliminate up to 95 percent of the carcinogens by flipping them every minute. And there's a bonus: these burgers are both juicy and cooked enough to kill any *E. coli* bacteria.

market much earlier than naturally raised cattle. Profit margins in the meat industry are very small, so these growth stimulants offer cost benefits that pretty much guarantee the hormones aren't likely to disappear any time soon—except for one new phenomenon that may be taking us back to great meat.

There's a major revolution happening in the meat world now, and in just a few years we'll be seeing widespread production of branded meat that's been grass-fed and raised humanely without growth stimulants and hormones and routine antibiotic dosing. In some supermarkets, these meats are already on sale, including buffalo, an excellent meat choice that's both low-fat and very tasty. Pasture-fed animals have a fat profile that's much more like wild ones, with lots of omega-3 and the antioxidant CLA (see page 123) in their fat, which counters the ill effects of omega-6 fats (which are much higher in grain-fed animals). Health food stores are a fine source of these meats, but they're also available at the price club outlets such as Sam's Club and Costco, imported from Australia and New Zealand. As we've learned from the low-fat era, meat producers will give us whatever we demand, so it's important to buy these meats and request more of them at your local market.

Beef

Corn-fed beef still rules the land, but for a number of cutting-edge chefs, grass-fed beef is the kind they want, for its complex flavor and superior texture. This meat needs aging, or it will be tough, but it has a much deeper flavor and it doesn't have a mushy consistency like so much supermarket beef. It doesn't taste quite as "beefy," so some ranchers grass-feed their cattle and "finish" them for 120 days on grain to get the beefy taste. Grass-fed beef is raised sustainably, unlike feedlot cattle, but it's not just a question of plunking a regular steer from a feedlot down on the grass and letting him go at it. It's a different kind of cattle, and there isn't enough stock available yet to have large-scale grass-fed cattle raising—and, in fact, there may never be a solution to problems of scale in this kind of meat production. Fortunately, however, there are other good sources, such as beef from Argentina. Pasture-raised beef has a season, of course, which ends in the fall, but that's just when Argentina is coming into its spring.

BEST

- Small-farm, pasture-raised, hormone-free aged beef, preferably dry-aged
- Grass-fed meat, which can be mail-ordered from the New England Livestock Alliance (413-477-6200) or purchased online at www.nelivestockalliance.org
- Grassland Beef (877-383-0051), a Missouri company, sells beef that's tested (by the University of Iowa) to make sure it has a ratio of 16 to 1 omega-3 to omega-6
- Another good source is River Run Farm (503-728-4561)
- And another is www.eatwild.com

GOOD

- Hormone-free organic beef

The Resting Roast Myth

Virtually all cookbooks recommend letting a cooked roast just out of the oven rest under a foil jacket for 20 minutes in order to redistribute the juices. However, in a report to the 2002 annual International Conference on Meat Science and Technology in Rome, a Danish group reported that in extensive testing that advice doesn't hold up. In fact, more juice is lost—twice as much—if the roast rests. Although evenness of color is slightly better when the roast rests, all other factors, such as taste and slicing, are unaffected (except for veal, which has a very slight metallic taste right out of the oven; this taste disappears on standing).

Lamb

Although it's much beloved elsewhere in the world, lamb has really never caught on as a favorite meat in America, especially in the Midwest. In general, we like our meat to be mild and sweet, and the very possibility of eating mutton (which isn't actually available without seeking it out) is disturbing. Although American lamb is very tasty and mild, it's a small part of the meat market. Chances are you'll find Australian or New Zealand lamb at the market, and if you compare a leg of these grass-fed animals with one from a grain-fed American lamb, you'll be amazed: the American lamb is twice the size, especially compared to New Zealand lamb, which tends to be the smallest except for Icelandic lamb, a new face in the meat market. The lamb from down under is also leaner, and aficionados have their own preferences about which is tastier, lamb from New Zealand or Australia. But in general, American lamb is more delicate tasting.

All lamb is a great source of niacin, zinc, iron, and B_{12}. It's also a lower-calorie meat if properly trimmed; you need just the thinnest layer of fat for a roast, and, in any case, the fat is greasy and not particularly pleasant tasting. Lamb can be delicious cold, but not if it has any fat lingering on it. If you're planning on serving it cold, use the leaner New Zealand lamb.

Lamb has the most Omega-3 fat of all meats.

BEST

- You can buy the same top-quality lamb served at the best restaurants all over the country from Jamison Farm in Pennsylvania, including sausages and even finished dishes, which arrive frozen: www.jamisonfarm.com.
- For high rollers, small, very delicious, completely natural Icelandic lamb arrives by next-day delivery from www.iceland-naturally.com, fresh from September to November, otherwise frozen. (Iceland is a bit like New Zealand, a pure place in the world, and their other food products are similarly exemplary.)

• Grass-fed hormone-free lamb from New Zealand and Australia

Pork

Despite religious strictures against it and qualms about the personal hygiene of pigs, porcophilia rules. We can't seem to get enough bacon, spareribs, or ham in America, and we're pretty big on sausages too. Although bacon consumption did obediently decline during the low-fat era, it started back up again in 1995, and ever since we've been eating more and more bacon, despite the rulings of the nutritional police. One of my hopes in researching this book was that I'd find there's something good about bacon—and there is. Bacon is basically lard with a little protein thrown in, and as we've seen, lard is a pretty good fat, with a profile not dissimilar to olive oil's. It belongs in the monounsaturated fat camp, not with the other saturated animal fats (in fact, it's a profile remarkably like our own, which suggests it would agree with us more than other animal fats). In the 1970s, there was huge concern about nitrates in pork products, specifically sodium nitrate, used as preservatives and to guard against botulism. Nitrates can convert into nitrites in the body, which can, under the right (or wrong) conditions, become nitrosamines, a carcinogen group that's not to be dismissed as unimportant. We also get nitrates from drinking water, leafy greens, and root vegetables (about 85 percent of our nitrates, because of fertilizers used on the produce), as well as cigarette smoke. It's a complex subject, according to Professor Robert G. Cassens of the University of Wisconsin, and although you certainly want to limit your exposure to nitrates, you can also disable them by drinking a glass of orange juice with your morning bacon or having your bacon on a BLT—the vitamin C of the tomato will inhibit the conversion into the dangerous form of nitrites. The industry has also responded to the concerns about nitrates and has lowered the levels to one-tenth of the amounts present in bacon in the Seventies, when concerns about nitrates were first raised.

More good things about pork: it's the best food source of thiamine, vitamin B$_1$, which works as part of a coenzyme to promote carbohydrate utilization, normal appetite (just the opposite of what you'd expect from something piggy), and normal nervous system function. Of the part of pork that's saturated fat (about 40 percent), a third of that is the very good stearic acid, which has a beneficial effect on cholesterol and relaxes blood vessels.

Although the fat grams listed on a package of bacon are very high, once the bacon is cooked crisp, 70 percent of the fat is left in the pan, a Danish study shows. Once you subtract the fat you won't actually be eating, bacon looks like a perfectly reasonable healthy choice.

Aside from breeding low-fat pork, a disaster from a flavor and texture point of view, pork producers are now starting to add omega-3 fats to pig feed. This seems like a very good idea, since pigs themselves are low in omega-3, but if they're fed flaxseed or fish oil, their fat can develop telltale flavors of paint or fish when aged or heated. If you find a good brand of omega-3 pork, stick with it.

BEST

- Niman Ranch pork and bacon—after conscientious bacon-tasting, I say the crown goes to Niman for their dry-cured applewood-smoked bacon. All Niman pork is raised humanely on small family farms with no antibiotics or growth stimulators. Other people love their hot dogs, but I don't; to me they have that British-sausage sawdusty flavor. Niman products are available in a lot of gourmet markets (www.nimanranch.com).
- Another great applewood-smoked bacon comes from Nueske's (800-392-2266)
- A widely distributed excellent brand of bacon is hickory-smoked bacon from Jones Dairy Farm in Wisconsin
- Very good lard can be mail-ordered from John F. Martin and Sons (717-336-2804)

GOOD

- Applegate Farms Sunday Bacon with no nitrates
- Organic pork with no hormones

- Pork labeled "extra-tender," which has been shot up with sodium phosphate and water to make it seem juicier
- Purplish bacon, which is brined instead of being dry-cured in the traditional way and has more nitrates; dry-cured is not only tastier, it won't splatter grease all over your kitchen as you cook

CHOCOLATE

Several years ago, a Harvard alumni study noted that alums who ate candy several times a month were much healthier and longer-lived than those who abstained. Chocolate was the prime suspect, and the hypothesis was that the simple pleasure of eating chocolate and other candy stimulated serotonin and otherwise set the stage for a feeling of well-being that played out physiologically in the body itself. A *British Medical Journal* study noticed the same phenomenon in a longevity study of men and traced it directly to chocolate—those who ate just a few pieces of chocolate a month lived significantly longer. What could it be about chocolate?

Now we know a lot more about this glorious substance that's been around since at least 600 B.C., and it's all good news. A 1999 study published in the *American Journal of Clinical Nutrition* reveals it's jammed with antioxidants, more than any other fruit or vegetable by a factor of at least two. Ongoing studies at the University of Scranton demonstrate that the antioxidants (very similar to the ones in red wine) are quickly absorbed into the blood, and they have a good effect on cholesterol levels. These antioxidants, mainly the polyphenols, are suspected of blocking cancer and heart disease, as well as slowing down aging. They have a different form in chocolate than in red wine or green tea; they appear in large, complex molecules not usually found in other foods—which may be why they're such antioxidant superstars. Most important is their action against the oxidation of LDL cholesterol, which initiates the process of atherosclerosis. They back that up with an increase in HDL, the good cholesterol, and action against blood platelet clumping, which triggers blood clots. The effects are observed in both men and women, and they're highest when the antioxidants are from cocoa powder. Next most effective is dark chocolate (which is rich in oleic acid, the good fat in olive oil), then milk chocolate—which is still much higher than any other antioxidant in foods tested to date. White chocolate is useless from a health point of view, and I don't think it tastes like much more than suntan oil.

A Dutch study demonstrated that chocolate's catechins—extremely important antioxidants that are the star player in green tea—are four times more potent than those in tea. And that's just in the chocolate part, the solids from the cacao bean (which is actually a fruit).

Part two of chocolate is its voluptuous fat, which is mainly stearic acid. The fat is so valuable for cosmetics that it's separated out during processing and sold; only dark chocolate and milk chocolate of very high quality have cocoa fat added back in. Low-quality chocolate usually contains cottonseed or soy oil. Although stearic acid is a saturated fat, in the body it acts like a monounsaturated fat, an omega-9 like olive oil. It has no cholesterol, raises no cholesterol, but protects, like the cocoa itself, against the oxidation of cholesterol in the body. Stearic acid is also good because it makes blood platelets less sticky and relaxes the blood vessels, which protects against blood clots and atherosclerosis.

There are some other interesting elements of chocolate, like its magnesium—a crucial mineral in which we're virtually all deficient—which some researchers think is the reason people tend to crave chocolate (to cure those cravings, 400 milligrams a day of magnesium citrate may do the job). Chocolate is also a great source of copper, and copper deficiency is a major suspect in heart disease. And by now almost everyone knows that chocolate is just the thing for a broken heart. That's because it contains phenylethylamine, a stimulant released in the brain when people fall in love; it stimulates the feel-good brain chemicals, serotonin and endorphins.

In case you think carob is a good idea, it has none of these benefits, doesn't taste very good, and has loads more sugar, more calories, more saturated fat—and it is five times more likely to cause tooth decay than chocolate, according to a University of Texas study.

In fact, chocolate's main problem is the sugar that's usually added. High-quality dark chocolate has much less sugar than other types, however, and if you're using cocoa powder, which has the most antioxidants of all the chocolate varieties, you can use just a little sugar or use alternative sweeteners.

The only possible serious negative about chocolate has been voiced by the American Environmental Safety Institute, a California group that's filed suit against a group of mass-produced chocolate manufacturers such as Hershey's and Mars for excessive amounts of lead and cadmium in their chocolate, a result of processing practices. Lead can lead to cognitive problems, while cadmium can collect in the kidneys and is suspected of causing kidney disease. The World Health Organization noted this problem long ago and set limits for the amounts of these dangerous heavy metals; AESI proposes limits that are one-fifth the levels allowed by WHO. For children especially, any excess metal could be a problem, but we don't actually know for sure. To steer clear of these heavy metals, choose organic chocolate or high-quality chocolate.

You don't need to main-line chocolate to get the benefits. The British study shows that just a little chocolate, maybe once a week, does the trick. We don't know yet whether more is better, but no doubt we soon will. We eat about ten pounds of chocolate per person a year in this country, and that's a lot more than a few pieces a month. Smokers and others likely to be in a state of oxidative stress, however, might want to enjoy a little chocolate every day.

BEST

- Organic chocolate such as Chocolove, a Belgian chocolate made in Boulder, Colorado, and widely distributed to natural foods stores
- High-quality dark or semisweet chocolate with a high percentage of cocoa solids

AVOID

- White chocolate, which has none of the benefits of chocolate
- Carob

~

CHAPTER FIVE

Helping Fats Do Their Good Work

ANTIOXIDANTS

The story of antioxidants is one of the most dramatic of cutting edge science. It's a very new field, and the research is exploding. Antioxidants are our nutritional heroes, the ones who give marauding free radicals what they want—an electron—and (some of them) go on to do the same for more free radicals, neutralizing these dangerous everyday substances that can change the DNA of our cells, and even kill cells. When we have many too many free radicals—and other than smoking, our greatest source is bad fats—for even the tireless antioxidants to defuse, the body goes into a state called oxidative stress—and that's when free radicals do their real damage, starting off with cancer and heart disease (lycopene alone has been shown to cut heart attack risk by 50 percent).

The most important element in visual deterioration such as macular degeneration is free-radical damage, which only antioxidants can thwart. Free-radical damage is also centrally involved in the memory loss we all have beginning in our middle years; it slows down blood flow to the brain and damages the brain cell connections. The body makes its own antioxidants to some degree, but that process slows down a great deal with aging. So it behooves us to ingest as many antioxidants as possible—you can't have too many.

Before we get into antioxidants from food, though, there are two other ways to disarm free radicals. One is to restrict calories drastically, which cuts free-radical activity so much that it increases longevity by 30 to 40 percent in animals. For many of us, however, a life without good food doesn't make a very long life worth having.

Another is to use alpha-lipoic acid, which researchers refer to as the universal antioxidant, because it's both fat-soluble and water-soluble. It can go wherever it's needed, even in the brain, and it's a powerful antioxidant on its own. Once it gives an electron to a free radical, thereby disarming it, alpha-lipoic acid just becomes stronger, and goes on to do more good work. It even patches up other antioxidants—vitamin C, vitamin E, and glutathione—once they've done their jobs and are used up, so they can go on to disable other free radicals. You get huge benefits for just 50 milligrams a day.

For decades now, research has shown that antioxidant supplements are valuable, especially vitamin E, vitamin C, and beta carotene. Recently, however, some small studies have shown not such good results for supplements. One researcher, Dr. Paul Thomas, thinks that possibly if antioxidants are good for our healthy cells, they may be very good for cancer cells too. That may explain why beta carotene supplements increase the cancer rate for smokers. Others speculate that antioxidants work as a team, and testing just one of them in isolation from the rest will skew the results. We haven't heard the last word on this subject, but we do know that every study ever done shows that antioxidants from food work like crazy—these levels can actually be measured in the blood. The antioxidants beyond vitamins break down into families, like the carotenoids (phytonutrients that give fruit and vegetables their colors), and flavonoids, such as quercetin, in apples and onions, and other elements in berries and red wine.

Research on antioxidants is apparently endless, and it's why you read those little news clips all the time about how blueberries can save you from cancer. The USDA maintains a list called ORAC (Oxygen Radical Absorbance Capacity) that rates the known levels of anti-free-radical activity of a given food. The most eye-popping are the newest champions: dark chocolate (best of all) and milk chocolate. Right below them are cranberries, at least until some other bit of produce displaces them. This doesn't mean you should be knocking back the Cosmopolitans; sweetened cranberry drinks and cocktails have the least antioxidants. And prunes (a.k.a. dried plums) are very high, much higher than plums. On the ORAC list, raspberries and spinach are roughly the same, and toward the top of the list. But the new champ, dark chocolate, has ten times more antioxidants than these good guys, and even milk chocolate has more than double the amount found in blueberries, for several years the reigning champ. (Actually, all berries are very high in antioxidants.) Among the herbs and spices, it's oregano, hands down, which has a thousand times more antioxidants than other spices and herbs, and four times more than blueberries, which are right at the top of the list. You'd be wise to choose broccoli, but even wiser to choose plums. Pomegranate juice has been shown to reduce oxidative stress, processes that lead to blood clotting, and the oxidation of LDL cholesterol by 90 percent, which is crucial for preventing atherosclerosis (from a study on sick mice reported in the *Journal of Clinical Nutrition* in 2000). Antioxidant possibilities offer a whole new fascinating way to make food choices, and we're sure to be hearing much more about the topic.

Raspberries and other berries are high on the antioxidant list, but some fascinating work on raspberries suggests they also offer special protection against cancer. They do this not as other antioxidants do, by attacking cancer cells, but rather by stimulating the immune system to go after cells that are just beginning to show early structural alterations that may lead to cancer. Dr. Daniel S. Nelson of the Hollings Cancer Center in Charleston, South Carolina, studies ellagitannin, a substance that appears in walnuts, strawberries, and pomegranates, among other foods. The seeds of red raspberries, especially the Meeker variety, are loaded with this compound. If the seeds are crushed, the body will extract a maximum amount of ellagitannins, but the berry itself also contains a lot. The answer to releasing this highly beneficial compound is to make raspberry puree. What could be wrong with raspberry puree over your morning yogurt, or a raspberry puree sauce on a dish of sliced peaches?

Especially intriguing to researchers is lycopene, a powerful antioxidant shown to fight prostate cancer, among other problems. Lycopene doesn't easily lend itself to supplements, but it's found in red fruits such as tomato, pink grapefruit, and, especially, watermelon. The watermelon can be seeded or seedless, but a ripe watermelon (the spot on the skin where it rested on the ground should be creamy yellow, not white, and its stem shouldn't be green) has more lycopene. Home-grown tomatoes have more lycopene than store-bought, because being ripened on the vine develops the maximum. In tomatoes, this antioxidant is found just under the skin, primarily, and needs to be heated to be released; the levels double after thirty minutes of cooking, which proves there's some nutritional justification for catsup.

If you've ever wondered if there's some point to the color of produce, there is: the darker green, the better—the brighter red, the more vivid yellow, the lushest purple, that's the carotenoids talking. The reds, yellows, and oranges are especially valuable, but there are also very high antioxidant levels in green vegetables. They have a basic yellow carotenoid color that's disguised by the deep green of chlorophyll, a product of photosynthesis. Broccoli, for instance, has the most nutrients when it's purplish or bluish purple. Even the colors of citrus fruits (assuming they haven't been artificially colored) are meaningful, because there's an antioxidant called limonene in the zest, the colored part of the skin. It may or may not turn out that antioxidant supplements are essential, but you can't go wrong choosing the most beautifully vivid produce at the market.

That's not to say white vegetables are to be avoided; garlic and onions have valuable nutrients, as do leeks, green grapes, and celery. Lots of these fruits and vegetables have their nutrients near or in the skin, so it's a good idea to eat, for instance, carrot skin and apple skin (yet another reason to buy organic).

Phytochemicals (plant-derived chemicals) are just beginning to be appreciated and explored. Already we know there are more than four thousand of them in vegetables and fruits—and animal sources such as meat and dairy products also have antioxidants. That's reason enough to keep eating a wide variety of good natural foods, so you get the nutrients we don't even know about yet.

SPECIAL SITUATIONS

Weight Loss

Why do we think that fat makes us fat? It seems logical enough: fat has more calories per gram than protein or carbohydrates, so it must make us fat . . . and it *is* itself fat, so, by magical thinking, it must jump right on our bones as fat. The first person to raise this idea was not a great scientist, however, but David Reuben, a pop-psych author turned self-proclaimed nutritionist. It was in 1976 that Reuben first intoned the words heard round the world: "Fat Makes You Fat." It has since become Scripture, but it's not at all true.

Quite the opposite is true: you must eat fat to lose fat. Dr. Robert Atkins first pointed out that brilliant fact, and it's one reason why his weight-loss program works so well for the millions who swear by it. Major tests of the Atkins diet are under way now, but early testing results show that compared to low-fat diets, the weight loss is double on the Atkins diet, and triglyceride levels come down as well. In a 2002 study reported in the *American Journal of Medicine,* not only did overweight patients who ate very low-carb (an average of 6 grams of carbs per day) for 6 months lose a lot of weight, their blood values improved as well. By now you know that fat is crucial to your health for all sorts of reasons, but it's especially important in maintaining your metabolic balance.

Some fats actually boost your metabolic rate—coconut is a surprising one. If you don't have enough fat, you won't make enough hormones, and that will drastically affect not only your general health but your ability to lose weight as well. The essential fatty acids actually reduce body weight and fat by stimulating the oxidation of fat and increasing the metabolic rate. (Several supplement products on the market increase the rate at which the mitochondria, the little cells that are the source of energy, burn. An especially good one is Pentabosol, available from www.eatprotein.com.) Some researchers are keen on the omega-6 fat GLA, usually in the form of evening primrose oil, to activate the brown fat, the metabolically active fat that surrounds your organs and turns excess fat from storage into energy. Not everyone agrees; Barry Sears wouldn't be in favor of more than a tiny amount of GLA, while researchers at the University of Guelph in Canada use evening primrose oil as a placebo in fats testing, since they find it so ineffective. Ann Louise Gittleman, author of *Eat Fat, Lose Weight,* has seen dramatic results in her patients, however, and points to a study that shows a 10 percent weight loss without actual dieting when GLA is supplemented. (If you want to try, she recommends 500 milligrams 4 to 6 times daily, with food.) Gittleman also has an excellent "Fat Flush" plan to get you started on weight loss by clearing out your liver. The liver has to process both your incoming fats and your burned fats from storage, and sometimes that burden can become so onerous that it sort of shuts down and does only a minimal job of keeping things together. Another great liver-cleansing option is BHB Plus, from Dews Research Laboratories (940-382-1849), especially useful for low-carb dieters who have stopped losing weight because their livers are clogged. In working with low-carb dieters, I've discovered that BHB Plus often makes the difference between success and failure. Alpha-lipoic acid also clears the liver and increases metabolic rate.

Although exercise won't make you thin, it's really important as part of any weight loss plan, not to mention very good for your general health. The absolutely best, easiest, most fun, most effective, exercise is the rebounder, a mini-trampoline that uses gravity to intensify the effects of the workout. Rebounders also clear out your lympathic drainage system, which is where the immune system sends toxic substances. Even if you're half dead, you can exercise on a rebounder—it's that easy. (To find out more, call the AIR rebounder company at 888–464-JUMP; or check their website at www.healthbounce.com.) Dr. Julian Whitaker recommends drinking two cups of coffee before exercising to help mobilize the stored fat, which will start being burned about half an hour into your exercise routine.

When you're burning fat, drinking plenty of water is essential, or you won't lose as much as you could. (Otherwise, says kidney specialist Dr. Heinz Valtin of Dartmouth, the body takes care of its own water needs. You don't need to force yourself to drink eight glasses a day unless you're dieting.)

But what's wrong with low-fat dieting? Isn't a calorie a calorie? Yes, to some degree that's true, though any dieter can tell you it also isn't true. Weight gain and loss is a very complicated and poorly understood process, but we've learned a few things that are important. If you overrestrict calories, you'll sabotage your diet by slowing your metabolism. The brain in particular will want to conserve the fat it needs, so the fat will be protected against harvesting by slowing everything down. When you begin to eat a normal diet again, your body will still be in shutdown for about two months— and you can gain a lot of weight in eight weeks if you're ravenous, your fat cells are clamoring to be refilled, and you have a sluggish metabolism.

Dr. Rudolph Leibel, an obesity researcher at Rockefeller University, notes that "research has found that after a while on little to no fat, the body begins to compensate for the absence of fat in the diet by becoming more efficient in converting other food sources into body fat." So by eating low-fat, you actually fine-tune your fat-storage mechanism so you can more efficiently store *more* fat.

In order to lose weight, you need to activate a hormone called glucagon, which is stimulated in the pancreas by lean protein, a great metabolic booster. Glucagon is the opposite of insulin; insulin is the fat-storage hormone and carbohydrates stimulate insulin, whereas glucagon, its fat-cell-emptying polar opposite, is stimulated by protein.

The most promising area in obesity research has to do with hormones, which control everything from our desire to eat to the fat storage system to the desire to stop eating. There are "new" hormones coming all the time; among the latest are grehlin, an appetite stimulator, and PYY, which can eclipse the desire to eat for up to twelve hours. Some researchers theorize that what we're eating now—a lot of processed foods, which usually means a combination of simple carbs (like high-fructose corn syrup) and trans fats—somehow garbles the brain's ability to respond to hormonal signals. When the insulin spike is up from the big dose of carbs, they're stored as fat and the body seems to think it's run out of fuel and needs more carbs. As we get fatter, the ability to read the signals deteriorates even further, so the hormonal change stimulates even more overeating. We're still a long way from knowing how these hormones really work, but in the meantime it's good to remember that for the benefit of all your hormones, eating good fat is vital.

Fat has some other characteristics as well. One of them is satiety, that good feeling of satisfaction dieters so rarely experience. If you're eating low-fat, you're automatically eating more carbohydrates, which leaves you not at all satisfied but actually craving more sugar, in a vicious addictive cycle that's almost impossible to break. When dieters crave sugar, Gittleman thinks, they're actually suffering from good-fats starvation. (Remember that coconut not only has fewer calories than all other fats, it also has a very positive effect on metabolism. It definitely has a good part to play in any weight-loss scheme, and it also offers a lot of pleasure to the dieter.) To use coconut as a diet aid, see Bruce Fife's *Eat Fat, Look Thin*. The fatter you are, says Fife, the more fat you burn if you consume medium-chain fats such as coconut, which is 65 percent medium-chain fat.

Because of biochemical individuality, not everyone thrives on the same regime. But for most of us with weight problems, the issue isn't dietary fat but dietary sugar, in the form of bread, pasta, potatoes, junk food, and sweets. A low-carb regime is the answer to that problem, with a strong emphasis on the good fats. Dr. Atkins, for decades now the villain of weight loss, is being proved absolutely correct in his prescription that low-fat and carbs are bad, protein and fat are good. Early studies show—even one from the American Heart Association—that the Atkins diet patients had good weight loss, with lower bad cholesterol, higher good cholesterol, very much lower triglycerides, and no safety concerns. Several long-term studies are in the works that should settle this question in the next few years.

If you have a lot of weight to lose and you hit the wall on standard low-carb diets, you might want to try a fascinating dietary scheme detailed in Dr. Melvin Anchell's unorthodox book, *The Steak Lover's Diet*. He bases his plan on the midcentury work of Dr. A. W. Pennington, who was the internist for the DuPont Company and set himself a project to slim down its executives. Dr. Pennington did some research and concluded that the problem was carbohydrates—but not all carbohydrates. The culprits, he felt, were the ones that stimulated the most production of pyruvic acid, which he identified as the major cause of obesity. Indeed, obese individuals have high levels of pyruvic acid, which prevents the utilization of both fatty acids and blood sugar and causes them to be stored in the fat cells. Obese people are especially sensitive to the actions of pyruvic acid. Pennington's diet, which consists of meat and other protein, allows just a few carbs, but they happen to be the ones we low-carbers are used to passing by: bananas and potatoes are both on the (very small) list. Other treats include white grapes, sweet potatoes, rice, pears, and watermelon. Obviously this flies in the face of generic low-carb dieting and the glycemic index (the listing of foods according to their ability to raise blood sugar, potatoes being at the top of the list). Going on the Pennington diet could be a good way to take a vacation from low-carb without undoing the good work you've done. In fact, this may be the diet that launched Dr. Atkins on his fortune, the one he read about in the *Journal of the American Medical Association,* where Pennington's work appeared.

In *Syndrome X* (Wiley), Burt Berkson, Jack Challem, and Melissa Diane Smith explain that insulin resistance has a relationship to alpha-lipoic acid, which is essential to break down pyruvic acid so that glucose can be used by the cells. I've had great success adding 600 milligrams of ALA to my diet. Berkson recommends the Bio-Tech brand of ALA, which is from a European source (inferior Asian ALA is white, not yellow), and says it's important to take a good B-vitamin-complex capsule and 200 micrograms of selenium with it.

Whichever dietary plan you choose, be sure to supplement with fish oil. Fish oil makes your insulin receptors work much better, so that you're not overproducing insulin and thereby setting yourself up for fat storage. It also has positive mood effects, which can be invaluable for dieting, and it makes everything work more efficiently. Calcium is another crucial weight loss tool, especially the calcium in dairy products.

And for dieters, it's even more important to ditch the bad fats, which encourage weight gain and have so many other bad effects. In one major three-country study, the *Trans* Lin E study, consumers of high trans gained up to 2 kg (4.4 pounds), while the low-trans group *lost* up to 4 kg (8.8 pounds) in 12 weeks while spontaneously increasing their fat consumption. Fat can, in fact, help make you thin—but watch that cheese and those nuts; it's very easy to overconsume them, and that will stop your weight loss in its tracks.

Pregnancy

If there's even a chance you might become pregnant, it's a good idea to supplement with DHA (Neuromins [see Sources] is probably the best source, but omega-3-enriched eggs are important too). That way, your baby will have the benefit of the best possible nutrients for the brain, the eyes, and the nervous system, right from the get go. Fish oil too is important, but DHA is crucial. As David Kyle, the inventor of the omega-3 supplement for infant formula, notes, the fetus is a perfect parasite. If you don't have enough DHA in your diet for the developing infant, it will steal yours—a theft that will take four years to replace. DHA is most important of all in the last trimester, when the brain is growing exponentially.

Kyle reports that studies that extended even up to the age of four show that babies with good levels of DHA have superior brain and neurological function and better visual acuity. The brain and the retina are actually made of this fat, and if they don't get it, the results are serious. Only DHA can stimulate growth of nerve cells, and it is preferentially transported across the placenta into the fetal circulation. So if you want a smart, neurologically fit baby with good vision, start with DHA supplementation before it's even conceived.

Omega-3 fats are very good for mom too. Incidence of pre-eclampsia and of gestational diabetes is much lower in women who get good amounts of omega-3. Epidemiological studies show that women who eat lots of omega-3 tend to carry babies longer and have a lower rate of premature births. After childbirth, DHA levels drop dramatically, and that's thought to be a major element in postpartum depression—so it's important to continue supplementation after the birth, even if you're not nursing. Bonus: A new study shows that newborn babies whose mothers ate good amounts of omega-3 in pregnancy slept much more soundly.

If you are nursing, it's vital to supplement with DHA. American women have the lowest levels in the entire world of DHA in their breast milk, says David Kyle. For good infant nutrition, the right amount is 10 milligrams DHA per pound of weight. If you're bottle-feeding, avoid soy milk formula, which may depress your baby's immune system. It contains genestein, a hormone-like element that, as reported in a study to the National Academy of Sciences in 2002, decreased the number of immune cells and caused changes in the thymus gland, the source of maturing immune cells. The study was done on mice, but the implications of decreased immune function for human babies have raised serious concern about soy formula. A 1997 study reported in the *Lancet* showed that soy-formula babies get enough phytoestrogen to produce blood hormone levels thousands of times higher than those of breast-fed babies. Soy is especially bad for premature and low-weight babies, because it doesn't supply enough nutrients to create bone mass. Unless you'd like your baby to have the equivalent of five birth control pills every day, stay away from soy.

Be sure to choose an infant formula with DHA and AA added, which means nearly all of them. Coconut oil is also a big plus in infant formula (it used to be the standard, since it's so close to mother's milk). The United States has had these valuable supplements in formula only since 2001, although more than fifty countries already had them, and the World Health Organization had recommended them in 1994. Preliminary studies by Dr. Joseph R. Hibbeln at NIH suggest that insufficiencies of DHA and AA early in life increase lifetime risk for depressive or aggressive disorders.

While you're pregnant and nursing, all good natural fats should be enjoyed in abundance, but especially eggs (for their choline and their lutein, another crucial eye nutrient, and their DHA, if they're omega-3-enriched) and small fish. The larger fish, like tuna, may have concentrations of heavy metals that you want to avoid, but you can eat all the sardines and anchovies you can stand (but avoid Mediterranean ones, which have a bit of mercury). Canned salmon is another great choice because it's always wild salmon and doesn't have as much chance of being contaminated with heavy metals as tuna. The bones, like the bones in canned sardines, are great for the third trimester, when the baby's bones are calcifying and you need extra calcium.

What about dioxin, which is known to be carcinogenic? In July 2003, an Institute of Medicine report, after a thorough study of the dioxin literature, suggested that no woman who might become pregnant—and no girls—should be consuming anything but a minimum amount of saturated fats until we have more data. However, there's no actual evidence to support this advice, and since the cancer rate for vegetarians is slightly higher than it is for meat eaters, it would seem premature to come to this conclusion. Dioxin is everywhere (even in penguins), it's unavoidable, and although it's declined 70 percent in the environment in the last couple of decades, levels in food have not changed.

I asked an internationally known expert on both cancer and

Whole Foods

I knew when I started work on this book that the core of good eating is whole foods: the real thing, as grown in the ground, caught on the hook, raised on the range, or laid in the nest. What I didn't know is how hard it is to find actual whole food in America today. We're in desperate need of a Rachel Carson to come along and tell us what's happened to our food supply.

Something has been done to nearly everything that comes fresh to the market, whether it's pesticides, hormones, growth stimulators, antibiotics, plastic hay (to add fiber to cattle diets), "food glue" in canned tuna, cooking oils treated with dry-cleaning chemicals, white coloring to take away the blue in skim milk and powdered milk to bulk it up, fruits picked green that will never ripen, fish raised on dog chow, flounder genes in the strawberries to keep them from freezing . . . the list goes on. This messing with the food supply began in the early 1970s, when the FDA allowed all sorts of interference with natural foods without bothering to get congressional approval. Some of the battles over food have already been lost; more than 70 percent of our food is now genetically altered, for better or worse, and we won't really know what the consequences are for decades.

Some are brewing now, such as the fight over irradiation. Udo Erasmus, a Canadian fats researcher, says that a single irradiated food contains "billions" of free radicals. There's no question the molecules in irradiated food have been altered; that's the whole point, the way the bacteria are killed. Radiation also destroys nutrients. According to a 2001 report in *Nutrition Week,* irradiated orange juice loses 48 percent of its beta carotene, 13 percent of its vitamin C, and 10 percent of its vitamin A. But that's a lost battle too: fruit and vegetable juices are approved for radiation now.

Irradiated foods must bear the international radiation icon, which is a quite perky looking abstract plant inside a broken circle that suggests rays of sunlight—offhand, you might think this is a particularly healthy food. But if a processed food contains some irradiated ingredients—some raisins, say, or spices, which are often irradiated—it won't say so on the label.

There are very few studies of irradiated foods and their effects on humans. In the early Seventies, an Indian study of children fed irradiated grain showed damage in the form of extra chromosomes. In the late Eighties, the Chinese conducted studies for three months on volunteers fed irradiated food. They announced a clean bill of health for these volunteers and China then embarked on a major radiation experiment with food for its megapopulation. So far we know that irradiated corn is a great environment for aflatoxin, the fungus that's deadly for the liver as well as a potent carcinogen, and the Chinese now die of liver cancer at a rate of 10 percent of all deaths; the rate in the United States is 0.5 percent. Irradiated food can contain several cancer-causing carcinogens, such as benzene and formaldehyde. For children, especially, it's important to avoid irradiated foods.

The simplest, most basic food of all is probably salt. But, once again, this looks like a whole food but very often isn't. Those big cardboard cylinders of salt—"When It Rains, It Pours"—are actually industrial products, and only 10 percent of this stuff reaches us in the marketplace. Which is a good thing: this refined salt has not only lost all its nutrients, its trace elements of minerals, it's also got plenty of additives it doesn't have to announce on the label. To keep it pouring, this salt is laced with silicates (a fine sand) and ferrocynide (another one). That might make you reach for the more expensive brand of sea salt in the supermarket, but check the label: it too has additives, and it isn't a very-high-quality product. These refined salts are high in potassium and low in magnesium, a mineral we desperately need more of.

Real sea salt is the answer, and a really good one is Maldon salt from England. It has a mild, briny, almost sweet flavor, and its crumbly flakes of salt melt onto food in a delicious way. It's the only sea salt you can just crumble in your hands; it doesn't require a salt mill. If you have good salt, you actually use less of it, and although this salt isn't cheap, it isn't expensive either. Maldon salt is available at gourmet stores and some supermarkets; its website is www.maldonsalt.kemc.co.uk.

Second choice would be kosher salt, the favorite of chefs, because they like to pick it up in their fingers and toss it into the pot. It's a little cruder and saltier and cut in a different way, but tastier than supermarket salt, which has been boiled and stripped of its nutrients.

Second Thoughts on Soy

You know why soy's good for you—anticancer, anti–heart disease, low saturated fat, good vegetarian protein, good for women, and so on—but you probably haven't heard too much about why it's bad for you. We don't definitively know that soy's a bad thing, but here are some things to consider before you chomp into your next soyburger.

- Soybeans contain a number of toxins, and they're not safe to eat raw or before they've been treated with harsh chemical processing—acid baths, high heat, as well as additives such as artificial flavorings, sweeteners, and nitrates, which can convert to carcinogens in the body. One toxin, a protease inhibitor, slows growth in rats; we don't know yet whether it has the same function in human children.
- Unless they're sprouted, soybeans have a bad omega-6 to omega-3 ratio, 20 to 1. And unless they're fermented, they're hard to digest. However, fermented soybeans have a good fatty-acid ratio.
- Eighty percent of the cooking oil used in America today is soy oil, and it's as much as 40 percent trans fat, the dangerous kind. According to Dr. Joseph R. Hibbeln, a National Institutes of Health researcher, virtually all french fries are cooked in soy oil now, which means we get way too much omega-6, associated with both aggression and depression, plus 8 to 9 grams of trans fat.
- Compared to animal-protein sources, soy protein is quite low quality, low in the essential amino acid methionine and in cysteine. It's deficient in vitamins E, K, D, and B_{12}, and in copper, zinc, magnesium, and calcium (and the phytates in soy bind these minerals, even if you get them from other sources).
- Although in 1999 the FDA allowed manufacturers to make claims for soy and heart health (four servings a day would give you that benefit, according to scientists at Tufts), it still hasn't added soy to the GRAS list, the highly selective Generally

Regarded as Safe list. Doctors inside the FDA have raised concerns about some of the issues noted here (which the FDA claims it was fully aware of when it made the heart health recommendation), and until there's a truly clean bill of health for soy, it's unlikely it will be invited into the inner circle of GRAS foods. (To see what's up at the FDA from a critical point of view, check out www.fdareview.org.)

- The isoflavones in soy are phytoestrogens, and they have powerful effects on our hormones, including antithyroid effects. The Japanese, who eat soy mainly in fermented forms, get about 28 milligrams of isoflavones a day. The FDA inexplicably recommends 75 milligrams a day for us, while infants being fed soy formula get a whopping 38 milligrams. According to Dr. Jonathan V. Wright, that's the equivalent of five birth control pills a day for infants!
- Although soy is supposed to be protective against breast cancer, a 1996 study found that soy-eating women had increased epithelial hyperplasia, an early form of malignancy. In 1997, a chemical found in soy was pinpointed as encouraging breast cells to metastasize.
- Soy is often touted as a good source of omega-3s, but in fact those are cancelled out by its very high ratio of omega-6s. Its omega-3 level is about to drop in half in any case, because new breeds of soy have eliminated a lot of the omega-3 as a way to enhance shelf life—but labels will still list the old values.
- Soy contains hemagglutinin, a substance that makes platelets stickier and more likely to clot.

I'm against soy on the grounds that it's not a traditional food (unlike the fermented forms eaten in Asia), it's toxic in its natural state (like rapeseed, from which canola oil is made), and it doesn't taste good. Whether its bad characteristics will turn out to outweigh its good ones we won't know for a long time. In the meantime, though, women with breast cancer should avoid soy and infants should be raised on soy-free formula if breast milk isn't a possibility.

For more bad news on soy, check out www.soyonlineservice.co.nz.

pesticides, Dr. Bruce N. Ames, professor of biochemistry and molecular biology at the University of California at Berkeley, what he thought. Ames says the science just doesn't support the alarms about the extreme danger of dioxin in food (occupational hazards are another question). The evidence *is* there, says Ames, for the nutritional losses we'd suffer if we stopped eating these good fats, which include chromosome breaking and damage to the developing brain. "These essential nutrients are hundreds and hundreds of times more important than any possible ill effects from dioxin," according to Ames. So don't get frightened into avoiding the very nutrients your baby needs most; choose whole milk, organic meats, and wild fish from a good source, such as SeaBear, which routinely passes rigorous inspection for dioxin, PCBs, and mercury (www.seabear.com).

By the third trimester, the baby has developed a capacity for taste, which probably explains why whole cultures, like the Mexicans, seem to be born loving hot chiles. So it's really important in those last few months to cut out sweets and emphasize the foods you hope your baby will gravitate toward all its life. There's some evidence to show that you can set the stage for both obesity and diabetes in your child's future during this trimester by eating too many sweets and starches. To learn more about "fetal programming," see Dr. David Barker's British book, *The Best Start in Life* (available on amazon.co.uk).

By now you should be well aware that fried food is off your menu, as are partially hydrogenated vegetable oils. These oils are our major source of trans fats, especially dangerous because they can cross the placenta and end up in the fetus. If you consume them while you're nursing, the trans fats go right into your milk, and studies show they will negatively affect the baby's visual acuity, says David Kyle. Olive oil is your best choice, along with coconut oil. This is a great time to buy organic butter, eggs, dairy products, and meat, if they are in your budget. For your own immune system and the baby's, eat coconut—in the form of coconut oil, milk, and fresh or dried coconut—regularly. And since you should be getting about 300 extra calories a day in any case, coconut and chocolate and nuts are a delightful and useful way to spend them.

Although we need antioxidants and trace elements from our food more than ever, guess what: our food is less nourishing than ever. In a fascinating study of the nutrients in food, British researcher David Thomas went to the British Library and found all the past editions of the British nutritional bible, *The Composition of Foods,* by McCance and Widdowson. Record keeping started in 1940, and going year by year, Thomas discovered some surprising figures: In all fruits and vegetables, the numbers are significantly down, some startlingly. Calcium is down 49 percent; copper is down 75 percent. Carrots have lost 75 percent of their magnesium, broccoli 75 percent of its calcium.

How has this happened? Thomas speculates it's agribusiness at work, with chemical fertilizers and mass-production techniques. Tim Lang, professor of food policy at Thames Valley University in England, thinks plant breeding is the culprit. As plants are developed for hardiness, resistance to disease, superior growth, and early maturity—everything but taste and nutrients—preserving the basic nutritional content of the food had become the last desirable breeding characteristic. Lang is also amazed that no one in the world of nutrition seems to have noticed this phenomenon. That's just British food, of course; possibly we've done better in America. (Seeds of Change, an American company based in New Mexico, does breed seeds for nutrient value and taste.)

Breeding has also played havoc with taste, so that those gorgeous supermodel fruits and vegetables you see in the market are almost without exception pretty tasteless. A perfect winter tomato hauled halfway across the planet is almost guaranteed to be mealy and dry. Instead of perfection, look for bright colors and heavy fruit, which will have the most juice and be the sweetest. Your best bet in this chaotic world of food is to buy organic whenever possible, to support your local small farms and dairies through farmers' markets (for locations, see www.ams.usda.gov), and, as much as possible, to cook your own food.

CHAPTER SIX

~

The Big Picture

WHAT SHOULD WE EAT?

If you just dip in and out of this book, you might get the idea that a Mounds bar and some sardines would be the perfect meal. As with everything else to do with the human body, however, it's all a question of balance.

If fat's good now, how much fat is good? Harvard's Dr. Walter Willett is comfortable with 40 percent fat in the diet, as long as it's good fat, and others, like Dr. Ron Rosedale of the Colorado Metabolic Center, would go even higher. (Both of them would minimize saturated fats.) After all, there are only three food groups, fat, protein, and carbohydrate, and all regimes involve some trade-off between the three of them. Protein is absolutely essential for building and repairing the body, so we can't cut there (though we can add more protein). But even protein can eventually be broken down into sugar and stored as fat if it's consumed to excess, so too much isn't really a good idea either. Since our biological need for carbs is zero, and they cause so many problems for us, that's the obvious place to cut and trade into the fat budget. But antioxidants usually come in carb packages, so we don't want to miss out on the good things in fruits and vegetables. Sugar and starch carbs, however, can and should be ditched, hard as that is to do. In my own experience, which is of course anecdotal, eating very few carbs means you can eat more fat (i.e., more calories if they're from a fat source) without gaining weight, whereas the carbs-plus-fat (think ice cream) combination is very likely to promote fat storage. Whatever you do, don't just add a bunch of fat to your regular diet, or you'll be very sorry down the road. Think about what you eat and what you want to eat, and work it out.

Our general goals should be to eat the way our grandparents ate—real food that has a good omega-3 to omega-6 ratio, with as few free radicals as possible, and as few trans fats as possible—and as many antioxidants as possible, which means plenty of vegetables and fruits (okay, and a little chocolate). If our grandparents were Mediterranean types, so much the better. That's a perfectly fine diet, especially if you add some coconut and avocado. Some researchers think the reason the Mediterranean diet has such a good health profile is that it's full of antioxidants from olive oil and fresh vegetables and fruits. Instead of the cod liver oil our grandparents took, we now have pharmaceutical-grade fish oil. We don't use much lard anymore—though we should—but we can add coconut oil to the fats pantry. Once you have these general ideas in mind, the trick is in the details: finding the good stuff amid all the dross.

The details of this whole new way of looking at fats can be hard to remember, especially since it seems so counterintuitive to embrace fat after our long low-fat brainwashing. So here's a list of the most valuable recommendations in order of importance.

- Stop using hydrogenated, partially hydrogenated, and fake fats: Crisco, margarine, Olestra, Benefat, etc. Don't buy anything with the words "hydrogenated" or "partially hydrogenated" on the label. This includes all margarines. Use butter, nonhydrogenated palm shortening, olive oil, or coconut oil instead. Soon these bad fats will be listed on food labels as trans.
- Stop using the tasteless vegetable and seed oils, which have too much omega-6 fat and are sources of free radicals and trans fats (up to 15 percent, and there's no way to tell which is which) and even rancid fats: vegetable oil, salad oil, corn oil, cottonseed oil, soy oil, canola oil, and all hydrogenated oils (it will say so on the label). Ditching them is one of the best things you can do for your family's health. Use coconut oil, extra virgin olive oil, and non-hydrogenated peanut oil, sesame oil, or high-oleic sunflower oil instead.
- Pass up commercial cookies, doughnuts, chips, and crackers and all processed foods (i.e., anything that's not homemade or in the

form in which nature delivered it), all of which are loaded with trans fats. In a USDA study of 214 foods, the highest percentage of trans fats were found in soy and canola margarine (50 percent), fruit-flavored breakfast cereal with cottonseed and soy oils (40 percent), saltines and snack crackers (39 percent), and refrigerated biscuit dough made with soy oil (36.5 percent). Inevitably you'll eat some foods containing trans fats, but eat them sparingly. Take an alpha-lipoic acid capsule (100 mg) as a powerful antioxidant to minimize the damage.

- Don't eat fried foods unless you fry them the good-fat way yourself; these are loaded with toxic trans fats, free radicals, and omega-6 fats. If you can't live without potato chips, choose a brand that's cooked in lard or peanut oil*, which is a healthier choice. If you're indulging, be sure to counter this flood of bad fats with some antioxidants—a capsule of alpha-lipoic acid, a few olives, a handful of dried cranberries, a prune or two, or a little piece of chocolate.

- If you're going to give up one food forever, make it soft-serve ice cream. This junk food had its origins in a wonderful American invention, frozen custard, made from eggs, creamy milk, vanilla, and a little sugar, then frozen on the spot in giant machines. But now it comes from prepackaged liquid mix, which is full of bad fat (vegetable oils), superbad oxidized fat (powdered eggs and powdered milk), and high-fructose corn syrup (superbad sugar that increases your triglyceride levels). Premium ice cream, such as Häagen-Dazs, is infinitely better as a health choice—as an occasional treat.

- To boost your omega-3 levels, eat lots of canned small fish— sardines and anchovies—as well as fresh, canned, or smoked mackerel, tuna, salmon, and trout. Shellfish is also great for you. If you really don't like fish, supplement with fish oil (pharmaceutical-grade if you can afford it) and/or DHA (Neuromins); see Sources. Omega-3-enriched eggs are a very good idea.

- Look for grass-fed beef and lamb (New Zealand is a great source) and other meat raised without growth hormones and antibiotics. Organic meat is more expensive, but you can econ-

*Herr's, Grandma Utz, New Orleans "Dirty," Tim's Cascade

omize by cutting your portion size to 4 or even 3 ounces—we may love to see that giant steak on a platter, but we don't need to eat half a pound of meat at a sitting, and this more delicious meat is so satisfying that less truly is more.

- Eat as organically as you can. There's no reason to buy organic avocados, which are one of the least contaminated foods, but apples (more than 36 different pesticide residues), strawberries (more than 30), spinach, grapes (Chilean grapes are the worst), cucumbers, cantaloupes, potatoes, celery, green beans, and all grains—they're best from an organic source. Check out the lists at www.igc.org/mothers. Stickered fruits and vegetables with five digits starting with "8" are organic, but be careful; five digits starting with "9" means genetically modified.

- If you snack, eat a handful of nuts, especially walnuts, every day. This will cost about 180 calories (trade them for something else in your food budget) and is—aside from eliminating bad oils and increasing omega-3 fats—one of the best things you can do for your heart.

- Eat more coconut, avocado, nuts, omega-3-enriched eggs, and full-fat dairy products. Eat less sugar and starch.

- Don't buy anything labeled "light," "lite," "low-fat," or "non-fat." At the minimum you're paying for air and water being added to the food (as with light mayonnaise); worse, you may be paying for spray-dried milk powder or egg powder, which is oxidized cholesterol (the kind that turns into plaque in your arteries), something you want to avoid at all costs.

- Eat a lot of antioxidants (mainly from fruits and vegetables). The major ones at the moment are chocolate (just a little), oregano, cranberries and other berries, and prunes. Seek out produce with lots of lycopene, such as watermelon, tomato (when cooked for 30 minutes), and pink grapefruit, which all need to be consumed with a little fat. To preserve your antioxidants, take a 400 IU natural vitamin E oil capsule with mixed tocopherols daily.

- Eat a wide variety of foods. We all get into ruts, eating the same thing over and over because that way we don't have to make decisions and we can do it in our sleep, from shopping to cooking. Each food, however, from oils to nuts to fish, offers different nutrients.

- Demand the quality of food you want and you'll get it, eventually. The same megacorporations that met the demand for low-fat foods with SnackWell's and fifteen thousand other low-fat products will be only too happy to bring you foods made with coconut oil if that's what you want. If you want more grass-fed meat that's humanely raised using sound environmental practices, tell your market and you'll get it, though this may take several years. If farmed salmon that swim in clean, PCB-free water and aren't raised on grain or given routine doses of antibiotics are what you want, they'll be in your market, with guarantees of the quality you want. If you consistently buy organic cream and pass up the ultrapasteurized version, there will be more to buy, and it will be cheaper down the road.

  Huge compromises have been made on the quality of food in the name of lots-of-it and cheap. We don't need so much food or so much variety and we should be willing to pay a little more for quality and environmentally sound practices. If that sort of indulgence isn't in your budget, buy locally raised food, especially from the farmers' market, which will probably be cheaper and tastier and more nutrient-dense in any case.

- Cook! The only way you're going to really know what's in your food is to buy it and cook it yourself. Cooking is one of the all-time great creative opportunities in everyday life, and sharing food is a huge primal pleasure. Check out the recipes; there's something here for everyone, from sophisticated cooks to complete kitchen tenderfoots.

And pleasure, of course, is what it's all about. Food that's really good for you tastes really good, and now that you don't have to worry anymore about every succulent morsel you put in your mouth, you can truly enjoy it. And that's *very* good for you.

PART II

Recipes

A Note on the Recipes

Some of these recipes are incredibly easy, some are more complicated; many are low-carb, some are not. The main point is to use
good fats and foods containing lots of antioxidants and to enjoy
what you cook and eat. I recommend using omega-3-enriched
eggs in all the recipes, though I haven't specified that.

For my own cooking, I try to buy the best food I can afford,
which isn't always the very best. I always buy organic eggs and
organic canned tomatoes and organic apple cider vinegar; for all
other foods, it's a budget toss-up. If I'm using the zest of citrus in a
recipe, I look for organic citrus; if the skin on a potato is to be eaten
(which is the only part of the potato I eat), I choose organic potatoes. I try to keep in mind the "big ten" fruits and vegetables with
the heaviest pesticide residue, but buying all organic can be very
expensive.

I do indulge in good salt, however; I use Maldon salt (see page
153) and during tomato season, fleur de sel, the best salt of all. My
salt extravagances might amount to the cost of buying an extra bottle or two of Scotch a year, or of fine estate-bottled olive oil—and
are very much worth it, I think.

I think dessert should usually be fruit (berries and cream for low-
carbers) and perhaps a bit of chocolate to follow with coffee, but
I've included a number of desserts that are definitely in the Big Treat
category because I know those occasions will arise—and if you can
feel good about using good fats or good antioxidants in an indulgent dessert, all the better. Don't assume that I mean you should
make and eat these on an everyday basis.

Appetizers

Toasted Walnuts with Oregano

You can make these nuts with either olive oil—a sort of Greek taste—or butter, as you like. They couldn't be easier and they're more than slightly irresistible, so you may want to make a double batch.

Makes 2 cups

> 2½ tablespoons olive oil or unsalted butter, melted
> 2 teaspoons dried oregano, crumbled
> 1 teaspoon salt
> ½ teaspoon cayenne pepper
> 2 cups raw walnuts

Preheat the oven to 350 degrees.

Mix everything except the walnuts together, then stir in the walnuts, coating them well. Scatter the nuts on a baking sheet.

Roast the nuts for about 10 minutes, stirring once. Remove from the oven when they smell good, and let them cool before serving or storing.

The nuts will keep for a few days in a tightly sealed tin if made with butter, longer if made with oil.

East Indian Pecans

Addictive is the right word for these hauntingly but sweetly spiced nuts. They're great for a party or the holidays, and they make good presents too.

Makes 4 cups

> 4 tablespoons (½ stick) unsalted butter
> 2 tablespoons mild olive oil
> 1 tablespoon Madras curry powder
> 1 teaspoon garam masala (a curry-like spice mix; see Cook's Note)
> ¼ teaspoon ground cumin
> 1 teaspoon ground cinnamon
> 2 teaspoons salt
> ¼ teaspoon cayenne pepper
> 1 pound (4 cups) raw pecans

Preheat the oven to 300 degrees.

In a small saucepan, mix all the ingredients except the nuts and heat over medium heat just until the salt dissolves. Pour the mixture into a large bowl and add the nuts. Toss to coat them thoroughly.

Line a baking sheet with foil and spread the nuts on it in a single layer. Bake for about 30 minutes, stirring well every 10 minutes, until the nuts are very brown. Slide the foil off the pan onto a cooling rack; let cool completely.

Store the nuts in a tightly sealed tin, where they'll keep for a couple of weeks at least.

COOK'S NOTE: Garam masala is available in many supermarkets, Indian markets, and some natural foods stores.

Olives with Orange Zest and Fennel Seeds

This Italian way with olives has two virtues: it can be subtle (without the garlic and rosemary) or punchy (with them) and it goes together in about three minutes. These can also be made ahead—must, in fact, be made several hours ahead—and keep for a couple of weeks.

Makes 2 cups

> Zest of 1 orange cut into very thin strips (see Cook's Note),
>   or half lemon/half orange zest
> 1½ teaspoons fennel seeds
> 2 cups oil-cured black olives
> 1 large garlic clove, chopped, optional
> 2 sprigs fresh rosemary, optional
> 1 to 3 tablespoons extra virgin olive oil

Several hours before you plan to serve the olives, mix all the ingredients together, using just enough olive oil to moisten everything. Let sit at room temperature until you're ready to serve (after about 4 hours, remove the garlic). Serve in a small bowl, with a little plate to collect the pits.

To keep the olives for up to 2 weeks, remove the garlic and rosemary, cover with plastic wrap, and refrigerate. Bring to room temperature before serving.

COOK'S NOTE: If you have a zester, that's the easiest way to pull the skinny strips of colored zest off the orange. If not, use a vegetable peeler, then cut the long strands into skinny strips with a sharp paring knife.

Olive Paste with Tuna

This punchy condiment can be purchased at gourmet stores, but it's much cheaper and better to make your own. It's good on toast or crackers or tucked into thick slices of red pepper to serve with drinks. Leave out the tuna and you have olivada, delicious smeared on salmon before broiling, and a good secret ingredient in soups and stews with Mediterranean flavors.

Makes 1 cup

> 1 cup imported brine-cured black olives, such as
>   Kalamatas, pitted (see Cook's Note)
> ¼ cup capers, rinsed and drained
> 2 small garlic cloves, minced
> ½ teaspoon dried thyme
> 1 to 2 tablespoons olive oil
> Grated zest of ½ lemon
> One 6-ounce can tuna packed in olive oil, drained

Taste the olives; if they're very salty, they may need rinsing or even soaking.

Combine the olives, capers, garlic, and thyme in a food processor and process until you have a rough paste. With the motor running, slowly drizzle in 1 tablespoon of the olive oil, processing until you have a loose paste; add the extra oil if you need it.

Scrape the olive paste into a bowl. Stir in the lemon zest and tuna.

Without the tuna, the olive paste will keep for about a month tightly sealed in the refrigerator. With the tuna, it will keep for just a day or two.

COOK'S NOTE: To pit the olives, arrange them close together on a cutting board and lay the flat side of a chef's knife over them. Press down on the knife with your fist to split the olives. Pull out the pits with your fingers.

Tapenade

This zesty Provençal spread always has capers in it, but it doesn't always have hot peppers. You can use them or not, as you like. It's great on crackers or little toasts. The anchovies won't have a fishy presence, but they add a lot to the complex taste of tapenade. And, of course, they up the good fat ante.

Both capers and olives can be quite salty, so taste them before you toss them into the mix. They may need rinsing or even soaking in cold water for 15 minutes or so to get rid of some of the salt.

Makes 2 cups

> 8 ounces Kalamata olives, pitted (see Cook's Note on page 172)
> ¼ cup capers, rinsed and drained
> 4 anchovies, rinsed and chopped
> 3 garlic cloves, finely chopped
> Grated zest and juice of 1 large lemon
> ¼ teaspoon red pepper flakes, optional
> Olive oil if needed

Put all the ingredients except the olive oil in the food processor and coarsely chop, adding a little olive oil if necessary to bind the mixture together.

Scrape the tapenade into a crock, cover with plastic wrap, and let sit for at least an hour to develop flavor. Serve at room temperature.

You can store the tapenade for a couple of weeks in the refrigerator, tightly sealed.

Guacamole

It's only the chips that go with guacamole that are questionable from a health point of view, but it's so delicious on its own that you can substitute other dippers, such as shrimp, big radish slices, or healthy chips made from stale tortillas that you fry yourself in good fat such as lard or olive oil.

This is a traditional guacamole—no lime or lemon juice, no mayonnaise, no sour cream, no hot chile sauce or other American "improvements."

Makes about 1 cup

2 tablespoons finely chopped onion
½ teaspoon salt, preferably coarse sea salt or kosher salt
1 serrano chile, seeded and minced
1 Hass avocado, halved, pitted, and peeled
2 tablespoons finely chopped cilantro
2 tablespoons chopped tomato

The best way to make guacamole is in a *molcajete,* the traditional Mexican volcanic rock mortar and pestle. A regular mortar and pestle will do fine, as will a fork and a shallow dish and some elbow grease. Put the onion in the mortar and grind the salt into it, mashing the onion a bit as you do. Do the same with the chile. Add the avocado and mash down roughly—you don't want a smooth puree (see Cook's Note). Add the cilantro and mix well.

Guacamole has to be served immediately, or the top surface will turn brown. You can interfere with this process slightly by covering it with plastic wrap, pressed right onto the surface. Just remove any brown patches before you serve it. Serve the guacamole in the mortar or in a serving bowl, topped with scattered tomato bits.

COOK'S NOTE: The easiest way to get the right texture if you don't have a *molcajete,* the ancient Mexican mortar and pestle, is to cut the avocado in half lengthwise, remove the pit with a spoon, and press each half of the avocado through a wire rack, such as a mesh cooling rack, into a bowl. This gives you the perfect texture.

A good way to serve guacamole that bypasses the what-to-dip issue is to stuff cherry tomatoes with it. Scoop out their seeds with a melon baller and stuff them with the guacamole. Stick a small cooked shrimp into each one and finish with a sprig of cilantro. These are great for a cocktail party.

Grilled Cheese with Oregano

This South American take on grilled cheese is not only delicious, it also features the stand-out antioxidant oregano. If you can't be bothered to grill, you can make it in the oven. This is one of those very sociable dishes like fondue where everyone dips into the same dish.

Serve it with toast—toasted baguette slices are perfect. Low-carbers can use low-carb toast or just skip the toast altogether and treat this as fork food.

Serves 6

> 2 tablespoons extra virgin olive oil
> 1 teaspoon dried crumbled oregano
> 1 large ½-inch-thick slice provolone, preferably imported

Combine the oil and oregano. Place the cheese in a small dish just large enough to hold it and pour the seasoned oil over it. Turn the cheese once to be sure it's covered on all surfaces. Marinate for at least 4 hours at room temperature, or overnight in the refrigerator. Bring to room temperature before grilling.

To grill, set the cheese on the grill over medium coals and grill just until it starts to sag into the grate. Immediately remove it and serve on a platter, with toast.

To roast the cheese, place it in a baking dish and bake in a preheated 350-degree oven until it's soft and starting to melt, about 15 minutes. Serve hot. If you can't serve the cheese right away and it starts to harden again, put it back in the oven for 8 minutes or so to soften it.

COOK'S NOTE: If you reheat the cheese, pour off the oil in the baking dish or it will reabsorb into the cheese.

If the provolone is huge, you may want only a half-moon slice, which will weigh about a pound and serve 8.

Melon with Black Olives

This is a Provençal way of serving melons and olives together—a good combination. Both the melon and olives should be icy cold. Chill them for at least half an hour and up to 4 hours before you serve them in glass bowls. Breadsticks with tapenade (page 173) to dip them into make a nice accompaniment.

Serves 4

> 2 cups melon balls, from 1 large melon, such as cantaloupe
> ½ cup Niçoise olives or other not-too-salty olive (unpitted)
> Freshly ground black pepper

Mix the melon balls and olives in a bowl, cover and refrigerate for at least 30 minutes, or up to 4 hours

Just before serving, dust the melon and olives with pepper. Serve in small glass bowls.

Watermelon Sandwiches with Goat Cheese

These succulent little morsels are full of lycopene, the potent antioxidant, but that's not the reason to make them—they're just irresistible. The only problem is deciding when to serve them. They're a good snack, they'd be fine on a barbecue buffet, or they can be passed along with other summer tidbits for cocktails. They're also nice after a meal.

For a party, mix yellow and red watermelon and cut the sandwiches into different shapes—triangles, rounds, squares.

Thin slices of seedless watermelon
Salt and freshly ground black pepper
Mild fresh goat cheese, at room temperature
A little cream, if needed
Minced mint or dill

Trim the watermelon slices so that you have matching pairs about the same size and shape. Lay one slice of each pair on a cutting board and salt and pepper it. Spread a thin layer of the goat cheese (if it's not spreadable, add a little cream and blend it until it's the right consistency) over the seasoned watermelon. Salt and pepper the remaining watermelon slice and place it seasoned side down over the cheese. Lightly press the sandwich together.

Sprinkle both sides of the sandwiches with the minced herbs and cut into serving shapes, using a knife or a cookie cutter.

The sandwiches are good at room temperature, but they taste best just slightly chilled. Wrap loosely in plastic wrap and refrigerate for up to 2 hours. Remove from the refrigerator half an hour before serving.

Taramasalata

This lovely Greek dip/spread is a classic that happens to be brimming with good fats. Because this version is made with nuts instead of bread, it has a completely different texture from the usual taramasalata—much creamier, and not at all gummy. Made this way, it's also a great low-carb dish.

Serves 6

> 1 cup blanched almonds (6 ounces)
> 1 garlic clove
> 5 ounces tarama (fish roe, either cod or carp), about ½ cup
> 4 scallions, chopped, including the light green parts
> 2 tablespoons chopped dill, plus more for garnish
> ½ cup extra virgin olive oil, or as needed, plus more to drizzle over the dish
> Juice of 2 lemons
> Salt

In the food processor, grind the almonds and garlic together, pulsing on and off, until you have fine crumbs; don't let the nuts turn into a paste. Add the fish roe and pulse until well combined. Add the scallions and dill; combine. Slowly add the olive oil, alternating with the lemon juice, pulsing until the mixture is creamy. If it's too thick, add a little more olive oil. Taste for salt; it may or may not need some. You can keep the spread for a day or two tightly sealed in the refrigerator.

Serve in a small dish, drizzled with more olive oil and garnished with dill. Serve with pita bread or sticks of fennel or red pepper.

COOK'S NOTE: Tarama keeps for about a year in the refrigerator because it's so salty, so it's a good idea to keep it around. The tubes of cod roe (see Sources) work well here and are exactly the amount you need for this recipe.

Smoked Trout Spread

Good for a cocktail party or to begin an elegant meal, this delectable spread goes together in the food processor, so it's a snap to make. There are just two tricks: you need to make it a day ahead (actually a bonus) and you must add the lemon juice judiciously, because too much will make the fish taste too salty. For great smoked trout, see Sources.

Makes about 1 cup

> 1 to 2 tablespoons fresh lemon juice
> 1 small shallot
> 8 ounces lean smoked trout, bones and skin removed
> 3 tablespoons mayonnaise, preferably homemade
>   (page 206)
> 3 tablespoons cream cheese
> Pinch of freshly ground white pepper
> Pinch of cayenne pepper
> 1 tablespoon finely chopped parsley, plus parsley sprigs for
>   garnish
> Crackers or crisp toast for serving

Combine everything (start with 1 tablespoon lemon juice) but the parsley sprigs and crackers in the food processor and process until smooth. Taste for seasoning; if it tastes a little salty, that's okay, because the spread will mellow out overnight. If it needs more lemon, however, add it by the teaspoon now, tasting as you go.

Pack the spread into a crock and cover with plastic wrap. Refrigerate overnight.

Serve slightly chilled, decorated with parsley sprigs, with the crackers or toast.

Soups

Tomato Soup
with Spanish Smoked Paprika

This is a lighter version of cream of tomato soup, with a haunting flavor: the smoked paprika. This exotic spice is available at many gourmet shops or by mail-order (see Sources), and it's so delightful to cook with that you really should make an effort to find it. If it's unavailable, though, good Hungarian paprika will be fine here.

This soup has some of the complexity of lobster bisque, for some reason, though it contains none of the same ingredients. The coconut milk may seem like a really unlikely element, but you won't taste the coconut and it contributes a light, creamy smoothness to the soup.

Serves 4

> 1 tablespoon olive oil
> ½ large onion, chopped
> 1 garlic clove, chopped
> Salt
> ½ teaspoon Spanish smoked paprika, sweet or hot, or Hungarian paprika
> ½ teaspoon dried oregano, crumbled, plus extra for garnish
> 1 pint cherry tomatoes, quartered, or one 14.5-ounce can of diced organic tomatoes, including their juice
> 3 cups chicken broth
> 1 cup unsweetened coconut milk, well stirred
> Freshly ground black pepper
> ¼ cup crumbled fresh goat cheese, such as Montrachet

Heat the olive oil in a soup pot. Add the onion and stir it well over medium heat until wilted, about 5 minutes. Add the garlic and ½ teaspoon salt and cook over medium-low heat for another few minutes, until the garlic is soft. Add the paprika and oregano, stir well, and cook for a few minutes more. Add the tomatoes and cook for a few minutes.

Add the chicken broth and bring to a simmer. Let simmer uncovered, for 15 minutes.

Pour the soup into a blender and puree it (or use an immersion blender right in the soup pot), leaving a few bits of tomato. Add the coconut milk and blend well. Return the soup to the pot (if necessary) and bring back to a simmer. Check the seasoning, adding pepper to taste.

Serve the soup in shallow soup plates, each garnished with a tablespoon of the goat cheese and a pinch of oregano. You can reheat any leftover soup the next day.

Zesty Cucumber Soup

Every summer I decide I'm not going to make this soup again, but somehow I do, just because it's so refreshing and almost addictive. You can up the good fat ante by adding some little poached shrimp to float on top of each serving.

Serves 6

    1 teaspoon Dijon mustard
    1 teaspoon sugar
    2 cucumbers, peeled (but not seeded) and grated
    1 small onion, grated
    1 cup sour cream
    1 quart buttermilk
    1 teaspoon salt
    Freshly ground black pepper
    Snipped chives for garnish
    4 ounces shelled cooked baby shrimp, optional

In a large bowl, mix the mustard and sugar well, then add the vegetables and sour cream. Stir in the buttermilk and add the salt and pepper to taste, mixing very well.

Cover the soup and let it chill for at least 2 hours, or up to 8 hours to develop flavor.

Serve chilled, topped with the chives and the optional shrimp.

Red Pepper Soup
with Moroccan Flavors

This intensely flavored soup is easy to make—assuming you don't mind roasting peppers—and it's good hot or cold. The avocado gets just gently warmed if it goes into hot soup, which brings out its buttery quality.

Serves 4

4 red bell peppers
4 garlic cloves, smashed and chopped
2½ teaspoons paprika
1½ teaspoons ground cumin
Big pinch of cayenne pepper
1 tablespoon plus 1 teaspoon extra virgin olive oil
One 14.5-ounce can chicken broth
½ cup water
Salt
1 Hass avocado
1 lemon, cut into wedges
¼ cup chopped cilantro

Stand a pepper stem side up on a cutting board. Hold the stem and, with a chef's knife, cut off the 4 sides close to the stem, leaving the spongy central core and the seeds behind. Pull out any remaining seeds. Repeat with the rest of the peppers.

Turn on the broiler. Arrange the peppers flesh side down on the foil-lined broiler pan and broil about 4 inches from the heat for about 4 minutes, or until the skin is blistered and blackened. Fold the foil up around the peppers and let them sit for about 15 minutes to steam and loosen the skins.

Open the foil and pull off the pepper skins. Set the peppers aside.

In a large saucepan, combine the garlic, paprika, cumin, cayenne, and olive oil and cook over low heat for 2 minutes, stirring all the time. Add the chicken broth, water, and the peppers and simmer for about 10 minutes. Let the soup cool a bit, then puree it with an immersion blender or in the blender until smooth.

If you're serving the soup hot, return it to the saucepan and heat just to a simmer. If you're serving it cold, chill the soup for at least 2 hours, or up to 8 hours. Taste the soup for salt before serving.

To serve, cut the avocado into small dice and squeeze a little lemon juice over it. Serve the soup with garnishes of the avocado and cilantro. Have a few lemon wedges available in case guests want to add some lemon to the soup.

Carrot and Parsnip Soup with Orange

This slightly sweet bright orange soup is a hit at Thanksgiving but it's also good served cold at other times of the year. You can add either cream or coconut milk, or you can leave most of it out; the soup can be thicker or thinner, but it always tastes good.

Serves 8

> 1 pound carrots, cut into 1-inch lengths
> 1 pound parsnips, peeled and cut into 1-inch lengths
> 4 tablespoons (½ stick) unsalted butter
> 1 medium onion, diced
> 3 cups chicken broth
> Salt and freshly ground black pepper
> Juice of 3 oranges
> ½ cup cream or canned unsweetened coconut milk

Boil the carrots and parsnips in salted water until tender, 15 to 20 minutes. Drain well and let cool.

Meanwhile, melt the butter in a medium skillet and sauté the onion over medium heat until soft, just a few minutes.

Working in batches, puree the carrots and parsnips with the onion and broth in a blender. Add salt and pepper to taste. Transfer to a bowl and add the orange juice and cream or coconut milk, working them into the soup.

Serve hot or cold. You can make the soup a day ahead and keep it refrigerated.

Cold Beet and Cucumber Soup with Ginger

This gorgeous magenta soup is sweet and punchy at the same time, with crisp little bites of cucumber to cool you off. If you can buy cooked beets in plastic packages, it goes really quickly, but microwaving raw ones doesn't take much time.

Serves 4

> 1 hothouse cucumber, peeled and seeded
> 5 small beets, cooked, peeled, and cut into chunks
> 1 cup buttermilk
> 1 cup yogurt
> 1 cup water
> ½ sweet onion, cut into chunks
> ½ to 1 teaspoon salt
> Freshly ground black pepper to taste
> 1-inch piece of fresh ginger, grated
> 1 tablespoon fresh lime juice
>
> GARNISH
> Crème fraîche
> Asian pickled ginger (for sushi), minced

Cut about a third of the cucumber into small dice and set aside. Cut the rest into chunks and add to a blender jar. Add the remaining soup ingredients and process until relatively smooth. Taste for seasoning and adjust as necessary.

Cover and chill the soup for at least 1 hour, or up to 4 hours. If it separates, blend it again before serving.

To serve, divide the diced cucumber among the soup bowls and pour the soup over. Finish with a dollop of crème fraîche in each bowl. Pass a small bowl of the minced pickled ginger for diners to stir into their soup, along with the crème fraîche.

Guacamole Soup

This is my version of a soup that California food writer Jacqueline McMahan found in a little café in Tonala, Mexico. The original version is made with homemade chicken broth—and in Mexico that usually includes chicken feet, as well as a lot of other tasty items—but I've cheated a bit and made it with an enriched canned broth. The soup is bland and comforting without the chile; with it, it's lively and zesty. When you serve the soup, tell diners to stir it very well, so the avocado is distributed all through the broth.

Making the soup begins just the way making guacamole begins, with mashed avocado and salt in the bottom of each soup bowl. With chicken, a little cheese, and a topping of crème fraîche or sour cream, this terrific low-carb soup is a meal in itself.

Serves 4

> Two 14.5-ounce cans or one 32-ounce package low-sodium
>   chicken broth
> 2 cups water
> ½ onion, cut in half
> 1 garlic clove, smashed
> Salt and pepper
> 1 double chicken breast, preferably with skin and bones
> 2 ripe avocados, cut in half
> 1 jalapeño chile, minced, optional
> Juice of 1 lime, plus lime wedges for serving
> About ½ cup chopped cilantro leaves
> 4 tablespoons of crème fraîche or sour cream, optional
> Crumbled Mexican white cheese, optional

Combine the chicken broth and water in a medium saucepan with the onion, garlic, and a little salt and pepper, and heat. Cut the chicken into 4 pieces and add to the broth. Bring the broth to a boil, then turn down the heat and cook at a slow simmer, partially covered, for about 12 minutes, or until the chicken is cooked through but still tender. Remove the chicken breast and let cool. Strain the broth.

When the chicken is cool enough to handle, remove the skin and bones and shred the meat. Correct the seasoning of the broth.

When ready to serve, reheat the chicken broth until it's piping hot. Meanwhile, scoop out the flesh from an avocado half and mash it roughly in the bottom of each of the four soup bowls, adding ¼ of the optional jalapeño. Add salt to taste and a little lime juice; mash well.

Pour the hot broth over the mashed avocado in the soup bowls, divide the shredded chicken among them, and top with cilantro leaves and a spoonful of crème fraîche. If you're using the cheese, scatter it over the top. Serve the soup immediately, with lime wedges on the side.

COOK'S NOTE: You can make the chicken several hours ahead and just assemble the soup at the last minute.

Chipotle chile (smoked jalapeño) is great in this soup. You can blend up a small can of chipotle in adobo and offer it on the table, so guests can take a little and swirl it into their soup. Or you can do as they do in Mexico: Float a whole chipotle in each soup bowl. Chile aficionados can take little bites of the chile as it softens in the soup.

Oyster Avgolemono Soup

The lovely Greek peasant soup gets taken to new heights in this brilliant combination, the brainchild of Southern cook James Villas. If you can make or acquire some homemade chicken broth, the soup will be celestial, but it you can't or won't, don't let that stop you—the soup will still be very good made with good canned broth.

Serves 6

> 4 large egg yolks
> Juice of 2 lemons
> 1½ pints shucked oysters, drained, liquor reserved
>   (see page 96)
> 4 cups chicken broth, preferably homemade
> ¼ cup orzo
> Salt and freshly ground black pepper
> Tabasco
> 2 parsley sprigs, chopped

Whisk the egg yolks in a medium bowl until creamy. Add the lemon juice and whisk until well blended.

Combine the reserved oyster liquor and the chicken broth in a large saucepan and bring to a boil. Gradually add the orzo. Reduce the heat, cover, and simmer until the pasta is cooked, about 15 minutes. Add salt, pepper, and Tabasco to taste. Stir well.

Whisk ½ cup of the hot broth mixture into the eggs. Add the oysters to the broth in the saucepan, and gradually mix in the egg mixture. Heat the soup through over medium heat—but don't let it boil. Just before serving, stir in the parsley.

Thai Seafood Chowder

Easy, fast, and exotic, this chowder is a meal in itself. Oily fish with the very good fat don't work well here, but the white fish also have some omega-3s, as do the shellfish.

Serves 4

> 2 tablespoons mild olive oil
> 3 large shallots, minced
> 3 garlic cloves, smashed and minced
> 1 stalk lemongrass, trimmed to the tender, silky inner layers and minced
> 2 quarter-sized slices fresh ginger, minced
> 1 small red chile, seeded and minced, or more to taste
> 2 teaspoons grated lime zest
> Salt and freshly ground black pepper
> 1 quart chicken broth, preferably homemade
> 2 cups bottled clam juice
> 1 tablespoon fresh lime juice
> 2 teaspoons *nam pla* (Thai fish sauce; see page 194)
> One 14-ounce can unsweetened coconut milk, well stirred
> 1 pound firm white fish fillets, such as halibut, cod, or bass, cut into 1-inch chunks
> 8 ounces peeled shellfish, such as shrimp, scallops, crab-meat, or lobstermeat, cut into 1-inch chunks
> Minced cilantro for garnish

Heat a deep soup pot and add the oil. When it's hot, sauté the shallots, garlic, lemongrass, ginger, and chile over medium heat for a few minutes, until soft. Add the lime zest and season lightly with salt and pepper. Stir in the chicken broth, clam juice, lime juice, nam pla, and coconut milk and bring to a simmer. Taste for seasoning and adjust if necessary.

Add the fish and shellfish and simmer the chowder gently over low heat until a chunk of the fish slides apart easily when poked with the tip of a spoon, just a few minutes. Taste again for seasoning.

Serve the chowder in heated soup bowls, and sprinkle each serving generously with cilantro.

COOK'S NOTE: If some of the shellfish is precooked, add it just before serving to heat through.

Asian Fish Sauce

This terrific condiment—basically fermented little fish—is the Asian version of *garum armoricum*, the fermented fish sauce the Romans were so fond of. We see it in two main varieties: Thai (*nam pla*) and Vietnamese (*nuoc mam*), but basically they're the same thing, as are all the other Asian fish sauces from other countries.

Fish sauce is a bit like anchovies: once released into other foods, it does magical things and tastes not at all fishy. If you just take a whiff of it, though, you'll be very skeptical about using it at all. Just persevere: don't smell it, and use it in all sorts of Asian dishes. It's great with fish (of course), chicken, duck, pork, and beef. Asian soups are much better with a dollop of fish sauce, and it also perks up rice and noodles.

A great brand of fish sauce is Thai King Lobster (which contains not an ounce of lobster). But most brands are good, at least the ones that come in glass bottles. This stuff lasts forever at room temperature, especially since such a little bit of it goes so far.

Salmon Chowder

This variation on New England clam chowder uses good-quality canned salmon with its usual favorite partner, dill. Low-carbers can substitute small young turnips or celery for the potatoes. This recipe is a good one to have up your sleeve for a hearty blustery-day soup that's a meal in itself.

Serves 4

>   3 slices bacon, diced
>   1 small onion, minced
>   1 teaspoon dried dill or 1 tablespoon chopped fresh
>   dill
>   1 small bay leaf
>   Freshly ground black pepper to taste
>   Pinch of cayenne pepper
>   3 medium new potatoes or 6 small turnips, peeled
>   and diced, or 1 cup diced celery
>   1½ cups chicken broth
>   Two 4-ounce cans or one 7.5-ounce can red salmon,
>   skin and bones removed, juices reserved
>   One 14-ounce can unsweetened coconut milk, well
>   stirred
>   2 tablespoons minced parsley or dill for garnish

Sauté the bacon with the onion, dill, bay leaf, pepper, and cayenne in a soup pot over medium-high heat until the bacon renders its fat and is slightly crisp. Remove all but a tablespoon of the bacon fat from the pan. (If the bacon is lean, there may be less than 1 tablespoon.)

Add the potatoes or turnips and chicken broth and simmer until the potatoes are almost cooked, about 6 minutes. Separate the salmon into chunks. Add the salmon and its juices and simmer for 5 more minutes.

Add the coconut milk and bring slowly to a boil. Reduce the heat and simmer for 5 minutes. Remove the bay leaf and serve warm in heated bowls, garnished with the parsley or dill.

Persian Meatball Soup

This meal-in-itself soup has some typical Persian touches, such as the generous amount of chopped fresh herbs. The leeks and spinach add more fresh green to the soup, and the two kinds of beans give it some body. The meatballs inevitably crumble a bit by the time it's served, so the soup is more like a stew. The last-minute flourish of butter brings it all together deliciously.

Serves 4

MEATBALLS
8 ounces ground beef
1 garlic clove, minced
1 medium onion, minced
1 large egg, beaten
¼ rounded teaspoon ground cinnamon
¼ teaspoon cumin
Sprinkling of salt and freshly ground black pepper

SOUP
1½ quarts water
1 cup canned chickpeas, rinsed and drained
1 cup lentils, picked over and rinsed
1 teaspoon salt
2 leeks (white and light green parts only), thickly sliced
8 ounces spinach, chopped
1 cup chopped herbs—use a combination of parsley, dill,
    mint, and cilantro
Salt and freshly ground black pepper
2 tablespoons unsalted butter, softened

Blend the ingredients for the meatballs together with your hands. Form into little meatballs about the size of a walnut.

In a soup pot, bring the water to a boil. Add the meatballs, chickpeas, lentils, and 1 teaspoon salt; reduce the heat and simmer, uncovered, for 30 minutes.

Add the leeks and spinach and simmer for another 20 minutes. Stir in the herbs and simmer for 10 more minutes. Remove from the heat, taste for seasoning, and swirl in the butter.

Serve in soup plates, garnished with extra herbs if you have some.

COOK'S NOTE: There will be some leftover chickpeas, which can be fried in a skillet in a little hot olive oil to garnish the soup.

Leftover dill and cilantro can go into Egg Salad with Herbs (page 205) the next day.

Salads

Red and Yellow Cherry Tomato Salad
with Blue Cheese and Basil

This simple but extraordinary salad is typical of the fare created by Irish chef James O'Shea at the West Street Grill in Litchfield, Connecticut. For about five minutes' work, you get an elegant dish that's unforgettable.

O'Shea uses only fleur de sel, the world's best salt, but I think Maldon salt or another fine sea salt works very well too. The Papillon blue cheese is a delicate one; if it's not available, ask your cheese counterperson for a good substitute, such as Berkshire Great Hill Blue. A strong blue would overwhelm the salad.

Serves 6

> 3 pints red and yellow cherry tomatoes, cut in half
> Fleur de sel or another fine sea salt, such as Maldon salt
> Freshly ground black pepper
> 6 basil leaves, cut into skinny ribbons, plus (optional)
>   6 basil crowns (tops of the plant)
> 4 ounces Papillon or other delicate blue cheese, crumbled
> 2 tablespoons extra virgin olive oil

Place the tomatoes in a bowl and sprinkle with salt and pepper to taste. Toss gently and allow to marinate for 20 minutes.

Add the basil ribbons to the tomatoes and toss to mix.

Mound the tomatoes in a deep serving dish. Top with the crumbled blue cheese and drizzle with the olive oil. Garnish with the basil crowns, if you have them, and serve.

Beet Salad with Roquefort and Walnuts

If you have some really good walnut oil, this is a great place to use it. But if you don't, you can just use all olive oil and the salad will still be very good.

This salad can be lunch or a light supper, and it goes well with sardines on toast (see page 89).

Serves 4

> 6 medium beets, cooked and peeled (see page 189)
> 5 tablespoons extra virgin olive oil
> 2 tablespoons walnut oil
> ¼ cup red wine vinegar
> Salt and freshly ground black pepper
> 4 cups baby arugula
> ½ cup crumbled Roquefort cheese
> ¾ cup walnut halves, toasted

Cut each beet into 8 wedges, and set aside.

To make the dressing, whisk together the two oils and the vinegar. Season with salt and pepper and whisk again.

Put the greens in a shallow salad bowl and toss with the dressing. Add the beets, cheese, and walnuts and toss again gently, just to combine. Serve immediately.

Parsley Salad with Avocado

This is a zesty, punchy, fresh-tasting salad that goes with almost everything. If a robust garlic taste isn't appropriate with your main course, just omit it, and the lemony qualities of the salad will take up the slack.

Much depends on the parsley here; you need pristine Italian parsley, the flat-leaf kind (the curly kind tends to stick in people's throats).

If you add some big curls of Parmesan cheese (cut with a potato peeler), the salad is hearty enough for a main course.

Serves 2

> 1 bunch parsley, stemmed and coarsely chopped
> 2 tablespoons olive oil
> 1 tablespoon fresh lemon juice
> 1 garlic clove, pressed
> Salt and freshly ground black pepper
> 2 oil-packed sun-dried tomatoes, patted dry and cut into
>   slivers
> 2 scallions (white and green parts), chopped
> ½ avocado, diced

Put the parsley in a salad bowl and set aside.

In a small bowl, mix together the olive oil, lemon juice, garlic, salt and pepper to taste, and sun-dried tomatoes. Scatter the scallions over the parsley and drizzle the dressing on top. Toss well, then add the avocado and toss again before serving.

Watermelon, Tomato, and Mint Salad
with Feta Cheese

If you like to serve dishes that raise eyebrows, here's a good one. The combination of watermelon (the lycopene champion) and tomato is not only startling, it's also really tasty and everything else just adds to the fun.

Salting the fruits (tomato's a fruit, remember) first and letting them sit for a bit before assembling the salad is crucial for developing the flavors, so don't skip that step. Between that presalting and the feta cheese, you shouldn't need to add any more salt.

Serves 2

> 1 cup seeded watermelon chunks—red or yellow or a
> mixture
> 1 cup tomato chunks—any color
> Sea salt, preferably Maldon salt
> 1 tablespoon olive oil
> 1 tablespoon fresh lemon juice
> Freshly ground black pepper
> About 4 mint leaves, snipped
> About 5 chives, snipped
> ¼ cup crumbled feta cheese

About half an hour before you plan to serve the salad, arrange the watermelon and tomato chunks in a single layer on a tray and salt them. Set aside.

To make the salad, drain the watermelon and tomatoes well. Place them in a serving bowl and toss with the olive oil, then add the lemon juice and a few grinds of pepper and toss again. Sprinkle with the mint and chives and scatter the feta cheese over the top. Just before serving, toss very lightly.

Egg Salad with Herbs

A really well made egg salad is a completely satisfying thing to eat, and one you hardly ever find. The eggs in this salad are fluffy and light, with no gray rings around the yolks and no tough parts. The dill and cilantro are great together, and the walnuts add a little more good fat to the mix.

Serves 4

8 large eggs, at room temperature
¼ cup chopped cilantro
¼ cup chopped dill
¼ cup chopped chives
¼ cup chopped walnuts, optional
¼ teaspoon salt, or more to taste
Freshly ground black pepper to taste
Big pinch of cayenne pepper
Big pinch of ground cumin
⅓ cup mayonnaise, preferably homemade (page 206), or
    more as needed
Baby watercress for serving

Bring a pot of water just large enough to hold the eggs to a boil. Lower the eggs slowly into the water in a big spoon, one by one. Turn the heat down to a simmer and cook the eggs for 10 minutes. Take them off the heat and drain; immediately put them in a bowl of ice water to cool.

When they're cool enough to handle, crack the eggs all over against the side of the bowl, and return them to it, adding ice if the water is now warm. Let the eggs sit in the cold water until you're ready to peel them.

To make the salad, peel the eggs and grate them on the large holes of a box grater into a mixing bowl. Add everything but the watercress and mix gently but well. Taste for seasoning.

To serve, make a little nest of watercress on each salad plate and arrange a mound of the egg salad on top. To garnish, you could snip some more dill over the top of the salads.

Just a Little Mayo

Because commercial mayonnaise contains damaging trans fats, it's a good idea to make your own—which is a snap. But most recipes require hauling out the food processor and making a large quantity, and it keeps for only a few days.

If you have a hand-held immersion blender, however, you can make half a cup of mayo in moments. Tailor the recipe to your own taste: if you like an intense Greek-style mayonnaise, use extra virgin olive oil; if a delicate mayonnaise is what's called for, use a light French extra virgin oil. You could also use pure olive oil, which will be less pronounced in flavor and cheaper, but missing a lot of the antioxidants for which we prize olive oil.

If you don't have an immersion blender, or you'd rather make the mayonnaise by hand, just whisk away, drizzling the oil in very slowly. If the mayonnaise breaks, add a spoonful of warm water to re-emulsify it.

You can also add minced garlic, herbs, curry, whatever suits your meal. Double the recipe if you like; use just one egg yolk.

Makes ½ cup

1 large egg yolk, whisked, minus 1 teaspoon
½ teaspoon dry mustard
1 tablespoon fresh lemon juice, or more to taste
½ cup olive oil (see note above)
Salt

In a small bowl just large enough to hold the immersion blender easily, blend the egg yolk, mustard, and lemon juice. With the blender on, pour in the olive oil in a slow stream, making an emulsion. Add salt, then taste to see if you need more salt and lemon juice, and add any seasonings (see note above).

Store the mayonnaise in a tightly sealed jar in the refrigerator for up to a week.

Some embellishments:

- chopped preserved lemon peel (page 267)
- minced anchovies and lemon juice
- fresh herbs: tarragon and chives, or cilantro and dill; add a little minced shallot
- for aïoli: mix in some crushed garlic; also a little roasted red pepper is good with aïoli

Shrimp and Avocado Salad

This light, fresh salad has Southeast Asian flavors that may remind you of spring rolls. Small salad shrimp work very well here—or use larger shrimp and cut them into bite-sized chunks. You can use almonds instead of macadamia nuts, but the herbs and the lime are key ingredients.

Make the mayonnaise and chop the ingredients ahead of time if you like, but toss the salad together just before you serve it. Those colored airy shrimp chips that look like painted Styrofoam are a good accompaniment.

Serves 2

> Salt and freshly ground black pepper
> Fresh lemon juice
> 1 pound small shrimp, peeled
> About 2 tablespoons mayonnaise, preferably homemade
>   (page 206)
> Fresh lime juice
> Big pinch of garam masala (a curry-like spice mix; see
>   Cook's Note on page 170)
> 3 scallions (including some of the green parts), chopped
> 2 celery ribs, chopped
> 2 tablespoons chopped cilantro
> 1 tablespoon chopped mint
> 1 avocado, cut into chunks
> 2 cups torn romaine leaves
> 2 tablespoons chopped macadamia nuts or toasted almonds

Set a pot of water to boil, and add some pepper and lemon juice. When the water is boiling, add some salt and return to the boil. Drop in the shrimp and cook just until they take on some color. Drain well and set aside to cool.

In a small bowl, thin the mayonnaise with a little lime juice. Add the garam masala, whisking it in well.

Place the cooled shrimp in a large bowl and add the mayonnaise and the remaining ingredients except the romaine leaves and the nuts. Toss well.

Serve the salad on torn romaine leaves and sprinkle the nuts over the top. Serve immediately.

Smoked Trout Salad
with Avocado and Grapefruit

This elegant salad is great for a spring lunch or light supper, and it goes together in minutes—which is good, since you do have to make it at the last minute.

Pink grapefruit is full of lycopene and wonderful with the avocado. Look for the large Star Ruby grapefruit from Florida or Texas—a heavy, small-pored grapefruit with a few mottled brown splotches on the skin means delectable fruit lurks inside.

Serves 4

½ bunch watercress, heavy stems removed
1 large head butter lettuce, leaves separated
1 large pink grapefruit, sectioned over a bowl, juice
    reserved (see page 309), and diced
1 Hass avocado, diced
1 smoked trout (about 12 ounces), skinned, boned, and
    broken into bite-sized pieces
Salt and freshly ground black pepper
¼ cup extra virgin olive oil
2 tablespoons champagne vinegar
2 tablespoons chopped chives
¼ cup toasted chopped pecans

Tear the watercress and lettuce into bite-sized pieces and add them to a salad bowl. Lay the grapefruit on top.

Toss the avocado with 2 tablespoons of the reserved grapefruit juice and set aside.

Add the trout to the salad bowl and season with salt and pepper to taste.

Mix the olive oil with the champagne vinegar and pour over the salad. Toss the salad well, add the avocado with the grapefruit juice, the chives, and pecans, and toss again. Serve immediately.

Not Too Fishy

Delicious as half the world thinks anchovies, sardines, and other fishy fish are, the other half squirms at the very idea. Now that we know how extraordinarily good for you these fish are, it's important to develop a taste for them. Here are some ideas for minimizing the fishy quality.

- Oily fish, the ones with the most omega-3 fats, must be eaten very fresh, or they're a real nightmare of fishiness. When you buy them, take a sniff: they should smell of the sea, not at all unpleasant. Cook them as soon as possible.
- To bring out the sweeter, less fishy aspect of everything from canned anchovies to swordfish, soak in milk for about 20 minutes before cooking or using.
- Canned sardines benefit from a little lemon juice bath before using them in a dish. The least fishy ones are skinless and boneless—but those also have less omega-3.

Salade Niçoise

In Nice, they love to argue about how to make a correct salade Niçoise—are there green beans or not? Both tuna and anchovies or only one of them? Potatoes or not? Artichokes or not? I think it's hard to make a bad salade Niçoise as long as you observe a few rules. Use only very good quality tuna packed in olive oil (not seared fresh tuna, as is the style in pretentious restaurants), preferably imported; use a fine extra virgin olive oil, and salt the tomatoes twice before adding them to the salad. The salad can be composed artfully or all tossed together, as you like.

The salad is a riot of good fats, not to mention antioxidants.

Serves 6

> 8 ripe tomatoes, quartered, or about 40 cherry tomatoes, halved
> Sea salt
> 1 head of butter lettuce, leaves separated
> Two 6-ounce cans chunk light tuna, packed in oil, preferably Italian, drained and flaked
> 12 anchovy fillets, soaked in milk (see page 211), drained, and cut in quarters
> 1 hothouse cucumber, peeled and thinly sliced
> 2 green bell peppers, cored, seeds and ribs removed, and thinly sliced
> 1 large sweet onion, very thinly sliced
> 24 Niçoise olives
> 3 hard-cooked eggs, quartered
>
> DRESSING
> 6 tablespoons extra virgin olive oil
> 6 basil leaves, cut into thin ribbons
> Sea salt and freshly ground black pepper to taste

To make the salad, arrange the tomato slices on a rimmed baking sheet and salt them; set aside for 20 minutes.

Line a large serving platter with the lettuce leaves. Arrange the remaining salad ingredients on the lettuce. Drain the tomatoes, salt them again, and add them to the platter.

To make the dressing, whisk the ingredients together. Drizzle over the salad and serve.

COOK'S NOTE: You can chill the salad for an hour, but no longer. If you'd prefer, you can cut the ingredients into bite-sized pieces and toss them in a salad bowl, then toss with the dressing.

Lemony Tuna Salad
with Green Apple and Dill

For an instant dinner on a hot night, few things beat a good tuna salad. This one has some unusual elements: lemon zest as well as lemon juice, the clean crunch of green apple, and good old dill. You can amplify all this with some chopped nuts or toasted flaxseed, or both.

Serves 3

Two 6-ounce cans chunk light tuna, packed in olive-oil,
    preferably Italian, drained well
2 tablespoons mayonnaise, preferably homemade
    (page 206), or more to taste
Grated zest and juice of ½ lemon, or more to taste
Salt and freshly ground black pepper
½ Granny Smith apple, cut into thin slices and then into
    little chunks
2 tablespoons snipped chives or minced sweet onion or
    scallions
1 tablespoon snipped dill, or more to taste
3 tablespoons chopped toasted pecans or walnuts, optional
1 tablespoon chopped toasted flaxseeds (see page 50),
    optional
Salad greens for serving

Put the tuna in a large bowl.

In a small bowl, whisk together the mayonnaise and lemon zest and juice. Add salt and pepper to taste. Mix the mayonnaise into the tuna, and add the remaining ingredients (except the greens), mixing well.

Let the salad sit for an hour to develop the flavors, in or out of the refrigerator, as you like. Serve over salad greens.

Curried Chicken Salad with Nuts

This chunky chicken salad can go in all kinds of directions. It can be packed with fresh herbs or brightened with dried fruit. It can be curried or not. The chicken itself can come from a take-out roast chicken, poached chicken breasts, or roasted chicken breasts that have been brined, which loads some lovely flavors into the chicken meat (see Cook's Note).

Serves 4

⅓ cup mayonnaise, preferably homemade (page 206), or
 more to taste
1 teaspoon curry powder
About 4 cups chunked cooked chicken
Fresh lemon juice
3 celery ribs, diced
½ cup chopped toasted walnuts or almonds
½ cup seedless grapes, cut in half, or dried cranberries or
 dried cherries
Salt and freshly ground black pepper
Snipped dill and parsley
Grated lemon zest, optional
Salad greens for serving

In a large bowl, stir together the mayonnaise and curry powder. Toss the chicken pieces with the mayonnaise just until lightly coated (or as you like it). Add lemon juice to taste. Mix in the celery, half the nuts, and the fruit. Add salt and pepper to taste, mixing well, then add herbs and lemon zest, if using. Cover and chill for at least 1 hour, or up to 4 hours.

Arrange the salad greens on a serving platter. Drain the salad if necessary, toss well, and arrange over the greens. Scatter the remaining toasted nuts on top and serve.

COOK'S NOTE: To brine and roast the chicken breasts: A day before roasting, bring 2 quarts water to a boil, and pour into a large bowl. Add ½ cup salt, ¼ cup packed brown sugar, 2 tablespoons Dijon mustard, and 1½ teaspoons red pepper flakes. Stir until the salt and sugar are dissolved, and let cool.

Submerge 4 chicken breasts on the bone in the brine, weighting the chicken down with a heavy plate if necessary. Cover tightly and refrigerate overnight.

The next day, remove the chicken from the brine, place skin side up on a rack in a roasting pan, and bring to room temperature. Preheat the oven to 350 degrees.

Roast the chicken for about 40 minutes, or until an instant-read thermometer registers 150 degrees. Remove from the oven and let cool. Skin and bone the chicken and cut the meat into chunks. You'll have about 4 cups of chicken.

Main Dishes

Massaman Curry
with Sweet Potatoes and Peanuts

This sweet-sour-salty-creamy curry is very easy to make once you have the curry paste, which is sold in little tins and jars in Asian markets and some upscale supermarkets. If you have a tin or two in your cupboard along with some canned coconut milk and Asian fish sauce, you're just moments away from a really delicious, fragrant curry.

You can make this curry with shrimp or tofu, as you like (since I'm not a soy fan, I vote for shrimp). You can also substitute butternut squash for the sweet potatoes.

Serves 4

3 cups canned unsweetened coconut milk
3 tablespoons Massaman curry paste
¼ cup roasted unsalted peanuts
2 medium sweet potatoes, cut into 1-inch chunks
3 shallots, each cut into 8 thin wedges
One 2-inch cinnamon stick
1 tablespoon light brown sugar, or more (or less) to taste
1 tablespoon Asian fish sauce (see page 194) or soy sauce,
    or more to taste
2 tablespoons fresh lime juice
1 pound peeled and deveined small shrimp or 1 pound
    extra-firm tofu, cut into 1-inch squares
4 cups steamed jasmine rice or basmati rice for serving

In a wok or large skillet, bring 1 cup of the coconut milk to a boil over medium-high heat. Add the curry paste and cook until fragrant (the oil will begin to separate from the paste), about 2 minutes.

Add the remaining 2 cups coconut milk, the peanuts, sweet

potatoes, shallots, cinnamon stick, sugar, fish or soy sauce, and 1 tablespoon of the lime juice. If using tofu, add it now (if using shrimp, add it after 10 minutes of cooking). Bring to a boil, reduce the heat to medium-low, and cook until the curry is thickened and the sweet potatoes and shallots are tender, about 15 minutes.

Stir in the remaining tablespoon of lime juice. Taste and then adjust the seasonings with sugar, lime juice, and/or fish sauce. Serve hot, spooning the curry over the rice.

Shrimp with Coconut and Lime

This is a zesty, creamy, succulent shrimp dish with a sort of Thai personality. Once the cooking begins it's ready in less than ten minutes, and it's versatile—you can serve it over plain rice or orzo or low-carb noodles. If you get stuck with no fresh chiles, you can use a pickled jalapeño that's been well rinsed, and the dish will still be very good.

Serves 2

    1 pound shrimp, peeled and deveined
    Grated zest and juice of 1 lime
    Sea salt
    2 teaspoons olive oil
    1 serrano or jalapeño chile, seeded and minced
    ¾ cup canned unsweetened coconut milk
    ⅓ cup chopped cilantro
    2 tablespoons chopped mint
    4 scallions (white and green parts), cut into 1-inch lengths
       and then lengthwise into shreds
    2 tablespoons chopped roasted peanuts
    2 cups cooked basmati rice for serving

In a bowl, toss the shrimp with the lime zest and juice and a pinch of salt, and let marinate for 15 minutes.

Heat the oil in a large skillet over medium heat. Sauté the shrimp until they turn pink and bouncy, 3 to 4 minutes. Set the shrimp aside. Add the chile to the skillet and cook for 1 minute. Add the coconut milk, half the herbs, half the scallions, and the peanuts. Cook for 1 more minute.

Stir in the shrimp. Serve over the basmati rice, sprinkled with the remaining herbs and scallions.

Hot Avocado
with Cheesy Shrimp

Offhand, hot avocado may not sound particularly appealing. But heat, just enough to heat it through, does something very interesting to this fruit—it brings out the buttery quality and the succulence. This recipe is basically a spin on the old avocado stuffed with shrimp salad and yet it won't remind you of that dish.

You can make up the avocados ahead of time and chill; just bring them to room temperature before heating them.

Serves 4

> 1 cup mayonnaise, preferably homemade (page 206)
> 1 teaspoon mild sweet curry powder
> 1 pound salad (small) shrimp, cooked
> 4 scallions (including the white and some of the green parts), minced
> 2 Hass avocados
> Juice of 2 lemons
> Salt
> ¼ cup grated Parmesan cheese
> Mesclun or baby watercress for serving

Preheat the oven to 400 degrees.

In a bowl, mix together the mayonnaise and curry powder. Add the shrimp and scallions and mix gently but well.

Cut the avocados in half and remove the pits. Scoop out a little of the interior so the shrimp filling will have more room; save the trimmings for the salad. Peel off the skins. Cut a very small slice off each avocado bottom so they'll sit flat in the baking dish. Brush the avocados all over with the lemon juice and sprinkle the insides with salt.

Set the avocado halves in a baking dish and mound the shrimp mixture into them. Sprinkle each avocado with 1 tablespoon of the Parmesan. Bake for 12 to 15 minutes, or until hot all the way through and slightly browned on top.

Serve hot, on a bed of greens.

Fried Shrimp

A pile of well-fried shrimp is irresistible and surprisingly easy to make. If you keep the temperature at exactly 365 degrees, the shrimp won't absorb any oil and they'll be wonderfully crisp. The technique of using granulated flour gives a thin but crunchy veil to the shrimp. This idea comes from David Pasternack, the chef at Manhattan's Esca, and it works on fish fillets shallow-fried in a skillet as well.

The good fat oil used here is peanut oil, so the temperature can stay high. Be sure to use a nonhydrogenated brand.

Unless you're lucky enough to live in the shrimp belt, you'll be using frozen shrimp, which have been thawed for the market. Buy them frozen and give them a little flavor boost by thawing them in salted ice water in the refrigerator.

Serves 6

> Nonhydrogenated peanut oil for deep-frying
> 2 pounds small shrimp, peeled and deveined
> 1 cup granulated flour, such as Wondra
> 1 teaspoon cayenne pepper, or more to taste
> 1 cup milk
> Salt
> 2 large lemons, cut into wedges

Add enough peanut oil to a Dutch oven, preferably enameled cast iron, to come to a depth of 3 inches. Slowly heat the temperature of the oil to 365 degrees.

Meanwhile set a rack over a baking sheet to drain the shrimp. Mix the flour and cayenne in a bowl. Pour the milk into another bowl. Add the shrimp to the flour and toss well to coat. Dip them in the milk, then return them to the flour and toss again to coat. Shake off any excess flour.

Add the shrimp, in batches if necessary—don't crowd them—to the hot oil and fry until golden, about a minute or two, turning them once.

Immediately remove from the oil and let drain on the rack. Salt the shrimp, and serve hot with the lemon wedges.

Safe Frying

This idea may seem like an oxymoron, but in fact those same healthy Mediterranean folks love their fried fish, fried potatoes, and a number of other fried treats. Properly fried foods—cooked at the right temperature—absorb virtually no fat (unless they're fried in soy or vegetable oil—read on). The real problem with fried foods is that in the process of ditching good natural frying fats, such as olive oil and lard, we've turned to highly processed, chemically altered fats, such as canola and soy, that not only contribute no flavor but also contain dangerous levels of free radicals and are absorbed by the frying foods, increasing their calories and free-radical content. Commercially fried foods are fried in inferior fat that's used over and over again, breaking down its chemical bonds and creating trans fat.

The solution is to fry your own food at home, using olive oil or coconut oil or nonhydrogenated peanut oil or (gasp) lard, which, just as olive oil does, has a high percentage of monounsaturated fat.

If you're frying with peanut oil or lard, you can fry at 365 degrees, which will give you perfectly crisp food that has absorbed no oil at all. This is arguably the healthiest way to fry because no oil enters the food. As frymeister Hoppin' John Taylor explains, as long as the food is hissing and sizzling, steam is coming out, so no oil can enter. Once the hiss and sizzle slows down, the food is done and should immediately be scooped out to drain.

Although the manufacturers of highly processed vegetable oils have put out statistics suggesting otherwise, olive oil is in fact a quite stable oil at high heat, and it can perform very well in frying, as long as you keep the temperature around 350 degrees (any lower, and you'll encourage fat absorption). The oil can usually take that heat but this varies from brand to brand and year to year. Olive oil also contains its own antioxidants, which help to minimize the dangerous TPM chemicals formed during the frying process—but even olive oil produces some of those undesirable chemicals. Although it might seem like a great (if expensive) idea to use the best cold-pressed olive oil for frying, in fact regular or light olive oil is better, because it has already been heated and has had those chemicals removed, so it's more stable at high heat. In the process, however, it's also lost many of its natural antioxidants.

Fry foods in olive oil at 350 degrees (check with a candy/frying thermometer) in a wok or a Dutch oven, preferably one with a nonstick surface. Bring the oil up to temperature slowly, have the foods completely dry when they go into the pot, and monitor the temperature to be sure it stays as close as possible to 350 degrees; if it goes much higher, say, to 365 degrees, you'll be frying in damaged fat.

Drain fried foods on a rack, salt, and serve immediately (or in the case of fried fish, you might let it sit for about 4 hours to develop flavor, as Manhattan fish chef David Pasternack's English grandmother always did).

Once the frying oil has cooled, heat it for a couple of minutes with a lemon slice to remove impurities, then strain it through a coffee filter and store, tightly covered, in the refrigerator. You can use it to fry one more time. Then discard it. Each time you fry in it, the smokepoint goes lower and the fat gets more damaged.

Whichever fat you use, don't use a frying pan. The right utensil, says Hoppin' John, is a deep cast-iron casserole, and it shouldn't be more than half-full of oil. In this pot with the oil at this depth, it can't boil over and start a fire. Always use a spatter screen when you're frying, not only to avoid grease spots but also to protect yourself from hot oil spatters.

Frying insurance: according to Greek olive oil researcher Paraskevas Tokousbalides, you can counteract the effects of any nasty chemicals developed in the course of frying by simply eating 5 olives along with your fried food. This may be one of the secrets of the healthy Mediterranean diet. A bowl of the tasty marinated olives on page 171, served with drinks, does the trick in a particularly delicious way.

Deep-Fried Coconut Shrimp

This delectable way of frying shrimp is one of the all-time classic favorites. It's also a bit retro, but seems like just what we want to eat right now. If you want to make the people around your table truly happy, cook them these coconutty shrimp.

If you want a little spice in the mix, add a couple of pinches of hot pepper to the flour or a jolt of hot pepper sauce to the egg.

Serve with a mustard sauce (such as the gravlax sauce on page 259, minus the dill) or a spicy Asian dipping sauce to balance the sweetness of the crust, and with lime wedges.

Serves 4

> 1 pound medium shrimp, peeled, tails left on, and deveined
> Granulated flour (Wondra) for dusting
> 1 large egg
> Kosher salt
> 1 cup shredded unsweetened dried, coconut
> ½ teaspoon sugar or Splenda
> 2 quarts light olive oil
> Lime wedges for serving

Rinse the shrimp under cool running water and blot dry on paper towels.

Sift or sieve a thin layer of flour onto a large plate. Beat the egg with 2 teaspoons water and a few grains of salt; pour it onto another plate. Onto a third plate, mix the coconut with the sugar.

Heat the oil in a deep heavy pot, such as a Dutch oven, until a thermometer reads 365 degrees. Meanwhile, lay out no more than half the shrimp on the plate of flour. Holding them by the tail, turn the shrimp over in the flour, shake off the excess, and then lay them up on the rim of the plate. Add more flour if needed, and repeat with the remaining shrimp.

Again holding them by the tail, dip the fleshy part of the shrimp into the beaten egg, then lay them out on the coconut, tossing some over the top and pressing down firmly to thoroughly coat the shrimp.

Line a baking sheet with paper towels and set a small grid mesh cooling rack over the pan. When the oil is hot, drop in no more than a third of the coated shrimp at a time. They will take only about 2 minutes to cook and develop a deep golden brown, crisp crust. With a slotted spoon, remove the shrimp to the cooling rack. They cook so quickly it's unnecessary to hold them in a warm oven while the remaining shrimp take their turn in the pot.

Serve with lime wedges.

Aïoli

Aïoli is both the name of the garlicky mayonnaise in which vegetables and shrimp are dipped and the name of the entire Provençal dish, the "grand aïoli," including the vegetables and shrimp. The dish is somewhere between a light meal, say a lunch, and something more substantial to have with wine in the evening, depending on whether you use the shrimp or not. The essential thing is to have really garden-fresh vegetables, homemade mayonnaise, and people to share it with—the communal-pot aspect is a good part of its charm.

Serves 4 to 6

> About 5 pounds (only 2½ pounds if you're serving the shrimp too) very fresh finger-sized vegetables, such as asparagus, green beans, scallions, baby carrots, fingerling potatoes, and artichokes
> 2 pounds shrimp, peeled, tails left on, and deveined, optional (see Cook's Note)
>
> AÏOLI
> 3 garlic cloves (unpeeled)
> Coarse sea salt
> 3 large egg yolks
> 1 cup extra virgin olive oil
> 1 tablespoon fresh lemon juice, or more to taste

Trim and clean all the vegetables. Bring a large pot of salted water to a boil. Cook the vegetables one kind at a time just until they're tender. Remove them with a slotted spoon and set aside to drain on a kitchen towel.

To make the aïoli, smack the garlic cloves with a meat mallet or the side of a chef's knife and peel off the skin. In a mortar and pestle, pound the garlic with a little salt until you have a paste. Transfer the paste to a medium bowl and whisk in the egg yolks. Keep whisking while you add the olive oil in a steady trickle. Taste the mayonnaise and add salt if necessary and lemon juice to taste.

Arrange the vegetables, and the shrimp, if using, on a platter surrounding a small bowl of the aïoli.

COOK'S NOTE: To prepare the shrimp, have ready a simmering pot of salted water that's been seasoned with ½ lemon, some peppercorns, a bay leaf, a pinch of hot pepper flakes, and a clove or two of garlic. Drop in the shrimp and cook just until they turn pink; drain well and chill until ready to serve.

You may be wondering why you can't use a food processor to make the aïoli. You can, but it won't have the same light, silky texture. A better shortcut is to use an immersion blender in a small bowl.

VARIATION: You can skip the garlic and make anchovy mayonnaise instead. Drain 4 anchovy fillets, chop them, and grind them in the mortar (skip the salt), then proceed with the recipe.

Steamed Mussels Jamaican-Style

Most of the mussels in the market now are farmed, which means they don't need much scrubbing and debearding. If they've been through a process called depuration (see page 97), they may need almost no attention beyond a good rinse in a colander under the tap. This means mussels are a speedy dinner, not to mention a tasty one. Few of us think, "Oh, let's have mussels for dinner," but it's a fine choice and after you've cooked them once, you'll probably make them often.

Serves 2 to 4

> One 5-pound bag mussels
> 1 tablespoon light olive oil
> 4 inner celery ribs, cut into 1-inch lengths
> 1 leek (white part only), thinly sliced
> 1 teaspoon minced fresh ginger
> Pinch of cayenne pepper
> Salt and freshly ground black pepper to taste
> 3 tablespoons brandy
> 1 cup chicken broth
> 1 cup canned unsweetened coconut milk

Rinse the mussels, then pick out and discard any dead ones, the ones that refuse to close if the shell is lightly tapped.

Heat the oil over medium heat in a deep soup pot large enough to hold all the mussels. Add the celery, leek, and ginger and sauté until they wilt and the celery is tender but not soft. Add the seasonings, stir to combine, and add the brandy. Allow to sizzle briefly to evaporate the alcohol. Add the broth and coconut milk, stir to combine, and bring to a simmer. Add the mussels and cover the pot. When the broth returns to the simmer, reduce the heat slightly, uncover and fish out any open mussels with tongs, then replace the lid. Check in another 30 seconds or so for more open shells. The mussels should all steam open in 3 to 4 minutes, but give the reluctant ones a little extra time before pronouncing them goners. When the pot looks full of open shells, transfer the mussels with a slotted spoon to heated rimmed soup plates. Discard any mussels that didn't open. Distribute the early openers among the servings and pour the broth equally over them.

Poached Oysters on Spinach

If you love oysters, this is a great way to enjoy them, and it offers not only omega-3s but the good things—lutein, antioxidants—in spinach as well. It's a meal in itself that needs only fruit for dessert.

Serves 4

> 4 slices smoky bacon
> 2 pounds flat-leaf spinach, thick stems removed
> 1 large shallot, minced
> 2 tablespoons heavy cream, plus extra for serving
> Salt and freshly ground black pepper
> Pinch of cayenne pepper
> 16 to 20 shucked oysters, with their liquor
> Freshly grated Parmesan cheese for sprinkling

In a large skillet, fry the bacon until crisp, reserving the bacon fat. When cool enough to handle, crumble the bacon and set aside.

Put the spinach in a large colander and rinse it very well under cool running water; don't shake it dry. Put it in a large deep skillet over medium-high heat, cover, and steam the spinach until it's wilted, just a few minutes. (Depending on the size of your skillet, you may have to do this in batches.) Drain the spinach very well and let cool. When cool enough to handle, squeeze out any additional liquid with your hands, then finely chop the spinach.

Melt 3 tablespoons of the bacon fat in the skillet. Add the minced shallot and sauté over medium heat until softened. Add the spinach, along with the cream, salt and pepper to taste, and the cayenne. Heat through.

Meanwhile, pour the oysters and their liquor into another sauté pan and bring to a simmer. Poach briefly just until the edges of the oysters curl. Drain, and freeze the liquor for another use.

Preheat the broiler.

To serve, make a nest of the spinach on a heatproof serving dish. Place the oysters in the center, drizzle a little more cream over them, and sprinkle with the bacon and cheese. Run the dish quickly under the broiler to brown it lightly. Serve immediately.

Plain Broiled Mackerel

Spanish mackerel are simply delicious, one of the great fish, and when they're impeccably fresh, as they should be, they're sweet and almost delicate. This is how the Irish do it and how the Japanese do it, so it's obviously the right way to do it. Not to mention the easiest, most delectable way.

The skin will get blackened and blistered, and the bone frames are a cinch to remove once the fish is cooked.

Serves 2

> Extra virgin olive oil
> About 6 sprigs mint
> Two 2- to 3-pound Spanish mackerel, cleaned and scaled
> Big pinch of ground coriander
> Salt
> Lemon wedges for serving

Preheat the broiler. Oil the broiler pan with olive oil, line it with a sheet of foil, and oil that as well. Place half of the mint sprigs inside each fish and lay the fish on the broiler pan. Score the fish every 1½ inches, and sprinkle with a bit of ground coriander and salt.

Broil the fish until the skin blackens. Turn and continue to broil, about 8 to 10 minutes altogether. Check the flesh where the skin is scored: it should be white and flaky.

Serve the fish hot, with lemon and salt. A sprinkling of chopped mint is good with this fish, or serve a romaine salad with mint on the side.

Mackerel with Teriyaki Sauce

If you find some absolutely fresh mackerel, have the fishmonger cut you some fillets and make this supersimple weeknight supper. If you want to, you can make your own teriyaki sauce (see Cook's Note), which will be a little less sweet than the commercial one I'm recommending, but if you're in a rush, the ready-made teriyaki sauce is really very good.

The mackerel is also delicious on the grill, but should be cooked in one of those special baskets for fish.

Serves 4

  4 mackerel fillets, skin on (about 6 ounces each)
  Kosher salt
  Soy Vey teriyaki sauce
  2 tablespoons toasted sesame seeds for garnish, optional

About 15 minutes to half an hour before you plan to cook the fish, rub it all over with a thick coating of kosher salt and let it sit.

Preheat the oven to 350 degrees.

Rinse the mackerel fillets very well and pat them dry. Run your fingers down the center of the fillets and remove any bones you find. Place the fillets skin side down on a foil-lined baking sheet and cover them with teriyaki sauce.

Bake the fish for 15 minutes. Scatter with toasted sesame seeds, if using, and serve.

COOK'S NOTE: To make your own teriyaki sauce, mix together ½ cup soy sauce, ¼ cup mirin (rice wine), ¼ cup water, 2 tablespoons dark brown sugar, a minced garlic clove, a teaspoon of fresh grated ginger, and a squeeze of orange juice, if you have any. This will make about 1 cup.

Mackerel in a Mayonnaise Coat

If the idea of cooking mackerel leaves you a little unsure of whether you'll like it, here's a good starter recipe that everyone will love. Wonderful things happen to mayonnaise in the heat: it makes a really nice crust that's a bit like a sauce too. You can add all sorts of flavorings to the mayonnaise, of course, but this one is simple and fail-safe. And you can grill the fish if you'd prefer—about 6 minutes, or until the fish flakes—don't bother turning it.

Serves 4

> 4 mackerel fillets, skin on (about 4 ounces each)
> Salt
> 2 roasted garlic cloves
> ½ cup mayonnaise, preferably homemade (page 206)
> 2 tablespoons freshly grated Parmesan cheese
> Freshly ground black pepper

Run your fingers over the mackerel to feel for any stray bones, and remove them. Salt the fillets and let them rest on a foil-covered baking sheet for about 15 minutes.

Preheat the oven to 350 degrees.

Meanwhile, make the seasoned mayonnaise. Mash the garlic cloves with a fork or in the food processor, and add the mayonnaise and cheese. Grind in a little fresh pepper to taste.

Spread the seasoned mayonnaise over the fish fillets and bake for 15 minutes, or until the crust is golden brown. Let rest for several minutes before serving.

Pasta with Anchovies

Don't run screaming out of the kitchen at the very idea of making pasta with a lot of stinky little fish. I guarantee that no one at your table will recognize the anchovy flavor here, and everyone will be delighted by this very interesting pasta. If the subject of anchovies bothers you, give them the milk soak treatment to tame them (page 211).

Serves 4 to 6

2 cups sun-dried tomatoes (not packed in oil)
½ cup extra virgin olive oil
8 ounces anchovy fillets packed in olive oil, drained
⅓ cup capers, rinsed and drained
4 garlic cloves, minced
Juice of 1 lemon
Salt
1 pound penne

Put the sun-dried tomatoes in a small bowl and cover with warm water to rehydrate. After the tomatoes are soft, about 15 minutes, drain them, reserving ½ cup of the soaking water.

Heat a large skillet and add the olive oil. When it's hot, add the anchovies, tomatoes, the reserved soaking water, the capers, garlic, and lemon juice and cook over medium heat for 15 minutes. Keep warm.

Meanwhile, boil a large pot of water for the pasta.

When the sauce is ready, add salt and the pasta to the boiling water and cook until al dente. Keep the sauce warm. Drain, and add a spoonful of the pasta water to the sauce.

In a serving bowl, dress the pasta with the sauce, and serve hot. Cheese isn't necessary.

Pasta with Sardines

This one is a bit different from the Sicilian classic pasta with sardines, though it has some of the same elements. The mystery ingredient here is very un-Sicilian: good old American bacon. If you think you don't like sardines, this pasta would be a good acid test, since almost everyone likes it very much.

Serves 4 to 6

> Three 4.5-ounce cans lightly smoked sardines packed in
>   olive oil, drained
> Juice of 1 lemon
> 1 teaspoon freshly ground black pepper
> 3 slices smoky bacon, finely chopped
> Salt
> 1 pound fettuccine
> 3 tablespoons extra virgin olive oil
> 3 large shallots, finely sliced
> 1 anchovy fillet, drained and finely chopped
> ½ cup chopped parsley
> 1 cup dry white wine
> 1 cup toasted walnut pieces

Set a big pot of water on to boil for the pasta.

Meanwhile, put the sardines in a bowl and toss with the lemon juice and pepper; set aside.

In a large skillet, fry the bacon until crisp. With a slotted spoon, transfer to paper towels to drain. Wipe almost all the bacon grease out of the pan with a paper towel, leaving just a fine coating.

When the water is boiling, add salt and the fettuccine. Cook until al dente; drain.

Meanwhile, reheat the pan you used for the bacon, and add the olive oil. Heat the oil over medium-low heat, and caramelize the shallots in the hot oil. Add the bacon, anchovy, and the sardine mixture, then add the parsley and white wine. Increase the heat to medium and cook, stirring, for 2 minutes, or until the wine has been absorbed. Add the walnuts. Mix the sauce into the fettuccine in the pasta pot. Transfer to a serving dish and serve hot, without cheese.

Grilled Sardines

You never know when you're going to see fresh sardines in the fish market, but if you do, this is a good way to fix them, using a quick marinade. Fresh sardines don't taste much like canned sardines at all; they're both delicate and oily at the same time. If you have some rosemary branches to throw on the coals, better yet.

The sardines are best hot, but you can also serve them at room temperature.

Serves 4

> 1 teaspoon sea salt
> 1 garlic clove, minced
> ¼ cup olive oil, plus extra for grilling
> ¼ cup finely chopped fennel, including fronds, optional
> Big pinch of red pepper flakes
> 1 tablespoon fresh lemon juice or white wine vinegar
> 12 fresh sardines, cleaned (the fish market will do this for you)
> Lemon wedges for garnish

Put everything but the sardines (and lemon wedges) in a food processor and pulse to make a rough-textured sauce. Place the sardines in a shallow dish and cover with the marinade. Let marinate for 30 minutes, turning frequently.

Prepare a hot fire in a grill.

When the fire is ready, oil a fish grilling rack with olive oil. Wipe the marinade off the fish and rub them with olive oil. Grill them, turning just once, and basting frequently with the marinade, for about 5 minutes per side. To test for doneness, poke along the backbone with the sharp point of a knife—the fish will be opaque when it's done. Serve hot, with lemon wedges.

Swordfish in a Crumb Crust with Tomatoes

This is a good dish for fish-phobes because the milk bath before cooking removes any trace of fishiness, leaving the swordfish with all its delicate sweetness intact. It's also just delicious.

Low-carbers can just leave off the bread crumbs or use a low-carb bread to make crumbs.

Serves 4 to 6

> 4 swordfish steaks (about 2 pounds), skin removed
> 1 quart whole milk
> 1 heaped cup fine dry bread crumbs
> Salt and freshly ground black pepper
> 6 medium ripe tomatoes, thinly sliced
> ¼ cup olive oil

Put the fish in a shallow dish and cover with the milk. Let soak for 1 hour at room temperature.

Preheat the oven to 350 degrees.

Drain the fish and pat dry. Put the bread crumbs on a plate and dredge the fish in the crumbs.

Oil an ovenproof dish large enough to hold the fish in one layer. Arrange the fish in the dish and sprinkle with salt and pepper. Arrange the tomato slices in a layer over the fish and trickle the olive oil over the tomatoes. Season with salt and pepper again.

Bake the fish for 30 minutes, or until it's opaque at the center. Serve hot.

Tuna Confit

Canned tuna isn't a modern invention made possible by the wonders of canning, but an ancient way of preserving tuna during the annual harvest. Tuna in olive oil has been preserved traditionally in Italy and France for many centuries, and making it yourself is a good way to guarantee great tuna. You can choose the best tuna—sashimi grade—for one thing, and you can use really good olive oil, flavoring it to your own taste. Using really good salt (see page 153) makes a difference too.

A salade Niçoise (page 212) made with your own tuna confit is an amazing thing, and it couldn't be simpler. It will take two days for the tuna to absorb the flavorings, so plan ahead.

Serves 4 to 6

> 1½ pounds tuna, preferably sashimi grade
> Salt and freshly ground black pepper
> 2 garlic cloves, smashed
> About 2 cups olive oil, as needed
> Several strips of lemon zest removed with a vegetable peeler
> Several branches of thyme or 1 branch rosemary

Cut the tuna into chunks, about 1½ inches. Season generously with salt and pepper.

Place the tuna in a medium saucepan and add the garlic cloves. Pour just enough olive oil over the tuna to cover it. Bring the oil to a gentle simmer over medium heat and cook for 10 minutes, being careful not to let it boil. Remove from the heat and add the lemon zest and thyme or rosemary. Let cool.

Transfer the tuna to a covered container just large enough to hold it—it should still be covered with oil. Refrigerate for at least 2 days, or up to 10 days. Bring to room temperature before using.

Tuna with Rice

Bob Lake, who owns Katy's Smokehouse with his wife, Judy, rattled this weeknight recipe off to me on the phone one day when we were schmoozing about tuna. He, of course, makes this dish with their extraordinary albacore tuna (see Sources), but you can use another high-quality tuna.

You can toss in all sorts of embellishments, such as thinly sliced red onion, capers, chopped parsley, or other fresh herbs. But try it first all by itself, the way Bob serves it—it's very satisfying, one of those dishes you'll turn to again and again because it's so simple and so good.

Serves 2

> 2 cups warm cooked basmati rice (see Cook's Note)
> One 6-ounce can albacore tuna, preferably Katy's brand, or two 3.5-ounce cans imported Italian tuna packed in olive oil
> Extra virgin olive oil
> High-quality balsamic vinegar, sherry vinegar, or fresh lemon juice
> Salt and freshly ground black pepper
>
> OPTIONAL GARNISHES
> Thinly sliced red onion
> Capers, rinsed and drained
> Chopped parsley

Divide the rice between two plates. If using Katy's tuna, turn the opened can upside down and scrape out the tuna onto the rice, including any liquid in the can. If using Italian tuna, drain the tuna well and arrange on the rice.

Drizzle olive oil over the tuna, then vinegar or lemon juice. Season with salt and pepper to taste, and add any or all of the optional ingredients. Serve while the rice is still warm.

COOK'S NOTE: You can use Texmati rice here or even Carolina rice if that's all you have on hand. My favorite version of this salad includes the red onion rings, capers, and coarsely chopped parsley, with the lemon juice option. A nice way to serve it is to arrange all those extra tidbits, including fresh lemon wedges, on a platter and let guests help themselves to the garnishes.

Marinated Tuna

This marinade works equally well with tuna or marlin, though marlin's a bit tricky to cook because it can easily dry out. The tuna's good in the oven or on the grill, and leftovers are still tasty the next day.

Serves 4

1½ pounds tuna steaks
8 garlic cloves, smashed
½ cup olive oil
Salt and freshly ground black pepper

SAUCE
3 tablespoons reserved garlic oil
1 teaspoon grated lemon zest
3 tablespoons fresh lemon juice
Pinch of red pepper flakes
2 tablespoons chopped fresh thyme or oregano or
    2 teaspoons dried thyme or oregano
Salt
2 tablespoons chopped parsley

Place the tuna in a dish just large enough to hold it. Scatter the garlic cloves over it and pour on the olive oil. Let marinate for 2 hours in the refrigerator, then remove the garlic and marinate overnight.

Bring the tuna to room temperature before cooking.

Preheat the oven to 475 degrees (or prepare a hot fire in the grill).

Reserve 3 tablespoons of the garlic oil for the sauce. Place the tuna in a shallow baking dish (or in a fish-grilling basket, for the grill), season with salt and pepper, and bake for 10 minutes (if grilling, turn the fish over after 5 minutes), no longer.

Let the fish rest while you make the sauce.

In a small saucepan, combine the reserved garlic oil, the lemon zest and juice, red pepper flakes, and thyme or oregano and bring to a boil over medium heat, stirring frequently. Boil the sauce until it thickens, then stir in salt to taste and the parsley.

Pour the sauce over the fish and serve immediately.

COOK'S NOTE: If using marlin, bake it in a 350-degree oven for 20 minutes, or until almost cooked through.

Tuna Burgers

Canned tuna doesn't easily form into burgers that hold together. Here the sticking medium is rice—if you have leftover rice and canned tuna, you're in business. The burgers are really delicious served in pita bread with a little salad spooned in.

Makes 8 burgers; serves 4

16 ounces canned tuna packed in olive oil, drained
1 garlic clove, minced
1 teaspoon ground ginger
1 cup cooked long-grain rice
2 large shallots, finely chopped
½ cup finely chopped parsley
Olive oil if panfrying

SIDE SALAD
½ seedless cucumber, peeled and diced
½ sweet onion, diced
2 small tomatoes, diced, or about 16 cherry tomatoes,
    cut into quarters
3 tablespoons extra virgin olive oil
3 tablespoons rice wine vinegar
1 teaspoon tamari soy sauce (found in natural foods stores
    and some supermarkets)
4 pita breads, warmed

Add half the tuna, along with garlic, ginger, and rice, to the food processor and process until well combined. Remove the mixture to a bowl and add the remaining tuna, the shallots, and parsley. Combine well, and form into 8 patties.

Grill the burgers briefly, or fry them in a little olive oil, just till they're crisp on the outside. Mix the salad vegetables in a bowl.

Whisk the olive oil, vinegar, and tamari together, and combine with the salad.

Serve in the warm pita breads, with the salad on the side, so diners can add it to the sandwich or not as they please.

Simple Wild Salmon

This superb West Coast fish is probably the only wild salmon you'll be offered anywhere—and you can only find it from May to September, its short season. Whether it's Copper River, king, or sockeye, it's the most delicious salmon imaginable, with a superb texture and buttery taste. It also has a hefty price tag, so you want to cook it carefully and simply, the better to appreciate its delectable qualities. Letting it cook in steamy vapors brings out its subtleties and compensates for its tendency to be dry.

The quantity here may seem small, but the fish is so rich that it makes sense to serve smaller pieces—which also makes the price a little more bearable.

Serves 4

> About 1¼ pounds wild salmon fillet, skin on
> Olive oil
> Sea salt, preferably Maldon salt
> Lemon wedges for serving

About 20 minutes before you plan to cook the fish, place it skin side down on a baking sheet lined with foil. Rub lightly with olive oil and sprinkle with salt.

Preheat the oven to 225 degrees. Place a shallow pan in the bottom of the oven and fill the pan with boiling water.

Slide the salmon into the oven and cook for 18 to 20 minutes, until the fish flakes perfectly and the color has changed in the center.

Serve the fish hot, cut into serving pieces, with lemon wedges on the side. Any leftovers are delicious the next day.

Succulent Baked Salmon

When you're looking for something completely different to do with the usual salmon fillet, try this recipe. The flavors are ones usually more associated with meat, but they work very well with the fish.

The combination is a little smoky, a little sweet, a little hot. You can bake the whole fillet or cut it into individual pieces, as you like. The recipe as given is for two servings, but you can easily double it for a whole fillet to serve four.

Serves 2

12 ounces salmon fillet, skinned, cut into 2 equal pieces
Olive oil
Salt
Hot and sweet mustard or any favorite mustard
1 slice bacon, chopped
2 shallots, chopped
2 garlic cloves, chopped
Big pinch of dried oregano
Freshly ground black pepper

Check the salmon for any stray bones and remove them. Line a baking sheet with foil and grease with olive oil. Place the salmon on the baking sheet, sprinkle with salt, and spread the mustard over the top. Set aside.

Preheat the oven to 350 degrees.

Sauté the bacon in a small skillet over medium heat until golden. Add the shallots and garlic, mix well, cover, and cook until the shallots and garlic have softened, about 5 minutes. Stir in the oregano and pepper to taste.

Stir the shallot mixture, and divide it between the salmon fillets, spreading it evenly over the top. Bake the salmon for 15 to 20 minutes, or until it flakes easily when poked with a knife tip. Serve immediately.

Born-Again Salmon Soup

Leftover salmon is never a problem, at least in theory, because it's always good cold and makes great salad or burgers. But here's a really interesting way to serve it, a traditional Japanese dish called *ochazuke,* which means "soaked in tea." It's a make-it-yourself soup with a green tea broth. You need a little packet of nori seasoning from an Asian market, but otherwise just green tea and wasabi, which are widely available, and some leftover vegetables or baby greens. Make a little mound of brown rice in the bottom of a soup bowl, add the salmon, vegetables, and the seasoning, then pour hot steeped green tea on top, as much as you like. Stir in wasabi to taste.

Speedy Salmon in Coconut Sauce

This is probably my favorite fast way to cook salmon: steamed in the microwave under a comforting blanket of coconut milk. It always comes out succulent and moist, and the coconut sauce contributes not only its good fat but also a delicate flavor that goes perfectly with salmon. Any leftovers are delicious the next day—just bring them to room temperature before serving.

You can use other flavorings besides curry powder. The smoked Spanish paprika called *pimenton* is always delicious too, as is cayenne or cumin or even some good chili powder. If you have some Thai Sriracha chili sauce on hand, a dash of that is terrific here.

Serves 4

> Four 6-ounce pieces salmon fillet, skinned
> About 1 cup canned unsweetened coconut milk, or more as needed
> 1 teaspoon mild sweet curry powder
> Cilantro leaves for garnish, optional

Arrange the salmon in a glass pie plate or other microwaveable container. Mix the coconut milk and curry powder together and spoon it over the salmon to cover—use a little more coconut milk if you need to. Cover the dish with plastic wrap and microwave for 5 minutes.

Pull back one side of the plastic wrap and spoon the coconut milk over the salmon again. Check for doneness; there should be just a tiny bit at the center of the fish that's not opaque. If it's not quite done, re-cover it and cook for 2 to 3 more minutes, being careful not to overcook.

Serve the salmon warm, drizzled with the coconut milk and garnished with the optional cilantro leaves.

Fillet of Salmon with Garlic and Dill

A different way of slow-cooking salmon, this recipe makes a fine dinner party salmon or perfectly cooked cold salmon to be served at room temperature the next day. It's steamed in its own juices, so it's especially moist and flavorful. When it's just cooked, it will hold for about an hour still warm, so it's a good choice for a party when you're not sure of the exact moment you'll be sitting down to dinner.

Serves 6 to 8

>2 tablespoons extra virgin olive oil
>2 to 3 garlic cloves, finely chopped
>1 whole salmon fillet (about 3 to 4 pounds)
>4 large sprigs fresh dill or 1 teaspoon dried dill
>Salt

Adjust an oven rack to the center position and preheat the oven to 300 degrees.

Put the olive oil and garlic in a 9- x 13-inch Pyrex or other ovenproof dish and put it in the warm oven for 5 minutes. Feel the salmon all over for any stray bones and remove them. Cut off a portion of the tail (set it aside) if you need to in order to fit the salmon in the dish. Place the salmon skin side up in the dish and move it around a little to cover it with the olive oil and pick up any little garlic bits, making sure the surface is covered with oil. Carefully turn it over, and arrange the dill over the top. Salt lightly. If there's a tail piece, repeat the procedure with the tail, tucking it into a corner of the pan.

Cover the dish with foil and put it into the oven. Check after 20 minutes: the fish won't be done, but you'll get an idea of how much longer it will take—it shouldn't take more than 40 minutes altogether. The fish is done when the flesh is opaque except for a line down the center that's still slightly pink. (It will continue to cook a bit after it's out of the oven.) Remove from the oven and let it rest for 15 minutes with the foil just loosely covering it.

Serve warm or within an hour.

COOK'S NOTE: The cool salmon can also be wrapped well in plastic wrap, chilled, and served later or the next day. Bring it to room temperature before serving with Aïoli (page 230) or a chopped cucumber–sour cream–fresh dill sauce. Arrange the salmon on a platter and, with a sharp knife, cut it into slices or squares so it's easy to serve. Decorate the platter with lemon slices and sprigs of dill.

Salmon Skin

Some cooks automatically pull off the salmon skin and discard it, but it's a delicacy in Japan and it should be for all of us, because it's delicious and full of good fat. The tastiest salmon skin is roasted or broiled. You can do this under the broiler, in the oven, or even in a toaster oven or over an outdoor grill. When it's done, in just a few minutes, it will be golden brown and crisp. A little salt is a good idea too.

Salmon Cakes

There are two versions here: one uses canned salmon and is ridiculously simple; the other uses leftover cooked fresh salmon and takes the salmon cakes in an Asian direction that's more complex in its flavors. They're both good, so the one you choose depends on what you have on hand.

Handle salmon cakes gently and don't overcook them—a nice golden brown is all they need.

Makes 8 salmon cakes; serves 4

Canned Salmon Version

16 ounces canned red salmon, drained (see page 80)
2 tablespoons prepared horseradish
½ cup minced sweet onion
½ cup chopped dill
1 large egg, beaten
Olive or peanut oil for shallow-frying
Cornmeal for dredging
Lemon wedges for serving

Combine the salmon, horseradish, onion, dill, and egg in a bowl. Form into 8 equal patties.

In a large nonstick skillet, heat 1 inch of oil over high heat. When the oil is hot, dredge the patties in cornmeal, place in the hot oil, and cook for about 3 minutes on each side, or until golden brown. Drain on paper towels.

Serve the cakes with lemon wedges on the side.

Leftover Grilled or Baked Salmon Version

SALMON CAKES

1 pound leftover cooked salmon

2-inch piece ginger, grated

½ cup minced scallions (including some of the green parts)

2 tablespoons tamari soy sauce (found in natural food stores and some supermarkets)

1 teaspoon Asian sesame oil

1 tablespoon wasabi powder

½ cup toasted bread crumbs or panko (Japanese bread crumbs)

WASABI MAYONNAISE

1 cup mayonnaise, preferably homemade (page 206)

1 tablespoon fresh lemon juice

1 teaspoon tamari soy sauce

1 tablespoon wasabi powder

Olive or peanut oil for shallow-frying

Combine all the salmon cake ingredients except the bread crumbs in a bowl. Form into 8 equal patties. Mix together all the wasabi mayonnaise ingredients in a small bowl; set aside.

Heat 1 inch of oil in a large nonstick skillet over high heat. When it's hot, dredge the patties in the bread crumbs and add them to the skillet. Cook for about 3 minutes on each side, or until golden brown. Drain on paper towels and serve with the wasabi mayonnaise.

Gravlax

There's a lot of confusion about gravlax, which is reminiscent of smoked salmon, though not smoked, just cured briefly to firm it a bit and infuse some flavor. While you might not think of making smoked salmon at home, gravlax is actually a snap, and it's very impressive for a party. The only trick is to slice it paper-thin—not hard at all if you have a sharp fillet knife (see Sources). Classic gravlax is cured with dill, as this one is, and served with a slightly sweet mustard-dill sauce, which I've also done here. Except for the slicing, this is about 15 minutes' work maximum for a knockout dish.

Gravlax keeps very well in the refrigerator, up to 2 weeks, so it's worth doubling the recipe if you think you'll eat that much salmon. Another reason to make more: grilled gravlax is a wonderful thing. Just cut thicker slices and cook them for just a few minutes on each side, until warmed through.

Note: It takes almost 2 whole days for the salmon to cure, so don't decide to make this the day before the party.

Serves 12 to 16

CURING MIXTURE
2 tablespoons kosher salt
1½ teaspoons cracked or ground white pepper
1½ tablespoons sugar
1 tablespoon brandy, aquavit, or vodka

1 bunch dill, thicker stems removed
1 large shallot, very thinly sliced
1½ pounds impeccably fresh center-cut salmon fillet,
    in one piece, skin on or off, any pinbones removed

MUSTARD-DILL SAUCE
1 large egg, at room temperature

1 tablespoon Dijon mustard
1 tablespoon honey Dijon mustard
1 tablespoon Colman's dry mustard
½ teaspoon freshly ground white pepper
¼ cup minced dill
2 tablespoons minced chives
¼ cup light olive oil

To make the curing mixture, combine all the ingredients in a small bowl. Set aside.

To make the gravlax, line a shallow rectangular glass or ceramic dish large enough to hold the salmon with plastic wrap, leaving enough overhanging the sides to generously cover the contents. Lay half the dill and shallots in the dish. Smear half of the curing mixture over the skin side of the salmon and lay it skin side down in the dish. Smear the rest of the curing mixture over the top of the salmon and cover with the remaining dill and shallots. Pull up the plastic wrap to snugly cover the fish.

To weight the fish, so that it will lose its liquid and become firm, you need to put something heavy on top of it. A foil-wrapped brick is a perfect choice, and so is a small cutting board with two heavy cans on top. Refrigerate the salmon under its weights for 36 to 48 hours, turning it over at least once a day.

When nearly ready to serve, make the sauce by combining all the ingredients except the oil in the food processor or blender. With the machine running, add the oil in a slow, steady stream, as though you were making mayonnaise. Chill the sauce briefly before you serve it.

Just before serving, remove the dill and shallots and rinse the salmon briefly under cool running water. Blot it dry and slice it very thin on the diagonal, angling your knife for the largest slices possible—but don't worry, even ragged pieces will taste delicious as long as they're paper-thin.

Serve the gravlax and sauce with dark bread. Other traditional accompaniments are thin slices of sweet onion, capers, chopped hard-cooked egg, and more chopped dill.

Chicken with Olives and Oranges

This sort-of-Greek chicken is very satisfying, the kind of dish you turn to on a weeknight when you want something simple but soulful. The Greeks love to match oranges with pork, but oranges are also really good with chicken in this robust dish.

If you have time to assemble the dish a few hours ahead before cooking it, the flavors will develop even more. Just an hour will make a difference, though.

Serves 4

> 8 chicken thighs
> 1 navel orange, well scrubbed
> 8 garlic cloves, peeled
> 2 teaspoons dried oregano
> Salt and freshly ground black pepper
> Extra virgin olive oil
> 16 Kalamata olives, rinsed or soaked if salty

Several hours before you plan to cook the chicken, place it in a glass baking dish large enough to hold the thighs skin side up in one layer. Cut the orange into 8 slices or chunks and add it to the chicken, squeezing a little juice over the chicken. Scatter the garlic cloves and oregano over the chicken, and sprinkle with salt and pepper. Drizzle olive oil over everything and toss well—add more oil if everything isn't coated with it. Distribute the olives over the dish, and redistribute the garlic if it's all in one place.

Preheat the oven to 425 degrees.

Turn the chicken pieces over and bake for 20 minutes, then turn them skin side up and bake for 20 more minutes, or until golden and crisp, turning the orange pieces and garlic cloves several times to be sure they don't burn. Serve immediately.

Cuban Roast Pork with Lime

This absurdly simple roast pork is one of my all-time favorite dishes. You need to start it at least a day ahead of time, and a headstart of several days will be even better.

Serve the pork with a simple fresh salsa, such as diced mango with some minced sweet onion, cilantro, and serrano or jalapeño chile, fresh lime juice, and salt.

Pray for leftovers, which are great inside tortillas or on a sandwich.

Serves 6

> One 4-pound boneless pork shoulder roast
> 1 head garlic, cloves separated, peeled, and sliced
>   lengthwise in half
> 1 cup fresh lime juice (from about 8 large limes)
> Salt

At least a day and up to a week ahead, make little slits about 1 inch deep all over the pork with a knife point. Insert a garlic sliver into each one. Place the roast in a nonreactive container and pour the lime juice over it, rolling it around several times to be sure all surfaces are covered. Cover tightly with plastic wrap and let the pork marinate in the refrigerator, turning from time to time.

To cook the pork, preheat the oven to 325 degrees.

Place the pork fat side up on a rack in a roasting pan. Salt it generously all over. Roast for about 3½ hours, or until an instant-read thermometer inserted into the thickest part of the roast registers 165 degrees. Let the pork rest, loosely covered with foil, for 20 minutes before slicing.

Pacific Rim Roast Lamb
in Spicy Coconut Sauce

A small (4- to 5-pound) boneless New Zealand lamb loin, available at most supermarkets and price clubs, is what you want for this great dinner party dish. These are mild and sweetly flavored, very lean but juicy. Unlike most lamb, which is too fatty to serve cold, thin slices of this roast will be delicious cold the next day.

You'll have a bit too much sauce, but that's good news, because it keeps for at least a week and is very tasty served over grilled or roasted chicken.

Serves 8 to 10

> One 4- to 5-pound boneless lamb loin, preferably from
> New Zealand
>
> SEASONING PASTE
> 1 medium sweet onion, chopped
> 6 garlic cloves, chopped
> A 1-inch chunk of ginger, chopped
> 2 large jalapeños, preferably red, seeded and chopped
> ½ teaspoon ground coriander
> 1 tablespoon coconut butter or olive oil
> ¼ teaspoon salt
> Juice of ½ lime
> Salt and freshly ground black pepper
>
> SPICY COCONUT SAUCE
> One 14-ounce can unsweetened coconut milk, well stirred
> Reserved ½ cup Seasoning Paste
> ½ teaspoon ground coriander
> ½ teaspoon salt

1 teaspoon tomato paste
8 cherry tomatoes, halved, squeezed over the sink
   to remove the seeds, and slivered
Cayenne pepper, optional
¼ cup packed minced cilantro, basil, or mint

Preheat the oven to 375 degrees.

Free the lamb from its netting, if it has one, and lay it out flat on your cutting board. Slash the thick parts with a sharp knife so the meat will cook more evenly.

In a blender or food processor, pulse all the seasoning paste ingredients into a thick paste—don't puree them; you want some texture. Reserve ½ cup of the paste for the sauce.

Spread the remaining paste over the meat with your fingers, rubbing it into the crevices where you slashed it. Roll the meat into its original shape and tie up it tightly in 3 or 4 places with kitchen twine; just a simple knot will do—don't worry if it doesn't look the way a butcher-tied roast does. If some of the paste squeezes out, push it back in with your fingers. Salt and pepper the meat and place it on a rack in a roasting pan. Roast for 1¼ hours, or until the internal temperature reaches 140 degrees. Lift it onto a serving platter and remove the strings. Cover loosely with foil while you make the sauce.

Pour off the clear fat from the roasting pan, leaving behind all the browned bits. Put the pan over medium-low heat and add all the sauce ingredients except the cayenne and herbs. Simmer for 5 minutes, carefully scraping up the pan drippings. Taste and adjust the seasoning if necessary. If it needs more heat, add a dash of cayenne pepper.

Carve the lamb into slices. Add the herbs to the sauce and spoon it over the lamb. (Store any leftover sauce in a screw-top jar in the refrigerator for at least a week.)

Amazing Lamb Stew

Many things are amazing about this stew, starting with its star-tlingly simple ingredients list. What happens when you combine this unusual group of ingredients and let them simmer happily for a couple of hours is truly amazing—a dish so good your guests will beg you for the recipe. This is great cold weather comfort food, and it's versatile. Leftovers are great, and you can double the recipe with no problems. The stew is good served over egg noodles or roasted potatoes.

Serves 6 to 8

> 1 cup olive oil
> 4 garlic cloves, minced
> 2½ pounds lamb stew meat, cut into 1- to 1½-inch cubes
> 8 ounces black olive paste (see Cook's Note)
> 8 ounces oil-packed sun-dried tomatoes, drained
> 1¾ cups chardonnay

Set a large ovenproof casserole over medium-high heat, add half the olive oil, and heat until hot. Add the garlic, then add the lamb and sear, turning as needed, until well browned all over.

Add the remaining oil and the rest of the ingredients to the pot and stir thoroughly to mix well. Turn the heat down to a simmer, cover the pot tightly, and simmer for 1½ to 2 hours, until the lamb is very tender. Serve.

COOK'S NOTE: This much olive paste (a.k.a. olivada or tapenade) will be expensive, so it's smarter to buy half a pound of olives, pit them yourself, and make the paste in the food processor (use the recipe on page 172, and leave out the tuna).

You can gild this lily by adding to the pot a few chopped anchovies, some thyme or oregano, maybe some minced preserved lemon zest (see below), or almost anything that sounds good with these intense flavors.

Preserved Lemon Zest

Moroccan preserved lemons are an exciting condiment to have around, but usually you have to make them yourself and wait a long time before you can use them. And sometimes they go bad before you can use them. If you're using a lot of lemons, though, for fresh lemonade or some other purpose, you can preserve just the zest very easily. Unwaxed lemons are best and organic are even better. Just peel off the zest (don't include any of the bitter white pith) with a potato peeler and put in a clean jar with a screw-top lid. Add a little kosher salt or sea salt, mix well, and cover with olive oil. You don't need to refrigerate these lemons, and they're ready to use in just a few days. Though fresh lemon zest is sensational all by itself (and full of the antioxidant limonene), this is more complex and adds an interesting note to stews, soups, and salads. Preserved zest is great slivered and whisked into mayonnaise along with a little fresh lemon juice for a quick fish sauce.

The preserved zest will keep for about a month.

Roast Leg of Lamb in a Nest

This is a favorite way of roasting lamb in New Zealand, where they know a thing or two about lamb. The nest is made out of rosemary branches and the "eggs" are garlic cloves, dozens and dozens of them. The result is an overwhelmingly fragrant lamb that you can put together in moments.

Obviously this recipe calls for a rosemary plant to harvest; if you don't have one, you'll need several supermarket packets of rosemary. And it's smart to buy already peeled garlic if time is tight.

Serves 6

> One 4- to 4½-pound boneless leg of lamb, preferably from
>   New Zealand
> Rosemary sprigs to line a roasting pan
> About 50 garlic cloves (unpeeled)
> Olive oil
> Salt and freshly ground black pepper

Bring the meat to room temperature.

Preheat the oven to 425 degrees.

Arrange the rosemary sprigs in the bottom of a roasting pan. Set the lamb on top of the rosemary and scatter the garlic cloves around it. Sprinkle the roast with a little olive oil and salt and pepper.

Roast the lamb for 10 minutes, then reduce the temperature to 325 degrees and cover the meat loosely with foil. Roast until an instant-read thermometer inserted into the center of the meat registers 130 degrees, about 1½ to 2 hours. Remove the foil and cook for 10 more minutes or until the temperature reaches 140 degrees. Let the roast rest 10 to 20 minutes, loosely covered with foil, before carving.

Carve the lamb and serve with the pan juices and the roasted garlic, which is delicious squeezed out of its skin and spread on bread, or stirred into mashed potatoes.

Roast Lamb
with Anchovies and Garlic Crust

The very lean grass-fed lamb from Australia and New Zealand takes very well to an anchovy treatment. Little bits of anchovies are tucked into slits all over the lamb, then it's covered with a mustard-mayonnaise-garlic-rosemary spread that turns into a golden crust in the oven. Your guests probably won't know what the flavor is, but they'll find this roast lamb especially succulent and tasty.

Save the oil the anchovies are packed in to make the Roasted Onions on page 292.

Serves 8

>One 4 to 4½-pound boneless leg of lamb, from Australia
>   or New Zealand
>One (3.35-ounce) jar anchovies packed in olive oil
>3 garlic cloves, pressed
>1 teaspoon dried rosemary, crumbled
>¼ cup Dijon mustard
>¼ cup mayonnaise, preferably homemade (page 206)

Bring the lamb roast to room temperature. Remove any netting, and slash the surface of the roast all over with ½-inch-deep cuts.

Reserve 4 of the anchovy fillets and chop the rest into quarters. Insert the anchovy pieces into the slits in the lamb. Place the lamb on a rack in a roasting pan. Mix the garlic, rosemary, mustard, and mayonnaise in a small bowl and spread over the surface of the lamb. Place the reserved anchovies diagonally across the top.

Preheat the oven to 425 degrees.

Roast the lamb for 30 minutes, then reduce the heat to 350 degrees and roast for about another hour, or until the internal temperature reads 130 degrees. Transfer the roast to a serving platter and let rest, covered loosely with foil, for 10 minutes.

Thinly slice the roast and serve.

COOK'S NOTE: If you make the Roasted Onions to serve with the lamb, they go into the oven when you reduce the temperature.

Buffalo Chili

Chili can be extremely rich, but this one is relatively low-fat, low-carb (if you skip the beans or hominy), and simple to put together. It's even better the next day, like all chili.

Buffalo is not only naturally lean, it's also grass-fed, which means it's full of good nutrients. It needs the help of a little bacon and a little cocoa powder (the very potent antioxidant), as well as some apple cider vinegar.

This chili is mellow and just faintly hot; for more heat, add hot pepper sauce to taste. And, of course, you can also make it with ground beef.

Serves 6 to 8 (with beans)

> 2 slices bacon, chopped
> 2 pounds ground buffalo or ground beef
> 1 large onion, chopped
> Olive oil, optional
> 4 garlic cloves, chopped
> Salt and freshly ground black pepper
> 1 tablespoon ground cumin
> 2 tablespoons good chili powder, such as Gebhardt's
> 1 teaspoon dried oregano
> 1 teaspoon paprika
> 2 cups water
> One 14.5-ounce can diced tomatoes, preferably organic, with their liquid
> 1 tablespoon unsweetened cocoa powder
> 1 tablespoon apple cider vinegar
> Two 4-ounce cans chopped green chiles, optional
> One 15-ounce can black beans, or hominy, drained and rinsed, optional
> 1 avocado, diced, and tossed with fresh lime juice, optional
> Chopped cilantro for garnish, optional

Cook the bacon in a Dutch oven over medium heat until lightly browned, just a few minutes. Add the meat in batches, browning it well and transferring to a bowl with a slotted spoon as it browns. When the meat is done, add the chopped onion to the pot (there should be enough fat; if not, add a little olive oil) and cook until lightly browned. Add the garlic, stirring well.

When the garlic starts to wilt a bit, return the meat to the pot and add salt and pepper to taste. Add the spices, water, and tomatoes and stir well. Cook over low heat, covered, for 1 hour, stirring from time to time to prevent sticking.

Add the cocoa powder and vinegar and stir well. Cook, covered, for another 20 minutes, stirring several times. Add the canned chiles and beans or hominy, if using, along with more water if necessary, and cook, uncovered, for 20 more minutes. Taste for seasoning.

Serve the chili hot, with the avocado and cilantro garnish, if desired.

Side Dishes

Greek Lemony Fried Potatoes

Here they are: pretty-good-for-you french fries. Because they're fried in olive oil, fewer harmful chemicals are formed during the frying process, though there will always be some (to counteract them, see the tips on page 226).

This very unusual version comes from Paraskevas Tokousbalides, a Greek olive oil researcher. You soak the potatoes all day in fresh lemon juice, so they're intensely lemony (and, of course, the lemon is also an antioxidant and pulls some of the starch out of the potatoes). If lemony potatoes sound unappealing, you can just leave out the lemon part and cook the fries according to the recipe.

If you have any fresh rosemary branches around, toss a couple of them into the pot during the last few minutes of frying. Drain and serve them as a rustic garnish for the fries.

The Belgians love fries with mayonnaise, and homemade mayonnaise (page 206) would be great with these.

Low-carb note: You can also fry zucchini slices without flouring them. Just slice zucchini very thin, pile into a colander, salt well, and let drain for half an hour. Rinse and dry very thoroughly before frying (skip the lemon treatment) until crisp and golden. Drain, toss with salt, and serve immediately.

Serves 2

> 1 russet potato, preferably organic
> About 6 lemons, optional
> 1 quart olive oil, preferably not extra virgin
> Salt

Cut the potato into thin rounds, like thick potato chips (leave the skin on if you like; that's where the nutrients are and it's got fiber as well).

Stack the potato slices in a narrow container—a glass measuring cup works well—as close together as possible, to minimize the amount of lemon juice you'll need. Juice the lemons and strain the juice. Pour it over the potatoes to cover, cover with plastic wrap, and set aside to marinate all day. Just before frying, drain the potatoes and pat them dry all over.

Pour the oil into a wok or a Dutch oven and set over medium-high heat until the temperature reaches 350 degrees (use a candy/frying thermometer to be sure; if you have no thermometer, there should be a slight haze coming off the surface when the oil's the right temperature and it should bubble up when you add a potato slice). When the temperature is right, add the potatoes in batches and fry until golden brown, stirring gently from time to time. Drain immediately on a rack or paper towels, and salt generously. Serve right away.

Broccoli
with Toasted Pecan Butter

You know how good broccoli is for you but sometimes the usual Italian olive-oil-and-garlic treatment gets tiresome. I think broccoli and pecans are wonderful together—though you could also use almonds—and butter is the perfect foil for these sweet tastes.

I like the high-fiber stalks almost better than the florets—just peel them and cut them into little chunks. They take a few more minutes to cook than the florets, but add them a couple of minutes before the florets and they'll cook perfectly. If you prefer, you can use only florets.

I'm giving a traditional simmered recipe here, but broccoli is also great in the microwave. The water that clings to the broccoli after rinsing will be enough to steam it. Put the broccoli in a microwave-safe bowl, and cover with plastic wrap. Make a couple of pokes in the plastic wrap to vent it and microwave the broccoli for about 1 minute, until tender.

Serves 2

Salt
2 cups broccoli florets and peeled stems cut into chunks
    (see note above)
2 tablespoons unsalted butter
¼ chopped raw pecans

Bring a large saucepan of water to a boil and add salt. Add the broccoli, stems first, if using, and then, a couple of minutes later, the florets. Simmer uncovered for 4 to 6 minutes, or until the broccoli is tender but still a bit firm. Drain well and return to the hot pan to keep warm.

Melt the butter in a small skillet over medium heat. When it's bubbling, add the pecans, stirring well. Let the pecans start to brown, but remove the skillet from the heat when the butter begins to color. Stir into the broccoli in the pan and serve immediately.

Roasted Figs
with Gorgonzola and Greens

When the first figs of the year arrive, try this delectable treat that works as well as an appetizer or, minus the greens, tidbit with cocktails. It's just the thing to perk up a grilled chicken breast, however, so I've included it with the sides.

Serves 4

> 12 fine fresh black figs
> 4 ounces Gorgonzola dolcelatte or fresh goat cheese,
>   crumbled
> Clarified butter or ghee (see page 70)
> Mâche, baby watercress, or other mild, tender greens
>   for serving

Preheat the oven to 375 degrees.

Cut a cross in the tops of the figs and push a little of the cheese into each one with your fingers—not so much that it's bulging out. Paint the tops of the stuffed figs with the clarified butter or ghee and set them in a gratin dish.

Roast the figs for 5 to 7 minutes, until they're just warmed through. Serve 3 figs per person on a small mound of mâche or other greens.

Dinosaur Kale with Pecans

Dinosaur kale is a gorgeous sweet kale, sometimes called *lacinato,* that's starting to appear in most supermarkets and natural foods stores. It's great in a skillet sauté, where in about ten minutes it will be reduced to a pile of succulence that goes well with fish or pork. Don't try this with regular kale, which is much tougher and stronger tasting, unless you drop it into boiling water for a few minutes to soften it, then drain it before starting the recipe.

Serves 2 to 3

1 bunch dinosaur kale (about 1 pound)
1½ tablespoons extra virgin olive oil
2 garlic cloves, minced
½ small sweet onion, chopped
Salt and freshly ground black pepper
2 tablespoons chopped toasted pecans

Slice along both sides of the heavy ribs of the kale and discard them. Chop the remainder into bite-sized pieces.

Heat a large skillet and add the olive oil. When it's hot, add the garlic and onion and cook until they begin to soften. Add the greens and sauté for about 10 minutes, or until wilted. Season, mix in the pecans, stir well, and serve hot.

Red Cabbage
with Juniper Berries and Gin

This slightly startling recipe comes from England, where gin is highly prized. The only difficult thing about this quick-fix dish is finding the juniper berries, but it's worth seeking them out just because this dish is always a hit (they can be mail-ordered as a last resort, see Cook's Note). The butter or walnut oil is a key ingredient that brings the other flavors together and offers its own voluptuous touch.

As you're crushing the juniper berries into the salt, you'll get an incredibly heady aroma of pure gin—and of course the gin that goes into the recipe just accentuates that flavor, as well as adding an ineffable taste of its own.

Ginned cabbage is great with pork, game, duck—almost any rich meat.

Serves 4 to 6

8 juniper berries
2 teaspoons salt
3 garlic cloves, crushed
4 tablespoons (½ stick) unsalted butter or ¼ cup walnut oil
½ medium red cabbage, shredded
¼ cup gin
Freshly ground black pepper

Grind the juniper berries with the salt in a mortar or in a mini food processor. Add the garlic to the mixture by hand.

Melt the butter (or heat the oil) in a sauté pan over medium-high heat. When it's sizzling, add the cabbage and the juniper berry mixture. Stir to coat the cabbage, add the gin, cover, and cook for 4 minutes, shaking the pan from time to time.

Raise the heat to high, uncover the pan, and stir the cabbage for another minute. Serve immediately.

COOK'S NOTE: Juniper berries can be mail-ordered from Dean & Deluca (see Sources). They keep a very long time.

New Takes on Corn on the Cob

Nothing in the world is quite so good as truly fresh corn with butter, salt, and pepper. However, once corn season strikes, the same old thing can get a little boring. Here are some fresh possibilities using other good fats.

The olive oil version depends on having great olive oil—which has a great affinity for corn—and great salt. The coconut butter version is much subtler, but it gets punched up with some minced cilantro. Either way, start with farm-fresh corn, dropped into boiling water just long enough for the water to return to the boil and heat the corn through.

Traditionalists may not want to try these ideas at all, so you should also have butter on hand. You can make the salting and peppering easier by crushing some sea salt or kosher salt and adding some freshly ground black pepper. Guests can simply pinch up some of the mixture and drift it over their corn.

Corn with Olive Oil and Salt

Freshly cooked ears of corn
Tuscan estate-bottled extra virgin olive oil or Spanish
    Arbequina oil, preferably unfiltered
Fleur de sel or other high-quality sea salt, such as Maldon
    salt

Have ready a small bowl of olive oil with a new paintbrush to paint on the oil. Pass a bowl of sea salt, and let guests oil and season their own corn.

Corn with Coconut Oil and Cilantro

Freshly cooked ears of corn
High-quality coconut oil (see page 65)
Sea salt
Minced cilantro

Since it's summer, the coconut oil should be liquid; if not, warm it briefly until it is. Put it in a small bowl with a new paintbrush to paint it on the corn. Pass small bowls of sea salt and cilantro, and let guests prepare their own ears.

Spinach with Greek Flavors

This dish is full of rustic flavors—very good with lamb or pork. If you buy baby spinach that's already cleaned, the dish is very simple to put together (and a bit more expensive). The flavors of spinach, feta, olives, and oregano—a great good-fat-and-antioxidant team—are wonderful together.

Serves 4

> 1½ pounds spinach, thick stems removed and well washed
> 2 to 4 tablespoons extra virgin olive oil
> ½ teaspoon dried oregano, crumbled
> ½ cup crumbled feta cheese
> ½ cup pitted Kalamata olives

In a large pot, cook the spinach (with just the water still clinging to its leaves after washing) over medium heat until wilted and soft. Drain well and let cool. Wipe the pot dry.

When cool enough to handle, squeeze the spinach to get as much water out of it as possible. Chop it and set aside.

Heat a spoonful of the olive oil in the same pot over medium heat, add the oregano, and stir and cook for a minute. Toss the spinach back into the pot and reheat. When the spinach is hot, turn off the heat, add the feta cheese and olives, and mix well. Trickle more olive oil over the spinach, just to moisten it well, and toss again. Serve hot.

Spinach with Indian Spices

This lovely dish—the turmeric gives the sauce a gorgeous mellow creamy orange against the dark green of the spinach—makes a perfect natural bridge between coconut milk and spinach. Although it has a lot of spices, they all contribute to the complex flavor. It's one of those side dishes it's hard to stop eating.

Serves 2

> 1 tablespoon unsalted butter
> ½ large onion, finely diced
> ½ teaspoon ground cumin
> ¼ teaspoon ground cardamom
> ¼ teaspoon ground turmeric
> ¼ teaspoon ground ginger
> ¼ teaspoon salt
> 10 ounces spinach, thick stems removed and well washed
> ½ cup canned unsweetened coconut milk

In a large skillet, melt the butter over medium heat. Add the onion and cook until soft, about 4 minutes. Add the cumin, cardamom, turmeric, ginger, and salt and cook until fragrant, about 1 minute.

Add the spinach, cover, and cook until slightly wilted, about 1 minute. Pour in the coconut milk and continue to cook, uncovered, until the spinach is completely wilted, another minute or two; do not overcook. Serve hot.

Spinach with Orange

A Greek friend told me about tasting this very unusual dish, and this is my attempt to come up with something similar to her description. The spinach-orange combination is so good—and good from an antioxidant perspective too—that it's surprising it's not more common.

Serves 2

¼ cup extra virgin olive oil
1 garlic clove, minced
2 scallions (white and green parts), chopped
10-ounce package cleaned flat-leaf spinach, about 1 pound uncleaned
1 teaspoon grated orange zest
A big squeeze of orange juice
Salt and freshly ground black pepper

Heat a large skillet over medium-high heat and add the olive oil. When it's warm, add the garlic and scallions and sauté until soft, about 5 minutes.

Off the heat, add the spinach. Cover and cook over medium heat until the spinach is wilted and soft, about 8 minutes, stirring once in the middle of the cooking.

Drain the spinach well and return it to the skillet, adding the orange zest and juice, along with salt and pepper to taste. Serve warm.

Chard Bleu

This very interesting way of cooking chard—a long time, to bring out lots of flavors you don't get in the usual ways of cooking it—comes from vegetarian cook Deborah Madison. A little blue cheese in the mix adds yet another level of flavor.

Serves 4

2 bunches chard (about 2 pounds), well washed
1 garlic clove, peeled
Salt
1 medium onion, finely diced
½ cup chopped cilantro
⅓ cup extra virgin olive oil
1 teaspoon paprika
¼ cup water
Freshly ground black pepper
2 tablespoons crumbled mild blue cheese, such as Danish
    blue

Trim the bottoms of the chard stems and cut out the big center stems. If the chard isn't young, peel off the fibrous outer skin of the stems with a paring knife. Dice the stems, and reserve 1½ cups (you can use the rest for soup). Stack the green leaves and cut them into ribbons about 1 inch wide.

Pound the garlic clove with 1 teaspoon salt in a mortar or mash to a paste with a fork.

Put the chard stems and greens in a wide heavy pot with a lid and add the onion, cilantro, olive oil, paprika, and garlic and salt mixture, plus a couple of pinches of salt. Add the water and mix thoroughly. Cover tightly and cook over low heat for about 45 minutes, stirring from time to time to be sure there's enough water and the chard isn't sticking—if it is, add a few tablespoons more water.

When it's done, the chard will have a silky quality. Taste for salt and add pepper.

Remove the chard from the heat and sprinkle the blue cheese on top. Cover and let sit for about 5 minutes.

Remove the lid and stir the chard well to distribute the cheese, which should be melted into the greens, and serve.

Fragrant Swahili Rice

This mellow rice dish is perfumed with sweet spices, cardamom, and cinnamon. The coconut milk gives it a luxurious quality, like a savory rice pudding.

The rice is excellent with fish, lamb, and chicken. It doesn't need butter, but you can add a bit to the cooked rice if you want to gild the lily.

Serves 4

> One 14-ounce can unsweetened coconut milk
> 3 cups water
> 2 cups basmati rice
> 1 teaspoon ground cardamom
> ½ cinnamon stick
> ½ teaspoon salt, or more to taste
> 1 tablespoon unsalted butter, softened, optional

Mix all the ingredients except the butter together in a saucepan and bring to a boil over medium heat. Lower the heat until the mixture is just simmering, cover, and cook for 10 minutes. Test to see if the rice is cooked; if not, cook a few minutes more.

Remove the cinnamon stick, stir in the optional butter, and serve hot.

Sweet Potato Gratin
with Shiitakes and Parmesan

This wonderfully savory sweet potato dish is perfect for the holidays—great with ham, great with turkey, great for traveling to a potluck supper. You can bake it ahead of time and reheat it, or simply assemble it hours ahead of baking it.

The combination of shiitakes and sweet potatoes is earthy and memorable.

Serves 10

3 tablespoons extra virgin olive oil
1 pound shiitake mushrooms, stemmed and sliced
3 pounds sweet potatoes
8 tablespoons (1 stick) unsalted butter, cut into chunks
Salt and freshly ground black pepper
½ cup freshly grated Parmesan cheese

Preheat the oven to 350 degrees.

Oil a 2-inch-deep 10-cup gratin dish.

Heat the oil in a sauté pan over medium-high heat and briefly cook the mushrooms, just long enough to soften them. Remove from the heat.

Peel the sweet potatoes and thinly slice them. Layer a third of them in the gratin dish, dot with one-third of the butter, and add salt and pepper to taste. Sprinkle a third of the Parmesan on top, followed by a layer of half the mushrooms. Repeat the process, and end with a layer of sweet potatoes on top with the last of the Parmesan sprinkled over them. Dot with the remaining butter.

Cover the dish with foil and bake for 40 minutes. Remove the foil and bake for another 20 minutes, or until golden brown. Serve hot.

Roasted Onions

If you're serving a roast, it's hard to beat an accompaniment of roasted onions, which take all of about two minutes to prepare and always taste delectable. I think red onions roast best, and I especially like the torpedo-shaped ones I sometimes find in the market.

Serves 4

> 4 medium red onions
> Olive, anchovy, or a nut oil
> Fresh or dried thyme or dried herbes de Provence
> Salt and freshly ground black pepper

Preheat the oven to 350 degrees (or cook the onions at the temperature you're using to roast the meat, adjusting the cooking time accordingly).

Peel away the papery outer skin of the onions down to the firm purple layer. Cut the onions in half—around their waists for round ones, lengthwise for torpedos. Arrange them cut side up in a baking dish.

Drizzle the oil over the onions, sprinkle with the herbs, and add salt and pepper to taste. Roast for about 1 hour, or until the onions are tender and slightly caramelized at the edges. Serve hot or warm.

Tomato, Coconut, and Mint Chutney

Chewy, crunchy, mildly spicy, and thumbs-up delicious, this unusual chutney is good with grilled lamb, chicken, or shellfish. It takes just a few minutes to make and keeps well in the refrigerator in a screw-top jar.

Makes 2 cups

¼ cup shredded unsweetened dried coconut
1 tablespoon coconut oil or olive oil
¼ teaspoon chili oil
2 medium shallots, chopped
4 garlic cloves, smashed and minced
½ teaspoon garam masala (a curry-like spice mix; see Cook's Note on page 170)
¼ teaspoon ground coriander
¼ teaspoon coarsely ground black pepper
¼ teaspoon kosher salt
1 cup halved grape tomatoes or cherry tomatoes
¼ cup canned unsweetened coconut milk
½ cup loosely packed chopped mint

Spread the coconut in a flat heatproof dish or small pan and toast lightly either in the microwave or the toaster oven, stirring often. Watch constantly, as coconut burns easily. Set aside.

In a medium nonstick skillet, heat the coconut oil and chili oil over medium heat. Add the shallots and garlic and sauté until softened. Sprinkle in the seasonings and stir to combine. Allow the mixture to cook for a minute or two to release the flavors.

Add the tomato halves and sauté until they wilt slightly. Add the coconut milk and simmer until the tomatoes exude their juice. Add the toasted coconut—the mixture will now have the spoonable consistency of chutney. Remove from the heat and let cool.

Add the mint after the chutney cools—or, better yet, just before serving—or it will turn dark.

Breakfast

The Smoothie

I never tire of this delightful start to the day, partly because you can vary the fruit to suit the season and your mood. And frozen fruit works just fine here. Low-carbers note: because your insulin receptors are keener in the morning after the long overnight fast, this is the time to indulge your longing for some forbidden fruit, such as bananas (a mini-banana or a half banana is the right amount) and mangoes.

But this isn't just a traditional protein shake. The coconut milk is a secret ingredient that makes it not only smooth and especially delicious, but also adds some truly powerful energy to your morning. And if you're trying to lose weight, the smoothie gives you a great start on your coconut allotment for the day.

Serves 1

½ cup canned unsweetened coconut milk
1 cup water
2 scoops Designer Protein (whey)
1 tablespoon honey or Splenda
1 cup fresh or frozen fruit, such as berries, sliced peaches
Dash of pure vanilla extract or almond extract
Dusting of grated nutmeg, optional

Blend all the ingredients in a blender until frothy.

Hot Chocolate with Coconut Milk

Coconut milk adds an incredibly smooth richness to hot chocolate as well as indefinable taste—you just want to keep sipping to figure out why it's so good. It's also good cold, as chocolate milk, or frozen, as Popsicles.

If you want to be completely decadent, you can use just a little water, ¼ cup, and a whole cup of coconut milk.

Serves 1

> 2 tablespoons sugar
> 1 tablespoon unsweetened cocoa powder
> Pinch of salt
> ½ cup water
> ½ cup canned unsweetened coconut milk
> ¼ teaspoon pure vanilla extract

Mix the sugar, cocoa, and salt in a saucepan. Add the water and heat, stirring, over medium heat until the mixture boils. Boil for 2 minutes, stirring all the while.

Add the coconut milk, stir well, and heat just enough to warm thoroughly; don't let the mixture boil. Add the vanilla and stir again. Strain the cocoa into a mug and serve hot, or let cool and refrigerate to serve cold.

COOK'S NOTE: You can make this hot chocolate with Splenda instead of sugar, but don't add it until the end, with the vanilla, or it will turn bitter.

Crisp Coconut Waffles

These amazing waffles are a study in contrasts—they're so light they're almost ethereal, yet they have a subtle richness and delicate flavor from our friend the coconut. You may have a hard time convincing anyone else at your table that they don't need butter, but they truly don't. They're best with a little warmed fruit—blueberries, chopped up peaches or mangoes, or a mixture. You can warm the fruit in the microwave just to soften it, then add a squeeze of lime and a bit of sugar or Splenda if you like.

There's no excuse not to make waffles now that there's an incredibly cheap vertically stored waffler on the market. If you don't have one, you can turn these into pancakes by increasing the regular flour to ½ cup and skipping the rice flour.

Makes 4 to 6 waffles

> 1 large egg
> 1½ cups canned unsweetened coconut milk
> 2 tablespoons unsalted butter, melted
> 1 teaspoon pure vanilla extract
> 3 to 4 drops natural coconut extract, optional
> ¼ cup rice flour
> ¼ cup all-purpose flour
> ½ cup shredded unsweetened dried coconut
> 1 teaspoon baking powder
> Pinch of salt
> ½ teaspoon sugar or Splenda

Preheat the waffle iron.

Whisk the egg, coconut milk, butter, vanilla, and coconut extract, if using, in a small bowl until well combined.

Whisk the remaining ingredients in a medium mixing bowl to distribute thoroughly. Pour the wet ingredients into the dry ones while stirring with the whisk or a wooden spoon until you can no longer see the flour—but don't stir assertively.

Make the waffles according to the waffle iron manufacturer's directions, and serve hot.

COOK'S NOTE: The waffles also freeze successfully, well wrapped. Put them in a toaster oven to rewarm.

Granola with Coconut and Berries

Granola's like money in the bank—good over yogurt, good over fruit, good just to have a handful for a snack. If you make your own, you can be sure it's made with good fats and high-quality ingredients, which isn't always the case with store-bought granola. This one has both coconut and coconut oil, as well as lots of nuts and good antioxidant berries.

Makes about 4 cups

½ cup shredded unsweetened dried coconut
¼ cup coconut oil
⅓ cup maple syrup
Grated zest of 1 lemon
2 cups old-fashioned rolled oats
½ cup sliced almonds
½ cup coarsely chopped pecans
1 teaspoon ground cinnamon
¼ teaspoon grated nutmeg
½ cup dried blueberries or cranberries

Place an oven rack in the middle of the oven. Preheat the oven to 375 degrees.

Spread the coconut out in a single layer on a baking sheet. Bake, stirring often, until it is just turning golden, about 10 minutes; watch carefully, because it burns easily. Transfer the coconut to a small bowl and set aside. Leave the oven on.

Bring the coconut oil, maple syrup, and lemon zest to a boil in a medium saucepan over medium heat; remove from the heat. Place the remaining ingredients except the coconut and the berries in a large bowl and mix well with your hands. Add the syrup mixture and mix until well combined. Spread the mixture in a ½-inch-thick layer on a baking sheet; set the bowl aside.

Bake, stirring often, until the granola is golden brown, about 15 minutes. Remove from the oven and let cool.

Return the granola to the large bowl, stir in the coconut and berries, and mix well. The granola will keep for a month, tightly sealed in a screw-top jar.

Scrambled Eggs with Smoked Salmon

This good brunch dish also works for supper, of course. It's rich and elegant, good with Champagne for an important breakfast or late-night supper. You can top it with red salmon eggs or even caviar to up the ante a bit.

The eggs are French-style, made in a double boiler. They're very creamy, so it may be best to serve them in shallow bowls rather than on plates. But if you don't want to fuss with the double boiler, just make regular scrambled eggs in a skillet with the same ingredients.

Serves 4 to 6

   2 tablespoons unsalted butter
   8 large eggs
   Salt and freshly ground black pepper
   4 ounces smoked salmon, cut into thin strips, at room
      temperature
   ⅔ cup crème fraîche or heavy cream
   2 tablespoons minced chives
   Salmon caviar or sturgeon caviar for garnish, optional

Melt the butter in the top of a double boiler over an inch or two of simmering water. Whisk the eggs just enough to combine them, then add salt and pepper to taste and the salmon strips. Pour the eggs into the hot butter. Cook, stirring with a wooden spoon, until very thick and creamy—it may take as much as half an hour.

Add the crème fraîche or cream and chives, stirring to combine well, and serve hot, with the optional caviar, passing the pepper grinder at the table.

Desserts

Ambrosia

This Southern holiday classic is simply wonderful on a buffet table or for a refreshing dessert after a rich meal, especially one featuring pork. Everyone in the South has his or her own recipe; in the North, we've pretty much forgotten about it.

You can make ambrosia a day ahead and its flavors will actually improve. You can add some sliced fresh mint leaves before serving, or some fresh pineapple chunks, or some sliced sweet kumquats or bits of candied ginger—improvisations are almost always appreciated. Some at your table may beg for baby marshmallows too, but they're on their own.

Serves 8

    1 coconut, cracked and grated (see page 62)
    10 navel oranges, peeled and sectioned, juices reserved
        (see Cook's Note)
    Sugar to taste

Mix everything together, including the juice from the oranges, in a big bowl. Cover tightly and chill, preferably overnight. Remove from the refrigerator half an hour before serving.

COOK'S NOTE: To section the navel oranges, peel them and cut away the bitter white inner pith. Using a small sharp knife, cut down along the sides of the membranes that hold each section and release the fruit, working over a bowl to catch the juices.

Bananas Steamed in Coconut Milk

A Southeast Asian take on dessert that's the perfect finish to an Asian meal—or a good breakfast on a hot day, for that matter. Burmese chef Michael Min Kinh had this bright idea and it's great, an unusual dessert that's made in moments.

This isn't a low-carb dish—though it would probably work for a low-carb breakfast, when the long overnight fast means you can handle a bit more carb without getting into trouble.

Serves 4 to 6

> 4 medium bananas, thinly sliced
> Two 14-ounce cans unsweetened coconut milk, well stirred
> Shredded fresh or dried unsweetened coconut for garnish
> Big pinch of ground cinnamon, grated nutmeg, or ground
>   cardamom

Pile the bananas into a microwaveable dish and pour the coconut milk over them. Cover the dish with plastic wrap and microwave on high for 10 minutes.

Let cool and refrigerate the bananas for at least several hours, or overnight; the coconut milk will thicken into a sauce.

Serve chilled or at room temperature. Scatter a little coconut over the top just before serving and sprinkle with a bit of spice.

Pink Grapefruit Foster

Bananas Foster is by now a Southern classic, though it's a fairly recent invention. Pink grapefruit takes the dish in an entirely different direction, and, of course, it has the advantage of fewer carbs and lots of lycopene. It's a simple dish to make, but it has to be put together at the last minute. You can have everything ready to go, though, and just spend a couple of minutes making the sauce.

Serves 2

    1 large ruby red grapefruit
    1 tablespoon unsalted butter
    3 tablespoons light brown sugar
    2 tablespoons dark rum
    Vanilla ice cream for serving

With a sharp knife, peel the grapefruit, removing all the bitter whole pith. Holding the grapefruit over a bowl to catch the juices, use a paring knife to slice between the membranes and release the segments whole. Transfer the segments to another bowl and set aside; drink the juice for a cook's treat.

Melt the butter in a large skillet over medium-low heat. Add the sugar and rum (it may splatter, so stand back, and use a splatter screen) and stir until smooth. Cook until the sugar just dissolves, 1 to 2 minutes. Remove from the heat and let cool slightly, about 2 minutes.

Fold the grapefruit sections into the sauce and serve immediately over ice cream.

Mexican Coconut Popsicles

Anyone who's ever had a *paleta,* one of the astoundingly good fruit Popsicles sold on city streets and in the parks in Mexico, will be overjoyed to be presented with one of these. There are *paleta* makers in Los Angeles and in Brooklyn, and always the favorite seems to be coconut; mine too. Kids will love these, and so will adults, especially if you add the rum.

These are ridiculously easy to make and wonderfully refreshing on a very hot day. All you need is a Popsicle maker (Martha Stewart–types can hunt down charming sturdy paper cups and Popsicle sticks) and you're set.

Makes eight 3-ounce pops

One 14-ounce can unsweetened coconut milk, well stirred
3 tablespoons light brown sugar
¼ cup shredded fresh coconut
1 tablespoon dark rum, optional

In a small bowl, combine the coconut milk and sugar, stirring until the sugar dissolves. Add the coconut and the rum, if using. Mix to combine well.

Pour the mixture evenly into eight Popsicle molds and freeze overnight, or until solid.

Peach Melba with Caramelized Pistachios

This classic dessert gets a bit dressed up with the caramelized pistachios and the crème fraîche instead of the usual ice cream. The raspberries have those great antioxidant qualities (see page 143), and there's not much sugar here. In a pinch, you could make this dessert with frozen peaches, which aren't terrible, and you could also substitute ripe apricots or nectarines for the peaches. If you can't be bothered making the nuts, just crumble a few of the Italian macaroons called amaretti over the fruit.

I like to keep the skin on the peaches because that's where the nutrients are, but of course you can peel them if you'd prefer.

Serves 4

> 1 tablespoon unsalted butter
> ¼ cup packed light brown sugar
> 1 tablespoon plus 1 teaspoon water
> ⅔ cup shelled unsalted pistachios
> 1½ cups raspberries
> 4 ripe peaches, pitted and cut into eighths, or 32 defrosted
>   frozen peach slices
> Pinch of sugar, or to taste
> Crème fraîche for serving

To make the nuts, line a baking sheet with foil. Heat the butter and sugar with the water in a nonstick skillet over medium-high heat until melted and clear. Reduce the heat to medium-low and stir in the nuts. Cook until the mixture is syrupy and the pistachios are completely coated, about 3 minutes. Pour the mixture onto the foil-lined baking sheet, spreading the pistachios out with a fork so they don't touch each other. Let cool completely, allowing the caramel to harden.

Break the coated pistachios up into individual nuts.

To serve, arrange half the raspberries and all the peaches in individual serving bowls.

Puree the remaining raspberries and add a little sugar to taste. Drizzle the fruit with the puree and top with crème fraîche. Scatter the caramelized pistachios over the top, and serve.

If you have any extra nuts, they'll keep for a few days, tightly sealed in a tin.

Hazelnut Meringue with Raspberries

If you like meringues, you'll really like this dessert, which is crunchy, nutty, and creamy, with sweet/sharp berries. It's basically a big, airy, nutty meringue sandwich with whipped cream and berries. Be sure to let the meringues cool completely, or they won't be crisp.

Serves 6 to 8

> 1 cup (6 ounces) hazelnuts
> ¾ cup plus 2 tablespoons superfine sugar
> 5 large egg whites
> ¼ teaspoon cream of tartar
> 1¼ cups heavy whipping cream
> 1 teaspoon pure vanilla extract
> 8 ounces raspberries
> Confectioners' sugar for garnish

Set the oven racks on the top and lower levels. Preheat the oven to 350 degrees.

Spread the hazelnuts on a rimmed baking sheet and toast on the top oven rack for 10 minutes, or until the nuts are golden and the skins are papery and crisp. Put the warm nuts in a kitchen towel and rub them to remove the skins—don't worry if every little bit doesn't come off. Reduce the oven heat to 275 degrees.

When the nuts are cool, transfer them to a food processor, add 1 tablespoon of the sugar, and process to a coarse powder.

In a large bowl, beat the egg whites until you have soft peaks. Start adding the ¾ cup sugar a tablespoon at a time as you continue to beat, adding the cream of tartar with the last tablespoon. Carefully fold in the ground hazelnuts.

Line a baking sheet with parchment paper and draw two 8-inch circles on it, using a pencil to trace around an 8-inch pan. Turn the paper over on the baking sheet, so the pencil side is down. Using the circles as a guide, pipe or spread the meringue into circles, smoothing it with a wooden spoon.

Bake the meringues on the top rack for 30 minutes, then move to the lower level and bake for another 30 minutes, or until pale golden and dry to the touch. Remove the meringues and let them cool completely on the parchment paper—they'll crisp as they cool.

Just before serving, whip the cream with the remaining tablespoon of sugar and the vanilla.

Put one meringue on a serving platter. Spread with the whipped cream, add the berries, and top with the remaining meringue. Dust with confectioners' sugar and serve right away, using a serrated knife to minimize the inevitable crumbling—the crumbs, however, are delicious.

COOK'S NOTE: You can make superfine sugar yourself by just whirling regular sugar in the food processor for a few seconds.

Apple, Pear, and Cranberry Crisp
with Walnuts

This is a good fall dessert—and not at all bad for breakfast either. It's a shortcut crisp—you melt the butter first instead of cutting bits of cold butter into the oats—but the topping still comes out crisp. Lots of people would want to have vanilla ice cream (superpremium full-fat, of course) with the crisp, which is fine, but plain heavy cream is wonderful with it.

Serves 6

CRISP
3 medium baking apples, such as Rome or Empire, cored
2 firm but ripe Bartlett pears, cored
⅓ cup dried cranberries
1 teaspoon grated lemon zest
1 tablespoon fresh lemon juice
1 tablespoon sugar

TOPPING
8 tablespoons (1 stick) unsalted butter, melted
½ cup chopped walnuts
1 cup old-fashioned rolled oats
½ cup shredded unsweetened dried coconut
½ cup all-purpose flour
½ cup packed light brown sugar
1 teaspoon ground cinnamon
½ teaspoon coarse sea or kosher salt

Vanilla ice cream or heavy cream for serving

Preheat the oven to 350 degrees.

Cut the apples and pears into 1-inch pieces and transfer to a large bowl. Add the remaining crisp ingredients and toss to combine. Pour the apples and pears into a 9-inch square glass baking dish. Combine all the topping ingredients and stir well. Spread the mixture evenly across the fruit.

Bake until the fruit is soft and the topping is crisp, about 25 minutes, watching carefully to be sure the topping doesn't brown too much.

Let cool for 15 minutes before serving with ice cream or cream.

Rhubarb-Orange Clafouti
with Coconut

This French dessert isn't really quite like anything American, except perhaps a cobbler made with a batter. But it's really delicious, and although the French wouldn't make it with rhubarb, let alone coconut, it's a great combination. If you have any strawberries around, you could throw in a few of those as well.

Serves 6 to 8

RHUBARB

1½ pounds fresh rhubarb, trimmed and cut on the diagonal
    into ¾-inch lengths
¼ cup sugar
Grated zest of 1 orange
⅓ cup shredded unsweetened fresh or dried coconut

CUSTARD

3 large eggs
½ cup plus 1 tablespoon sugar
½ teaspoon salt
1 cup heavy cream
6 tablespoons (¾ stick) unsalted butter, melted
Seeds from ½ vanilla bean or 1 teaspoon pure vanilla
    extract
1 tablespoon Cognac or rum, optional
⅔ cup all-purpose flour

Preheat the oven to 350 degrees. Butter a 1-quart ceramic gratin or baking dish.

Toss the rhubarb with the sugar and orange zest in the gratin dish. Bake for 20 minutes, or until the rhubarb is soft, stirring occasionally and watching to make sure the sugar does not burn. Remove from the oven, sprinkle with the coconut, and set aside. Raise the oven temperature to 450 degrees.

Combine the eggs, the ½ cup sugar, the salt, cream, melted butter, vanilla, and Cognac, if using, in a blender. Blend until thoroughly combined, then add the flour and process just until smooth.

Pour the batter over the rhubarb and coconut, and sprinkle with the remaining tablespoon of sugar. Bake for 20 minutes, or until the top is lightly golden and the sides are set. Let rest for 10 minutes before serving.

Coconut Custard

This is a homey dessert, made in moments but a lot more fun than just plain custard, especially if you include the rum option. You can play around with it—add the seeds from a vanilla bean instead of the vanilla extract, or toss in some grated fresh ginger. The custard isn't terribly sweet, but low-carbers can make it even less sweet by using Splenda.

A small bowl of chilled coconut custard is delicious for breakfast on a really hot day.

Serves 8

>   5 large eggs
>   ½ cup sugar
>   1 tablespoon pure vanilla extract
>   One 14-ounce can unsweetened coconut milk, well stirred
>   ½ cup whole milk
>   2 tablespoons dark rum, optional
>   ½ cup shredded unsweetened dried coconut
>   Grated nutmeg, optional

Preheat the oven to 325 degrees. Put a kettle of water on to boil and have a small roasting pan ready to make a water bath.

In a large bowl with a pouring spout, mix the eggs well with a whisk. Whisk in the sugar and vanilla until well combined. Add the two milks and combine thoroughly. Add the optional rum.

Strain the mixture into a 1½-quart soufflé dish or glass custard dish. Stir in the coconut and sprinkle the top with the optional nutmeg.

Set the custard inside the roasting pan in the oven and carefully pour boiling water into the pan to come halfway up the side of the custard dish. Bake the custard for about 30 minutes, or until not quite set in the very center. Remove from the oven and allow to cool. Serve at room temperature or chilled.

The custard will keep for a couple of days tightly covered with plastic wrap and refrigerated.

Lemon Posset

This old-timey British dessert is magical. It takes just three ingredients and just a few minutes to produce a sweet so divinely rich you'll have to give up the recipe to your guests. The raspberries are a wonderful foil for the decadent cream, a fine fat.

Serves 4

2 lemons, preferably unwaxed, scrubbed
2 cups heavy cream
¼ cup sugar
Raspberries for serving, optional

Peel the zest off the lemons with a vegetable peeler—long strips are fine, but don't include any of the white pith. Juice the lemons, and set the juice aside.

Put the lemon zest, cream, and sugar in a large saucepan, bring to a boil over medium heat, and boil for exactly 3 minutes, no longer (an egg timer is perfect for this job).

Remove the saucepan from the heat and whisk in the lemon juice. Pour the mixture through a strainer into a pitcher, then divide it among four small serving dishes or ramekins. Cover the dishes with plastic wrap and let cool, then chill for at least 4 hours, or as much as 8 hours.

Serve chilled, with raspberries or not, as you like.

Orange-Almond Cake with Coconut

This cake has no flour—it is instead thickened with ground almonds and whole oranges, skin and all. It's a great keeper cake, and in fact it's better the second day.

You need thin-skinned juice oranges here, not the giant pebbly skinned ones. You could use either blanched almonds or unskinned ones; I prefer the unskinned for their extra fiber.

Dress the cake up a bit, if you like, by drizzling melted chocolate over the top once it's cooled or giving it a light dusting of confectioners' sugar.

Serves 8 to 10

> 2 medium thin-skinned oranges, such as Valencias,
>   preferably organic, scrubbed
> 6 large eggs
> 1 cup sugar
> 1½ teaspoons baking powder
> 1½ cups ground almonds
> 1 cup shredded unsweetened dried coconut

Put the oranges in a medium saucepan, cover with water, and bring to a boil. Reduce the heat and simmer for 2 hours, covered, checking every now and then to see that the water isn't getting too low—if it is, add a little boiling water. Drain the oranges and let cool.

Preheat the oven to 350 degrees. Grease and flour a 10-inch springform pan and line it with parchment paper.

When the oranges are cool, cut them in half and remove the seeds. Put the orange halves, peel and all, in a food processor and puree. You need 1¼ cups.

In a large bowl, beat the eggs with the sugar and baking powder with a mixer at medium-high speed until thick and lemon colored, a few minutes. Add the almonds and coconut and mix well. Stir in the orange puree, in several batches.

Pour the batter into the prepared pan and bake for 1 hour, or until the cake is firm and a toothpick inserted in the center comes out clean. Cool the cake on a wire rack in its pan for 10 minutes, then remove the rim and let the cake cool completely.

To store, wrap the cake in plastic wrap; it will keep for almost a week.

Carrot Cake

Familiar and predictable as carrot cake is, it's usually the first dessert to disappear on a buffet table. Possibly people think it's health food, which it certainly isn't; on the other hand, the carrots are good, the nuts are good, the olive oil's good, and the eggs are good, and that's a big improvement over most cakes.

You may roll your eyes at the very idea of using olive oil in a cake, but it's delicious and produces a lovely crumb. This is a keeper cake, one you'll have around for a while if you don't eat it up right away.

If you want to up the omega-3 ante, you can add a handful of chopped flaxseeds to the batter.

Makes 1 large cake, serves 16

 2 cups sugar
 1½ cups extra virgin olive oil
 4 large eggs
 2 cups all-purpose flour
 2 teaspoons ground cinnamon
 1 teaspoon baking soda
 ½ teaspoon salt
 3 cups grated carrots (from about 1 pound carrots)
 1 cup chopped pecans or walnuts
 A handful of chopped flaxseeds, about ¼ cup, optional

 ICING
 6 ounces Philadelphia cream cheese, at room temperature
 6 tablespoons (¾ stick) unsalted butter, at room
    temperature
 3 cups (¾ package) confectioners' sugar, or more if needed
 1 teaspoon pure vanilla extract
 A little milk if needed

Cinnamon for dusting
12 nut halves for decorating

Set an oven rack in the middle of the oven and preheat the oven to 350 degrees. Butter and flour a large Bundt pan.

In a large bowl, beat the sugar with the olive oil until thick and well blended. Add the eggs and beat until thoroughly incorporated.

Using a whisk, mix together the flour, cinnamon, soda, and salt in a small bowl. Add to the egg and sugar mixture, beating well to incorporate. Add the carrots, pecans, and flaxseeds, if using, stirring well.

Pour the batter into the prepared pan. Bake for 45 minutes, or until a toothpick inserted in the center comes out clean. Cool the cake in the pan on a wire rack. After 15 minutes, loosen the cake from the pan by running a knife around the inner edge of the pan and the center tube. Carefully invert the pan and ease the cake onto a cake platter.

To make the icing, beat all the ingredients together until smooth and spreadable. If it's too thick, add a little milk.

Frost the cake. Dust with cinnamon and arrange the nut halves around the top of the cake.

To store the cake, wrap it loosely in foil—it will keep up to a week; it also freezes well, tightly sealed in foil.

Coconut Cheesecake
with a Mac Nut Ginger Crust

Coconut milk does great things for cheesecake—for some reason, the tops never crack, and the texture is very silky. Macadamia nuts are the perfect foil for the coconut, zipped up with a little ginger. Mac nuts are very good omega-3 bargains—their omega-3 to omega-6 ratio is one to one, just about ideal.

Serves 12 to 16

CRUST

1 cup crushed gingersnaps (4 ounces)
½ cup (2½ ounces) chopped macadamia nuts
½ cup shredded unsweetened dried coconut flakes
3 tablespoons coconut oil or unsalted butter

FILLING

Three 8-ounce packages Philadelphia cream cheese, at
    room temperature
¾ cup sugar
1 tablespoon cornstarch
3 large eggs
1 cup canned unsweetened coconut milk, well stirred
¼ cup fresh lime juice
1 teaspoon pure vanilla extract

Preheat the oven to 325 degrees. Grease a 10-inch springform pan.

To make the crust, spread the gingersnap crumbs, nuts, and coconut on a baking sheet and bake for about 15 minutes, stirring twice, until golden. Remove from the oven and let cool. Leave the oven on.

Mix the crumbs, nuts, and coconut with the coconut oil in a bowl, making sure they are thoroughly combined. Press the crumb mixture evenly over the bottom and about 1 inch up the sides of the prepared pan. Raise the oven temperature to 350 degrees.

To make the filling, beat the cream cheese in a large bowl with an electric mixer until smooth. Slowly beat in the sugar and cornstarch, mixing until the sugar dissolves. Add the eggs one at a time, mixing well after each addition. Add the remaining ingredients and mix well.

Pour the filling into the crust and bake for 15 minutes. Turn the oven temperature down to 275 degrees and bake for about 30 minutes more, or until the filling is set. Turn off the oven, open the oven door just a crack, and let the cheesecake rest in the oven for 30 minutes (this will prevent the surface from cracking).

Remove from the oven, cool completely, and chill thoroughly before serving.

Any leftovers will keep well, tightly wrapped, in the refrigerator for several days; the cheesecake also freezes well.

VARIATION: Add a roasted banana to the cheesecake. Roast an unpeeled banana on a baking sheet at 400 degrees until blackened all over, about 12 minutes or so. Let cool, then peel and mash very well. Mix into the cheesecake filling after you add the eggs. Substitute a tablespoon of grated fresh ginger for the lime juice.

Avocado Cheesecake

A friend told me about this California specialty of the Seventies and even though it made me think of canasta parties, of course I had to try it. After a little fiddling with the basic recipe, I ended up with a more contemporary version that will remind you more of Key lime cheesecake than avocados—but of course it's rich and smooth, with avocados substituted for half the cream cheese in a traditional cheesecake.

Don't skip the sour cream topping. Although it seems like overkill, it's essential—delicious as it is, this cheesecake is not to be seen in the nude.

Serves 12

CRUST
2 cups walnut pieces
2 tablespoons sugar
¼ teaspoon ground cinnamon
4 tablespoons (½ stick) unsalted butter, softened

FILLING
Two 8-ounce packages Philadelphia cream cheese, at room
    temperature
1 cup sugar
Grated zest of 1 lime
4 large eggs, at room temperature
2 Hass avocados, cut into chunks
1 tablespoon fresh lime juice
¼ cup sour cream

TOPPING
1 cup sour cream
1 teaspoon grated lime zest
1 teaspoon fresh lime juice
1 tablespoon sugar

Preheat the oven to 475 degrees.

To make the crust, grind the walnuts in the food processor until you have fine crumbs, which is just before you would have walnut butter—be careful not to let it reach that consistency. In a small bowl, mix the nuts with the sugar, cinnamon, and softened butter with a fork. Press the nut mixture into the bottom of a 9-inch springform pan.

To make the filling, in a large bowl, beat the cream cheese with an electric mixer on low speed until smooth, scraping down the sides of the bowl and the beater from time to time; be careful not to over-beat. Add the sugar and lime zest and mix well. Add the eggs one at a time, beating well after each addition and scraping down the bowl and beater.

In a food processor, blend the avocados and lime juice until completely smooth—if you have any doubts, push the mixture through a fine-mesh strainer. Whisk in the sour cream. Add to the cream cheese mixture and incorporate thoroughly.

Pour the filling into the prepared pan and bake for 20 minutes. Lower the heat to 200 degrees and bake for about 40 more minutes. The center of the cheesecake should be just slightly jiggly.

Transfer the cheesecake to a wire rack, away from drafts, to cool completely, about 3 hours.

Mix the topping ingredients and spread over the top of the cooled cheesecake (still in the pan). Cover the cheesecake with plastic wrap and refrigerate for at least 3 hours, or overnight, before serving. Serve slightly chilled.

COOK'S NOTE: It's important to have everything at room temperature when you're making cheesecake. If you're in a hurry, just drop the cream cheese, still in its foil package, into warm water for a few minutes. The eggs will respond to the same treatment.

Wall-to-Wall Walnut Brownies

These indulgent brownies—so loaded with good fats and anti-oxidants—can be whipped up in about five minutes. Because they're made with such good chocolate, they're very pure tasting. But you could also make a less expensive version using 4 ounces of baking chocolate instead of a fancy chocolate bar. Chocolate maniacs may want to double the amount of chocolate for a truly intense, fudgy brownie that's a bit less sweet.

Other nuts that work well here include pecans, hazelnuts, and macadamias.

Makes 16 brownies

> One 3.5-ounce bar premium bittersweet chocolate,
>   chopped
> 8 tablespoons (1 stick) unsalted butter, cut into bits
> 1 cup sugar
> 3 large eggs
> ⅓ cup all-purpose flour
> Pinch of salt
> 1 teaspoon pure vanilla extract
> 1½ cups toasted walnuts

Preheat the oven to 350 degrees. Generously butter an 8-inch square baking pan.

In a heavy saucepan over low heat, or in the microwave, melt the chocolate and butter with the sugar, stirring well from time to time. Set aside to cool.

Beat the eggs well in a medium bowl. Whisk in the flour, salt, and vanilla. Add all but ¼ cup of the nuts and stir well. Add the chocolate mixture and stir thoroughly to incorporate.

Scrape the brownie batter into the prepared pan and smooth the top with a metal spatula. Scatter the remaining ¼ cup nuts over the top. Bake for 30 minutes, or until a toothpick tester comes out with wet crumbs—if it comes out clean, the brownies are overbaked.

Transfer the brownies in their pan to a wire rack to cool for at least 3 hours before cutting into 16 squares.

The brownies keep well for up to 5 days layered in wax paper and sealed in a tin; they also freeze very well.

COOK'S NOTE: My friend Faith Heller Willinger, a born-again Tuscan cook, uses olive oil (½ cup) instead of butter in brownies and swears by the result. She's right; olive oil and chocolate are surprisingly wonderful together.

Almond Paste Macaroons

Here's a more-or-less instant food processor cookie you can make on the spur of the moment as long as you have almond paste in your cupboard—and since it keeps forever, that shouldn't be a problem. These are great with after-dinner coffee or with fruit desserts.

Makes about 2 dozen cookies

One 8-ounce can almond paste, preferably Odense brand
½ cup confectioners' sugar
2 large egg whites
Pinch of salt
½ teaspoon pure vanilla extract

Preheat the oven to 350 degrees. Line a baking sheet with parchment paper.

Crumble the almond paste into the bowl of a food processor. Add the remaining ingredients and process until smooth.

Using a pastry tube or a heavy-duty plastic freezer bag with a corner cut off, pipe 1-inch mounds of the cookie dough onto the parchment paper–lined baking sheet, keeping them well apart.

Bake the cookies for 15 to 20 minutes, or until lightly colored. Transfer the cookies, still on the parchment paper, to a wire rack and let cool.

These cookies are good keepers; store them in an airtight container in the refrigerator, and they'll last for weeks.

Toasted Coconut–Almond Macaroons

These little treats are full of good things, but they're not a fancy cookie to serve at a dinner party. They're chewy, not crisp on the outside, and they're soft inside. You could dust them with confectioners' sugar to make them look prettier. You could also dip their bottoms in melted dark chocolate to emphasize the chocolate flavor, not to mention the antioxidant value.

Makes 18 small cookies

  1 cup shredded unsweetened dried coconut
  ⅓ cup ground almonds
  1 tablespoon unsweetened cocoa powder
  6 tablespoons sugar
  2 large egg whites
  ½ teaspoon pure vanilla extract
  ¼ teaspoon pure almond extract
  Pinch of salt

Preheat the oven to 325 degrees. Line a cookie sheet with parchment paper or foil and lightly oil it.

Combine the coconut and almonds and spread on another cookie sheet. Toast until light golden, just a few minutes—watch carefully, since both the nuts and the coconut can easily burn. Turn the mixture out into a medium bowl to cool completely.

Whisk the rest of the ingredients in a small bowl, then stir into the coconut and nuts, mixing well. Place mounded teaspoons of the mixture on the lined cookie sheet, keeping the cookies about an inch apart (the cookies won't spread or change their shape as they bake).

Bake for 10 to 12 minutes, or until the cookies just start to turn golden. Slide the parchment off the baking pan and onto a cooling rack. The cookies will release themselves from the paper when they're cool.

They'll keep for several days, layered in wax paper in a sealed container.

Kourambiedes
(Greek Shortbread Cookies)

Classic kourambiedes are butter cookies, delectably short and melt-in-your-mouth, with a dusting of confectioners' sugar to give a little sweetness to each bite, since the cookies themselves are not very sweet at all. In Greece, at the Avia olive oil collective in Kalamata, a group of olive oil aficionados from around the world fell upon and devoured these superb cookies, made with olive oil instead of the traditional butter. We wanted to eat them for breakfast as well as at virtually every other hour of the day, and fortunately, they keep very well, so we could.

I've messed around with the recipe a bit, using walnuts instead of almonds, and more of them, and adding a bit of lemon zest. These aren't really improvements (except nutritionally), just a different way to prepare them.

Makes about 6 dozen cookies

2 cups pure or extra virgin olive oil
⅔ cup sugar
⅓ cup brandy, Scotch, or orange liqueur
Chopped zest of 2 lemons, optional
½ teaspoon baking soda
2 tablespoons fresh lemon juice
1 cup finely chopped walnuts or almonds, plus ½ cup
    coarsely chopped nuts
4 to 5 cups all-purpose flour
3 to 4 cups confectioners' sugar for coating

Preheat the oven to 350 degrees. Line two baking sheets with parchment paper or foil.

In a large mixing bowl, beat the oil and sugar together at high speed with an electric mixer or an immersion blender until well combined. Add the brandy and lemon zest, if using. Dissolve the baking soda in the lemon juice and add that to the mixture, mixing well.

With a wooden spoon, stir in the fine and coarse nuts and mix well. Add 3 cups of the flour, a little at a time, mixing with the spoon until a dough starts to form. Add more flour in increments, kneading as you go, for 10 to 15 minutes, until the dough is stiff; if it's still too sticky after you've added 4 cups of flour, refrigerate it for an hour. You still may need more flour.

Take a heaping tablespoon of the dough and shape it into a small mounded oblong or 1½-inch round cookie and place on one of the prepared baking sheets. Continue with the remaining dough, making the cookies all the same shape so they bake evenly, and spacing them about 1 inch apart.

Bake for 12 to 15 minutes, until very lightly colored. Remove from the oven and slide the paper with the cookies on it onto a rack to cool.

When the cookies are cool, sift the confectioners' sugar over them, turning them to coat all sides.

Store in a tightly sealed tin; they should keep for a week.

COOK'S NOTE: A 50-milliliter airline bottle of brandy won't be quite enough.

Coconut Cookies
with Chocolate Chips

Sweet chewy coconut and melting bittersweet chocolate make an addictive combination. These wonderfully good cookies will disappear immediately from a cookie plate—you can't eat just one.

Don't bother peeling the brown skin off the coconut; it adds some fiber and completely disappears in the baking. If fresh coconut is out of the question, just use unsweetened dried coconut.

Makes about 3 dozen cookies

½ pound (2 sticks) unsalted butter, softened
¼ cup granulated sugar
1 cup packed light brown sugar
1 teaspoon salt
2 teaspoons pure vanilla extract
1 large egg
½ teaspoon baking soda
1 cup all-purpose flour
1 cup ground almonds
2 cups grated fresh coconut
12 ounces bittersweet chocolate, in chips or chunks

Preheat the oven to 375 degrees. Line two baking sheets with parchment paper.

In the bowl of an electric mixer or with a hand mixer, beat the butter until soft and light. Add both sugars, the salt, and vanilla and beat well to combine. Add the egg and baking soda and beat until combined. On low speed, add the flour and almonds, mixing until just combined. Stir in the coconut and chocolate bits.

Using moistened hands, roll about 1 heaping tablespoon of the dough into a ball. Place on one of the baking sheets and flatten with the palm of your hand. Repeat with the remaining dough, spacing the cookies 2 inches apart.

Bake for about 10 minutes, until evenly browned, rotating the sheets halfway through baking. Transfer the cookies to a wire rack to cool.

Chocolate Haystacks

These sweetmeats are nice to serve with after-dinner coffee or on a buffet table. They're also a snap to make from ingredients you can easily keep on hand, and although they don't keep a long time, that shouldn't be a problem.

The darker the chocolate (i.e., premium bittersweet), the more good cocoa butter it will contain—and the lower-carb it will be. Regular chocolate chips will be sweeter as well; made with the good stuff, these have a sophisticated not-very-sweet taste that may not please all palates. Semisweet chocolate is a good compromise. Chocolate chips come in all sorts of varieties, but even most supermarkets now carry "gourmet" varieties such as Ghirardelli.

You can prepare the toasted almonds and toasted coconut whenever you have a minute during the day, then just melt the chocolate and put the haystacks together shortly before you serve them.

Makes about 30 haystacks

1⅓ cups (6 ounces) slivered almonds
3 tablespoons shredded unsweetened dried coconut, optional
1 cup bittersweet or semisweet chocolate chips

Preheat the oven to 350 degrees.

Spread the almonds on a baking sheet in a single layer and bake for 5 to 10 minutes, stirring them a couple of times, until they smell toasty and are golden brown. Let cool.

In a small heavy skillet, toast the optional coconut over low heat—carefully, because it can easily burn. Watch it like a hawk and stir it around frequently. When it's golden, in just a few minutes, remove from the skillet and let cool.

When you're ready to assemble the haystacks, cover a baking sheet with wax paper. Melt the chocolate in a microwave or in a small saucepan over low heat. Stir well to be sure it's all melted, then mix it with the almonds in a bowl, covering them all.

Using tongs, make little 1-inch piles of the chocolate-almond mixture on the wax paper, pulling them up into a haystack shape. Sprinkle a little toasted coconut over each pile, if using. Let the haystacks cool and set before serving, which will take a couple of hours. (If time is an issue, you can harden the chocolate by putting them in the refrigerator for about 20 minutes.)

The haystacks don't keep well, and they're best the day you make them, so don't plan on leftovers.

Sources: Food and Food Products

FISH AND SEAFOOD

Audubon's Living Oceans: www.seafood.audubon.org
Good fish choices from an environmental point of view.

Cap'n Mike's Holy Smoke: 707-585-2000; www.holysmokedsalmon.com
An amazing array of smoked fish products, including lox, Indian smoked salmon, smoked tuna, smoked cod, smoked trout and jerky. Salmon candy, the unfortunately named old Indian treat, is cured in honey and smoked three days.

Citarella: 212-874-0833 (ext. 1); www.citarella.com
Sicilian anchovies (from Talatta).

Dean & Deluca: 800-221-7714; www.deandeluca.com
Swedish cod roe caviar and smoked herring spread in tubes.

Taylor Shellfish Farms: 360-426-6178; www.taylorshellfish.com
Mediterranean mussels, plump and sweet (summer).

Tsar Nicoulai Caviar: 415-543-3007; www.tsarnicoulai.com
American whitefish caviar.

Tustumena Smokehouse: 907-260-3401;
www.tustumenasmokehouse.com
Hot-smoked wild Alaska salmon.

Walden Foods: 800-64-TROUT; www.waldenfoods.com
Smoked trout. The best smoked trout imaginable comes from Walden Foods in Virginia. It's chemical-free, antibiotic-free, artisanal, old-fashioned, apple-wood-smoked trout. The trout keeps at least twenty-one days in the refrigerator.

MEAT

Green Circle Organics: 540-675-2627; www.greencircle.com
Organic beef (Angus and Wagyu) from small ranches.

Iceland Naturally: www.icelandnaturally.com
Icelandic lamb, a true novelty.

Jamison Farm: 800-237-5262; www.jamisonfarm.com
Lamb from Jamison Farm appears on many of the finest restaurant tables in America.

Niman Ranch: www.nimanranch.com
Beef and pork, especially terrific dry-aged bacon; small-farm animals are grass-fed without hormones, then are finished on grain. The name of the farm where the animal was raised is on the package.

Pipestone Family Farms: 866-767-8875; www.pipestonefamilyfarms.com
Pork; the animals are raised on small family farms with no hormones or antibiotics.

GRASS-FED MEAT

Eat Well Guide: www.iatp.org/eatwell
Sustainably raised meat without antibiotics, in state-by-state listings.

Eat Wild: www.eatwild.com
Wild game and supplies of animals raised on pasture-based farming.

Grassland Beef: 877-383-0051; www.grasslandbeef.com
Beef certified by the University of Iowa to have a high omega-3 content, with a ratio of 16 to 1 of omega-3 to omega-6.

The New England Livestock Alliance: nelivestockalliance.org

Prather Ranch: 877-570-2333; www.pratherranch.com
Grass-fed lamb and beef from animals that also have eaten some fruit, pork from pigs that have eaten watermelon—all these animals are raised in the Sierra, so they're available during late summer to winter, the opposite of the season of most grass-fed meat.

NUTS

Ann's House o' Nuts: 410-813-0080
Very fresh, high-quality nuts.

Columbia Empire Farms: 888-252-0699; www.yournw.com
Hazelnuts direct from the source, Oregon (where they're called filberts).

Magee's Nut House: 323-938-4127
Fresh and delicious nut butters: peanut, almond, cashew, macadamia.

CHEESE

Cowgirl Creamery: 415-663-9335; www.cowgirlcreamery.com
Superb handmade cheeses from Ireland, France, and California. There's an artisan-cheese-of-the-every-other-month club.

www.fromages.com
The real thing—European raw milk cheeses delivered to your door.

OILS

Armando Manni: www.manni.biz
For high rollers, this is ambrosial olive oil from Tuscany.

Omega Nutrition: 800-661-3529; www.omeganutrition.com
Coconut oil.

Coconut Oil Supreme: 800-922-1744; www.coconutoil-online.com
Superb oil at a relative bargain.

The Republic of Tea: 800-298-4832; www.therepublicoftea.com
A boutique tea oil with a lovely light flavor.

COCONUT

Red Mill Farms: www.redmillfarms.com
Jennie's macaroons are high in lauric acid and are available in natural foods stores or through the website.

SALT

The Grain & Salt Society: 800-867-7258; www.celtic-seasalt.com
Celtic Sea Salt: completely unrefined, nutrient-dense salt; intensely salty.

La Cuisine: 800-521-1176; www.lacuisineus.com
Spanish salt, Brittany salt, Maldon salt, and fleur de sel.

The Maldon Crystal Salt Company, Ltd.; www.maldonsalt.kemc.co.uk
Flaky Maldon salt from England.

MARKETS

Formaggio Kitchen: 888-212-3224; www.formaggiokitchen.com
Highest-quality imported cheeses, Italian tuna and anchovies, smoked fish, caviar, and fine nut oils from the J. Leblanc factory in the French Dordogne.

The Spanish Table: www.tablespan.com
Excellent Spanish olive oils, nuts (the almonds are outstanding), tuna and sardines, plus wonderful smoked Spanish paprika.

Zingerman's: 888-636-8162; www.zingermans.com
A great source for everything from olive oil to nuts to imported tuna and anchovies.

OMEGA-3 OIL SUPPLEMENTS

Life Extension Foundation: 800-544-4440; www.lef.org
A vegetable source of omega-3 fat, perilla oil is much more stable than flax oil. Available in soft gels.

Natrol: 800-326-1520; www.natrol.com
Neuromins (DHA) supplements are available from several sources, but some of them contain other undesirable fats, such as sunflower oil. To avoid these, get the Natrol brand.

OmegaBrite: 800-383-2030; www.omegabrite.com
Developed by Dr. Andrew Stoll, these pharmaceutical-grade fish oil soft-gel capsules are especially designed for use in mood disorders and contain very little DHA.

www.scientificnutrition.com
www.healthyskinshop.com
Eskimo-3 fish oil is a high-quality oil that has no contaminants and is exceptionally stable. It also has no fishy aftertaste. Available in capsules (from Scientific Nutrition) and in liquid form.

Sears Labs: 800-404-8171; www.drsears.com
Dr. Barry Sears designed Liquid OmegaRx, a high-quality oil, which has a pleasant taste and no contaminants. This pharmaceutical-grade fish oil liquid is especially convenient for the large doses that Dr. Sears often recommends to correct a medical problem.

FLAXSEED

Low-Carb Corner: 800-965-9008; www.lowcarbcorner.com
Dakota Flax Seed, an exceptionally clean, high-quality organic golden flax raised in the cold North Dakota country. Available from Nutritional Associates, who also sell low-carb products, such as their terrific cranberry nut protein crunch cereal and a new pure wheat protein that's delicious.

WEIGHT-LOSS SUPPLEMENTS

Bio-Tech: 800-345-1199
The best quality alpha-lipoic acid, according to Dr. Burt Berkson.

Dews Research Laboratories: 940-382-1849
The liver cleanser BHB Plus is especially useful when starting a diet or hitting a plateau.

Pentabosol: 800-264-8446; www.pentabosol.com
Pentabosol is a very effective weight-loss accelerator designed to work with the Protein Power program (www.eatprotein.com).

FATTY-ACID TESTING

Great Smokies Diagnostic Laboratory: 800-522-4762; www.gsdl.com
You'll need a prescription for this test, which will be sent to you in the form of a kit in the mail. After you return the test, you will receive a very detailed profile of your fatty acids.

Sears Labs: 877-468-6934; www.drsears.com
You don't need a doctor's prescription for this fatty-acid profile, which will be returned to you with recommendations.

TOOLS

Art Pottery Coffignal: http://perso.club-internet.fr/hccoffig
Butter keepers are a clever idea, immersing butter in water inside a crock, and give you room-temperature butter that's always spreadable but not exposed to the air or the refrigerator. The original butter keeper comes from Normandy, and you can order (in English) a gorgeous handmade blue crock from Art Pottery Coffignal.

Chef's Catalog: 800-884-CHEF; www.chefscatalog.com
Williams-Sonoma: 877-812-6235. www.williams-sonoma.com
Once you start using a lot of avocados, an avocado slicer makes slicing them an instant process. You get eleven exact slices, and all the fruit leaves the peel in one fell swoop. Dishwasher safe.

The Australian Coconut Knife: mike.foale@csiro.au
This gorgeous handmade tool will get you right into a coconut, husk and all.

American Institute of Reboundology, Inc.: 888-464-JUMP; www.health-bounce.com
The rebounder, a mini-trampoline, is the best of all exercise equipment. The Ultimate Rebounder and the ReboundAIR fold up easily and are highly portable.

FURTHER INFORMATION

Agricultural Marketing Service: www.ams.usda.gov
To find a farmers' market near you.

Center for Research on Lauric Oils, Inc.: www.lauric.org
To see which coconut products contain the most lauric acid.

The Independent Institute: www.fdareview.org
To see the latest information on what the FDA is up to from a critical point of view.

Institute for Global Communications: www.igc.org/mothers
Check out the latest information on pesticides and the most contaminated produce.

National Institutes of Health: http://efaeducation.nih.gov
This website on essential fatty acids is very informative and has an interactive program called KIM; you enter the details of your diet and learn how much omega-3 and omega-6 you are depositing in your tissues.

The Omega-3 Information Service: www.omega-3info.com
Keep up with the latest details on omega-3 news.

Seafood Choices Alliances: www.seafoodchoices.com
The endangered fish list on this site changes constantly, so it's a good idea to frequently check this website.

The Weston A. Price Foundation: www.westonaprice.org
A fascinating website devoted to the healthfulness of traditional foods. See the Soy Alert page and Mary Enig and Sally Fallon's "The Oiling of America."

Ban Trans Fats.com, Inc.: www.bantransfats.com
This nonprofit organization sued Nabisco to remove the trans fat in Oreos.

Further Reading

Albert, Christine M., et al. "Blood Levels of Long-chain n-3 Fatty Acids and the Risk of Sudden Death." *New England Journal of Medicine* 346 (2002): 1113–18.

Anchell, Melvin. *The Steak Lover's Diet*. Atlanta: Second Opinion Publishing, 1998.

Barnes, Broda O., M.D., and Lawrence Galton. *Hypothyroidism: The Unsuspected Illness*. New York: Harper & Row, 1964.

Berkson, Burt. *The Alpha Lipoic Acid Breakthrough: The Superb Antioxidant That May Slow Aging, Repair Liver Damage, and Reduce the Risk of Cancer, Heart Disease, and Diabetes*. Roseville, Calif.: Prima, 1998.

———, Jack Challem, and Melissa Diane Smith. *Syndrome X: The Complete Nutritional Program to Prevent and Reverse Insulin Resistance*. New York: Wiley, 2000.

Cordain, Loren. *The Paleo Diet*. New York: Wiley, 2002.

deLorgeril, M., et al. "Mediterranean Diet, Traditional Risk Factors, and the Rate of Cardiovascular Complications After Myocardial Infarction: Final Report of Lyon Diet Heart Study." *Circulation* 99 (1999): 779–85.

Eades, Michael, and Mary Dan. *The Protein Power Lifeplan*. New York: Ballantine, 2000.

Enig, Mary G. *Know Your Fats*. Silver Spring, Md.: Bethesda Press, 2000.

———. "The Oiling of America." Available at www.westonaprice.org.

Erasmus, Udo. *Fats That Heal, Fats That Kill*. Burnaby, British Columbia: Alive Books, 1993.

Fife, Bruce. *Eat Fat, Look Thin*. Colorado Springs: Piccadilly Books, 2002.

———. *The Healing Miracles of Coconut*. Colorado Springs: Piccadilly Books, 2001.

———. *Saturated Fat May Save Your Life*. Colorado Springs: Piccadilly Books, 1999.

Gittleman, Ann Louise, with Dina Nunziato. *Eat Fat, Lose Weight*. Los Angeles: Keats Publishing, 1999.

Hertoghe, Thierry. *The Hormone Solution*. New York: Harmony, 2002.

Hibbeln, J. R. "Fish Consumption and Major Depression." *The Lancet* 351 (1998): 1213.

Pennington, A. W. "A Reorientation on Obesity." *New England Journal of Medicine* 248 (1953): 959–64.

Pereria, M. A., et al.: "Dairy Consumption, Obesity, and the Insulin Resistance Syndrome in Young Adults, the CARDIA Study." *Journal of the American Medical Association* 287 (2002): 2081.

Perricone, Nicholas. *The Wrinkle Cure.* New York: Warner, 2001.

Ravnskov, Uffe. *The Cholesterol Myths.* Washington: New Trends, 2000.

Schmid, Ronald F. *Traditional Foods Are Your Best Medicine.* Rochester, Vt.: Healing Arts Press, 1997.

Sears, Barry. *The Omega Rx Zone.* New York: ReganBooks, 2002.

Siguel, Edward N. *Essential Fatty Acids in Health and Disease.* Brookline, Mass.: Nutrek Press, 1994.

Stoll, Andrew L. *The Omega-3 Connection.* New York: Simon & Schuster, 2001.

Taubes, Gary. "The Soft Science of Dietary Fat." *Science* (March 2002): 2536–45.

———. "What If It's All Been a Big Fat Lie?" *New York Times Magazine,* July 7, 2002.

Westman, Eric C., et al. "Effect of 6-Month Adherence to a Very Low Carbohydrate Diet Program" (Clinical study). *The American Journal of Medicine* 113, no. 1 (July 2002): 30–36.

Willett, Walter C. *Eat, Drink, and Be Healthy.* New York: Simon & Schuster, 2001.

Williams, Roger J. *Biochemical Individuality.* New Canaan, Ct.: Keats Publishing, 1998.

Conversion Charts

Approximate Temperature Conversions

	FAHRENHEIT	CELSIUS OR CENTIGRADE	
Water freezes	32°	0°	To convert Fahrenheit into Centigrade, subtract 32,
Water boils—at sea level	212°	100°	multiply by 5, divide by 9.
Very low oven	250°–275°	121°–133°	To convert Centigrade
Low oven	300°–325°	149°–163°	into Fahrenheit, go into reverse: multiply by 9,
Moderate oven	350°–375°	177°–190°	divide by 5, add 32.
Hot oven	400°–425°	204°–218°	100°C × 9 = 900
Very hot oven	450°–475°	232°–246°	900 ÷ 5 = 180
Extremely hot oven	500°–525°	260°–274°	180 + 32 = 212°F

Linear Measures

1 centimeter	= 0.394 inch	1/2 inch	= 12 millimeters
1/4 inch	= 6 millimeters	1 inch	= 2.54 centimeters

U.S.–Metric Mass (Weight)

	OUNCES	POUNDS	GRAMS	KILOGRAMS
1 Ounce	1	1/16	28.35	.028
1 Pound	16	1	454	.454
1 Gram	.032	.002	1	.001
1 Kilogram	.000032	2.2	1000	1

U.S. and British Dry Volume Measures

One 8-ounce U.S. measuring cup = 16 U.S. tablespoons or 48 U.S. teaspoons

One 10-ounce English measuring cup = 20 4/5 U.S. tablespoons or 62 1/2 U.S. teaspoons

U.S.–Metric Fluid Volume Measures

	TEA-SPOONS	TABLE-SPOONS	OUNCES	1/4 CUPS	GILLS 1/2 CUPS	CUPS	QUARTS	MILLI-LITERS	LITERS
1 Teaspoon	1	1/3	1/16	1/12	1/24	1/48	1/192	5	.005
1 Tablespoon	3	1	1/2	1/4	1/8	1/16	1/64	15	.015
1 Ounce	6	2	1	1/2	1/4	1/8	1/32	29.56	.030
1/4 Cup	12	4	2	1	1/2	1/4	1/16	59.125	.059
1 Gill 1/2 Cup	24	8	4	2	1	1/2	1/8	118.25	.118
1 Cup	48	16	8	4	2	1	1/4	236	.236
1 Quart	192	64	32	16	8	4	1	946	.946
1 Milliliter	.203 or 1/5	.068	.034	.017	.008	.004	.001	1	.001 or 1/1000
1 Liter	203.04	67.68	33.814	16.906	8.453	4.227	1.057	1000	1

Acknowledgments

This book was conceived as a result of several spirited conversations with my editor, Beth Wareham, who was savvy enough to see its outlines in our mutual fascination with the subject. As a former book editor, I know that the hardest thing is to catch the wave while it's still so far away that few other people can see it, which is the only way to have the lead time it takes to produce a book on a timely subject. So I owe huge thanks to Beth and to Susan Moldow, the publisher at Scribner, for taking this leap with me. Rica Allannic at Scribner magically made my manuscript much more organized and saved me from a lot of gaffes, another great gift. Thank you, all.

Once the idea of the book was a gleam in all our eyes, Irene Skolnick, my agent, made it all happen the way I hoped it would, for which I'm deeply grateful.

Craig Winston, my researcher, did a great job, often turning up obscure material, sometimes in a matter of moments. His ability to find the right keys and unlock doors is uncanny.

I deeply wish that Dr. Mary Enig's website had not been down during the entire period I was writing this book, and that I had been successful in my efforts to reach her. Still, her books and articles have been invaluable to this project, and she should be recognized as a heroine in her courageous work to bring us the truth about trans fats and other unhealthy oils in the face of vigorous opposition from agribusiness, government, and the self-interested, career-promoting media "experts" who have so seriously endangered our national health. I've since met with Dr. Enig and she's shared her vast expertise on fats generously.

I'm especially grateful to the leading lipid researchers who patiently guided me through the extremely complicated world of fats and answered my endless questions: Bruce Fife, N.D., the coconut expert; Bruce Holub at the University of Guelph in Canada, a longtime fats researcher; Joseph Hibbeln and Bill Lands at the National Institutes of Health; Dr. Jon J. Kabara, the lipid pharmacologist who pioneered the work on coconut and monolaurin; David Kyle, the creator of the omega-3 supplement for infant formula; Dr. Georges Mouton, a leading fats expert in Europe; and Dr. Barry Sears, the lipid chemist who pioneered our understanding of how fats influence our hormonal system. Molecular cell specialist David King at the Howard Hughes Medical Institute has been brilliant at explaining extremely complicated subjects in language so evocative and clear that even I can understand them. Thanks to Dr. Bruce N. Ames, professor of biochemistry and molecular biology at the University of California, Berkeley, for shedding light on the difficult topic of dioxin. Three conferences were crucial for my understanding of this subject: the Rockefeller University Conference on Childhood Obesity (thanks to Wendy Lane), the Oldways Preservation and Exchange Trust conference on aquaculture (thanks to Dun Gifford), and the annual Endocrinology Conference of the Broda O. Barnes, M.D., Foundation (thanks to Pat Puglio). Paraskevas Tokousbalides in Greece, an olive oil researcher, explained some very important chemical processes to me and also gave me a wonderful recipe. Special thanks to nutritionists Rosie Schwartz and Lauren Braun and hormone expert Pat Puglio, as well as Doris Hicks of the Sea Grant program and seafood expert Lori Howell. Michael and Vivian Straus of the Straus dairy family were very helpful, as was Mike Daniels, who steered me in the right direction for pork information. Doctors Mike and Mary Dan Eades, who originally opened my eyes to the wisdom of low-carb eating, are always my go-to people when I don't understand something biochemical or medical, and they're unfailingly helpful and cheerful about it.

This book isn't just about science, it's also about food, and I owe a great debt to my recipe developers, kitchen testers, and friends who've offered invaluable help. Irish chef James O'Shea of the West Street Grill can't seem to stop himself from rattling off impromptu recipes into my ear during our long phone conversations, and he's taught me a huge amount about the cooking process itself, especially the cooking of fish. I can't thank him enough. Other professionals who've made important contributions include Bruce Aidells, Jo Bettoja, Niloufer Ichaporia King, Martha Rose Shulman, Molly Stevens, Annie Somerville, John Martin Taylor, James Villas, Eileen Weinberg, Faith Heller Willinger, Paula Wolfert, and Diane Worthington. Cooks whose recipes make me seem like a much better cook than I am include David Barnes, Jennifer Herman, Bob Lake, Julie Monson, Steve and Melissa Sorman, and Barbara Witt.

My friends have been a great support throughout the researching and writing of this book and some of them have also made contributions. I particularly want to thank Rick Kot, Maggie McCarthy, Patty O'Neill, Alice Rosengard, Le Anne Schreiber, and Karolyn Wrightson.

My family has been not only long-suffering but also incredibly helpful. My son, Ben, has dealt with innumerable tech crises (including a lightning strike) and endless idiotic questions without a whimper. My daughter, Katy, and her husband, Darian Cork, have jumped right in to help with everything from research to last-minute recipe testing. For my husband, David, it's been a long vacationless year of chaos and stress, not to mention way too many coconut custard experiments, all undertaken in good spirits and with unfailing support.

My great thanks to you, everyone. All in all, I'm a very lucky duck.

Index

lignans, 51, 53
lime:
    Cuban roast pork with, 263
    shrimp with coconut and, 221
    zest, in Thai seafood chowder,
      193–94
limonene, 144
linoleic acid:
    cancer and, 5, 23, 32, 44, 59
    heart disease and, 23, 32, 59
    in walnut oil, 115
linseed oil, *see* flaxseeds, flaxseed oil
lipoprotein(a) (Lp*a*), trans fats and,
    36–37
liver, cleansing of, 145–46
liver cancer, 109, 153
Living Low-Carb (McCullough), 4
Low-Carb Cookbook, The (McCul-
    lough), 4
low-carb diets, 4, 144–49
    finding ideal balance in, 159–60
    insulin resistance (Syndrome X)
      and, 27, 123, 149
    Pennington alternative to, 148–49
low density lipoproteins (LDLs), 12,
    20, 60, 100, 138, 143, 148
low-fat diets, 6–7, 39
    cardiovascular disease and, 4, 12,
      15, 27
    children on, 6–7, 31
    cravings on, 147–48
    forces colluding in promotion of,
      1, 5–7, 11, 12, 13–17, 18, 20,
      21, 24, 25, 33, 57–58
    health consequences of, 6–7, 11,
      13, 20, 27, 31, 146–47
    insulin resistance (Syndrome X)
      and, 27, 147–48
    longevity and, 13
    problems of, 146–47
lutein, 110, 127–28, 151
lycopene, 32, 141, 143–44, 162
Lyon Diet Heart Study, 19

macadamia nut butter, 109
macadamia nuts, 109
    in coconut cheesecake with a mac
      nut ginger crust, 326–27

    health benefits of, 108, 326
    in shrimp and avocado salad,
      208–9
macaroons:
    almond paste, 332
    Jennie's, 60
    toasted coconut-almond,
      333–34
McDonald's fries, 22–24
Macdougall, John, 20
mackerel, 87–89
    king, 76, 88
    in a mayonnaise coat, 238
    omega-3s in, 87, 88
    plain broiled, 236
    preparation and cooking of,
      87–88
    recommendations for, 88
    Spanish, *see* Spanish mackerel
    with teriyaki sauce, 237
    toxins in, 76, 88
McMahan, Jacqueline, 190
macrobiotic diets, 4
macular degeneration, 141
Madison, Deborah, 288
magnesium, 15, 139
main dishes, 217–72
    aïoli, 230–31
    amazing lamb stew, 266–67
    buffalo chili, 271–72
    chicken with olives and oranges,
      262
    Cuban roast pork with lime, 263
    deep-fried coconut shrimp,
      228–29
    fillet of salmon with garlic and
      dill, 255–56
    fried shrimp, 224–25
    gravlax, 259–61
    grilled sardines, 242
    hot avocado with cheesy shrimp,
      222–23
    mackerel in a mayonnaise coat,
      238
    mackerel with teriyaki sauce, 237
    marinated tuna, 247–48
    Massaman curry with sweet pota-
      toes and peanuts, 219–20

About the Author

Fran McCullough won a James Beard Award for *Great Food Without Fuss*. She wrote the best-selling *Low-Carb Cookbook* and followed it with *Living Low-Carb*. She is also a well-known editor of cookbooks, literary books, and general nonfiction, including Sylvia Plath's *The Bell Jar* and—with Ted Hughes—Plath's journals. She was the first recipient of the Roger Klein Award for Creative Editing and currently edits *The Best American Recipes* series.